FISHING GUIDE TO
WESTERN
AUSTRALIA

by
Kurt Blanksby and Frank Prokop

GW00908508

AUSTRALIAN FISHING NETWORK

FRONT COVER: Sam Canella with a massive giant trevally taken from the shore at Exmouth. PHOTO: KURT BLANKSBY

DEDICATION

Kurt would like to thank his wife Caroline and children
Brendon and Mitchell for their support during the lengthy
birthing process associated with a book of this magnitude.

Frank would like to thank Sonja as well as Frank and Natasha
for their similar indulgence.

First published in 2003 by
Australian Fishing Network
48 Centre Way
South Croydon, Vic. 3136
Australia
Tel: (03) 9761 4044
Fax: (03) 9761 4055
Email: sales@afn.com.au
Web: www.afn.com.au

Copyright © Kurt Blanksby, Frank Prokop and AFN 2003
Designed by Eckermann Art & Design

ISBN 1 86513 035 4 (Paperback edition)
ISBN 1 86513 047 8 (Hardcase edition)

This book is copyright. Apart from any fair dealing for the
purposes of private study, research, criticism or review as
permitted under the Copyright Act, no part may be reproduced,
stored in a retrieval system or transmitted, in any form or by any
means, without prior written permission. Inquiries should be
addressed to Australian Fishing Network

DISCLAIMER

Anglers should note that details of fishing regulations
applying to Western Australian waters have not been
incorporated into this publication as they were under review
and changed during the course of its publication.

However, details of WA's fishing regulations plus those
relating to protected areas and protected species can be
readily obtained via the Department of Fisheries website:
www.fish.wa.gov.au/rec or by telephoning it on (08) 9482
7333.

The publisher accepts no responsibility, either directly or
indirectly, for the actions of anglers or other persons engaging
in fishing / boating activities who fail to abide by the WA
Department of Fisheries information and by the Department
of Transport regulations that apply to the waters mentioned in
this publication.

CONTENTS

ACKNOWLEDGMENTS

There are many people who kindly donated a wealth of information and some stunning photographs that are used in this publication. We also thank Mike Roennfeldt for his work on the Fish Species sections of this book. A few of the many people who helped include Bill and Helen Classon, Quintin Skippings, Bob Cox, Ian Sewell, Steve Correia, Gary Shugg, Peter Golding and Tamlin Little. Without you our job would have been near on impossible.

Kurt Blanksby & Frank Prokop

INTRODUCTION

Welcome to Western Australia. For those of you visiting and fishing this great State for the first time, it is an adventure into a diversity of recreational angling experiences to last you until, well, your next visit. One thing is for certain, if you are after angling frontiers, there are more to be found in Western Australia than anywhere else in Australia.

If you are a resident of WA and want some additional information on areas, species availability and a few tips to improve your fishing in your back yard or holiday destination, then sit back and enjoy the book.

There are a couple of little tips that will help you to enjoy both your stay and your fishing. Firstly, it is important to realise just how big a place Western Australia actually is! This State can offer everything from fishing for the biggest Australian salmon to barramundi fishing, from trout and marron in the southwest to sooty grunter, giant catfish and cherabin in the northwest. A trip from Perth to Carnarvon is equivalent to a run from Melbourne to Sydney, and you would only be half way to Broome. A drive from Kununurra to Esperance can and does take many people several months to negotiate.

When a road sign says last fuel for 200 km, this is not a trap for tourists. While fuel and some supplies might be pretty expensive, it can be very remote country. This necessitates some careful planning so that you will enjoy your trip and minimise your capacity for avoidable catastrophe. From Kalbarri northwards and Esperance eastwards, always carry spare fuel and water. Spare tyres should be checked and if you are towing a boat, sufficient spares need to be carried for even a major structural failure. Otherwise your boat could sit on the side of the road for a few days while you chase a spare part, and quality fishing time may drift past.

Most of Western Australia is desert. Once you leave the far northern end of Perth's northern suburbs until you reach the true Kimberley just south of Broome, or out on the Nullarbor, you will be struggling to find what most people would call a big tree. There are some truly spectacular plants and the wildflower season can make the drive and scenery memorable, but long distance driving bears little resemblance to a drive up the East Coast north of Brisbane. It can be dry, dusty and hard country but the fishing, oh the fishing can easily compensate.

Most visitors on a long time visit to Western Australia start in the north in the winter and end up on the south coast in summer. There is also much to be said for starting in the south in the summer and heading up north as autumn approaches. The down side to this pattern is that many others will be doing the same thing. Okay, it's nothing like the Pacific Highway near Taree in New South Wales on a long weekend, but to the locals it represents tourist season.

Not surprisingly, fishing is not really at its best in the tropics in winter. While it feels balmy to most people, it is relatively much colder than usual and this results in fish feeling more sluggish. As the dry season advances the waters recede and the fish become finicky about feeding. Much better fishing for fish like barramundi can be found in spring before 'the wet' and in autumn when 'the dry' just starts. Taking a 4WD, caravan and car topper dinghy rig that is commonly seen isn't recommended on still-wet bush tracks immediately after the wet. You will need a strong digging arm and be able to use a snatch 'em strap in a mangrove swamp and also have a satellite phone to ring for help if things get really bad.

Bait is available almost everywhere. However, a throw net can be used in most places in WA with the exception of estuaries south of the twenty-sixth parallel. A throw net is fun to use and once learned you will never forget the feeling of mangrove mud dripping down your arms.

Leave your gill net behind. Even though recreational netting is allowed in a number of locations in WA, the rules are complicated and general sentiments are increasingly opposed to recreational gill netting.

You don't need to worry about ciguatera poisoning in Western Australia. This means that locals rightly not only value chinaman fish for their strong fight, they also value their excellent eating qualities. There have been two recorded cases of ciguatera in Western Australia (one probably a flashback from an initial infection picked up in Queensland) so within the bounds of the reasonable you can safely eat large reef fish in this State.

But don't get too cocky that all the WA fish are 'safe'. The northwest blowfish, which in addition to containing the same toxins as the related toad or puffer fish, can grow to around 5 kg and easily munch through an indiscrete finger placed too close to the fused teeth.

Finally, Western Australians are fiercely proud of their State and their fishing. The fisheries are generally well managed and the recreational and commercial fishers get along pretty well, all things considered.

This does mean that there are a few individuals who don't really want you to find out how great it is in case you want to come here and live, increasing the competition for the great fishing at their 'special' place. Overall, you will find Western Australians friendly and helpful and the local tackle stores talk the same language as that spoken around the country.

A word of warning for visitors, however. If the Eagles or Dockers, or the Glory or the Wildcats have lost, pointing out their failings will not generally endear you to proud locals. And if you have strong opinions on why there shouldn't be more Western Australians in the Test cricket team, hold onto them until you get to the border unless you really know your company well.

This is great big State with fishing quality to match its size. Please take only what you need so that your kids will be able to enjoy the same fishing quality. Good fishing.

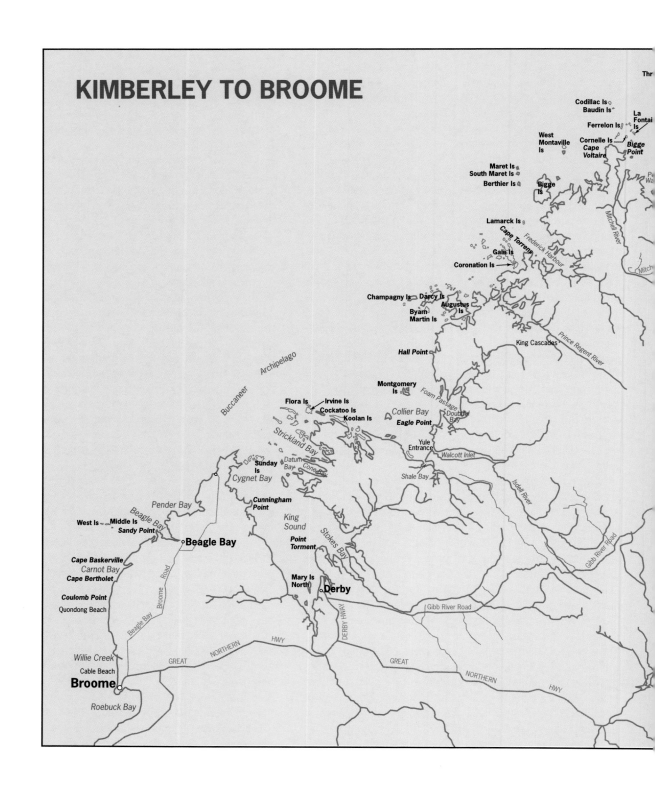

CHAPTER 1
KIMBERLEY TO BROOME

REMOTE KIMBERLEY FISHING

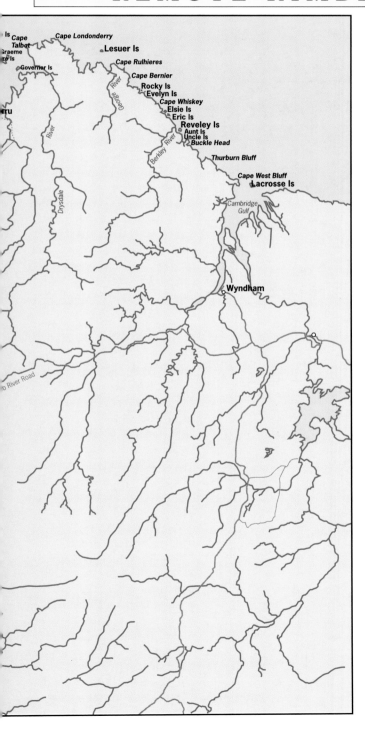

Remoteness, ruggedness and real wild beauty are hallmarks of the Kimberley and these features have protected the Kimberley from overfishing and development. Many anglers get their first taste of Western Australia in the tropical Kimberley.

From a base in either Kununurra, Broome, Derby or Fitzroy Crossing, anglers can access the many rivers and bays of this fish-rich area but they will need to be totally self-sufficient. The distances that have to be travelled, often down extremely testing tracks followed by a lengthy trip by boat, ensure that all supplies must be carried in, including fuel and water.

There is world-class fishing on offer all through this area, especially for the mighty barramundi in the many creeks and rivers. Indeed, many travellers on a round Australia trip catch their first barramundi in Western Australia. Combine this with the fantastic scenery and you can see why the Kimberley is becoming increasingly popular.

From a travelling angler's perspective, hiring a guide will cut many corners and takes much of the worry and planning out of a visit. Local knowledge and expertise, including in the provision of quality tackle and the right lures, is well worth the cost for your first exploration. The guides are colourful, well known and provide a quality service. Anyone asking for 'Hairy Dog' or 'Macca' in Kununurra or 'Bluey' Vaughan in Broome will soon be able to make the right contact. Don't worry too much about the cost, many people make subsequent trips to the Kimberley to experience the fantastic adventures.

If you are attempting a Kimberley fishing safari without local guided help it would pay to do your homework well in advance, and learn about the local weather, tides and navigational hazards you could face. Other issues to research include the requirements of local aboriginal communities if you are fishing in their areas and the basic ways to avoid too close an encounter with a saltwater crocodile.

The remoteness of this area means that getting help could be days away. It is important to advise people of your movements so take along adequate two-way radio or satellite communication equipment to keep in touch. You should have a good knowledge of first aid and carry a well-equipped first aid kit. After visiting, you will have no difficulty in making a decent contribution to the Royal Flying Doctor Service that does such a good job in these remote areas.

A Kimberley trip at the right time of year will be something that will remain a part of your best fishing memories for a lifetime. It is a place that any keen angler should visit at least once to experience the wild and remote side of Western Australia.

UPPER ORD RIVER

The Ord River is the jewel in the crown of the east Kimberleys. The Ord is now a regulated river with the construction of the massive Lake Argyle and downstream, the smaller Lake Kununurra. Lake Argyle is most famous for its huge catfish, sold as silver cobbler throughout Australia. While not regarded as a sportfish, these fish can grow to nearly 15 kg and put up a good fight. There is a good quality fishery for sooty grunter upstream of the dam for hikers.

Lake Kununurra also has catfish and sooty grunter, and represents one of the best opportunities for barramundi stocking anywhere in Australia. Lake Kununurra is right on the edge of Kununurra township and boasts a good caravan park and numerous eco-tour adventures to look at the wildlife and freshwater crocodiles. The township offers a wide range of amenities so you can base yourself there when accessing the upper and lower Ord River. Kununurra is also home to the Argyle diamonds, and the first part of Western Australia's mineral trilogy of diamonds, pearls and gold. Two of these three are sourced primarily from the Kimberley and many tourists make a diamond or pearl purchase on their holiday.

LOWER ORD RIVER

It is the lower Ord River that is most highly regarded. The terrific fishing starts from the rock bar immediately downstream of the Lake Kununurra dam wall. The area can be unsafe when discharge velocities are changed and care must be taken when fishing immediately downstream of the wall, but there are always a few barramundi to be found, even if most may not be larger than the 55 cm minimum size.

There is a good boat ramp just downstream from the wall, but never clean fish in the vicinity as the area downstream of the wall is saltwater crocodile habitat and they have been sighted at this boat ramp. There is very good fishing with surface lures, diving lures, bait and fly in this area for barramundi, sooty grunter, archer fish, oxeye herring and the under-rated catfish. Fishing is particularly good where the irrigation canals designated D1, D2, D3 and D4 enter the Ord on the northern bank and at the junction of the Ord and the Dunham rivers.

One of the most famous fishing spots is at Ivanhoe Crossing, which is signposted only a short way from town. Some very large barramundi have been taken from this crossing, but wading is strongly discouraged as large crocodiles have been regularly sighted both upstream and downstream of the crossing.

Until recently, access to the lower Ord was limited to a few guides (due to a quarantine restriction for Noogurra burr) but this has now been lifted. A good quality dirt road, Parry Creek Road, follows the river on the southern bank and gives reasonable access to the water by foot and better access for car topper boats. Commercial fishing for barramundi is also now prohibited upstream of Adolphus Island.

The lower Ord River system has a west and an east arm. The west arm of the Ord can be accessed from Wyndham, which provides the travelling angler with supplies, services and accommodation. The west arm also includes the Pentecost River that provides good barra fishing.

Even in the middle reaches of the Ord, a tidal bore of 30–60 cm can be experienced. While 'surfing the bore' is an exciting once-a-day experience in the

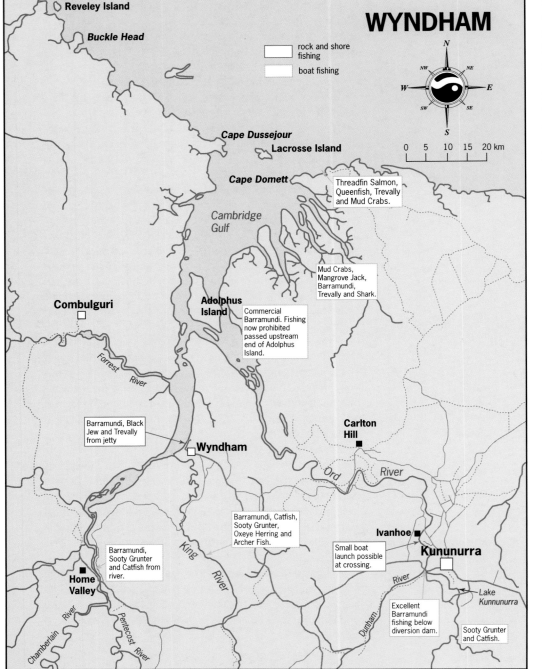

FISH FACTS

BARRAMUNDI

Without doubt the barramundi is the most popular fish amongst many anglers visiting the Pilbara and Kimberley regions of Western Australia. These fish live in the inshore waters and estuaries of northern Australia and are easily targeted with lure, fly or bait.

These fish are well equipped to hunt and ambush small baitfish and prawns that frequent the shallows, especially around rocks and mangroves. Their large mouths and powerful paddle-shaped tails enable them to surge forward and suck in their prey with surprising speed and accuracy, even in murky water.

Most anglers chasing barramundi do so from small boats or dinghies that are able to negotiate the shallow creeks and estuaries where barramundi are found. Tackle is usually a short but tough baitcasting outfit fitted with 4–6 kg monofilament or gelspun line. This is used to cast minnow lures or rubbertail jigs into likely looking ambush points. Another popular method is to drop a live mullet or other small fish into the deeper holes or near rockbars in the larger rivers. Once hooked, a barramundi will usually jump several times and follow this with short but powerful runs back into any cover that is available. Often anglers have to use all of their skill to keep the fish from busting the line around mangrove roots and sharp rocks, and a skilled skipper driving the boat can help keep the fish out of cover.

A large landing net is an advantage once these fish are brought close to the boat, as they have very sharp gill covers and spiky fins that makes grabbing them very hazardous. A landing net allows easy capture of most fish so that the hooks can be removed and the fish put in an Esky or released back into the water.

As bag and size limits are often altered—due to research and fishing pressure on barramundi stocks—check with the Fisheries Department (website: www.fish.wa.gov.au/rec/ or telephone 08 9482 7333) before venturing out after these fish. Eating qualities vary greatly depending on where the fish have been caught, but as a general rule barramundi are considered a fine eating species.

Big tides in the Kimberley cause the water to flow at more than 10 knots near this small rock island.

and then the Carlton Hill Station Road just after you cross the D4 drain to the north of Kununurra. The Cape Domett track takes you to the Cape while the Cave Springs Road gives access to the Keep River that flows into the Northern Territory. Just before Carlton Hill Station is a track which takes you to Skull Rock and some fine barramundi fishing on the Ord River itself.

Cape Domett is where the locals go to fish for threadfin salmon, trevally, queenfish, mangrove jacks and mud crabs. The local leaseholder maintains the area and charges a small fee for camping. To the east of Cape Domett, near Westwood Creek, you can gain access to the top part of the Gulf if you have a boat that can be beach-launched; otherwise the only public ramp is situated in Wyndham.

There is good fishing from the jetty in Wyndham, with some good barramundi coming from here when fish are moving down stream. The water is dirty here and live bait takes the most fish.

Offshore anglers fish small reef systems for the extremely hard-fighting black jewfish, a relative of the southern mulloway, or golden snapper. Both these species are highly prized table and sportfish.

EL QUESTRO

East of Kununurra off the Gibb River Road is El Questro station on the Pentecost River. El Questro provides accommodation ranging from basic camping sites through to special hideaways for stressed out international stars. The fishing is generally arranged through the accommodation venue and reasonable quality barramundi fishing is provided.

KALUMBURU

Access to the coast beyond Cambridge Gulf is now purely by boat or air all the way through to Kalumburu, and anglers must to be self-sufficient to explore and fish the area. The remoteness and possibility of big barramundi attract many keen anglers each year.

Kalumburu is an aboriginal settlement located 265 km north of the Gibb River Road along a 4WD access road. There is dry-season access for 4WD vehicles to Napier Broome Bay, but this trek often proves to be too demanding on vehicles and passengers to be worth the effort. For the Kimberley, dry-season access refers to access during the middle or late dry season, with early-season access only for those with special skills at

river, the tidal fluctuations can still be extremely large and barra fishing luck can change dramatically as the tide changes. While lure fishing is very successful and the favoured method for barramundi, the water is quite turbid.

CAMBRIDGE GULF/WYNDHAM

The mouth of the Ord is located at the base of Cambridge Gulf, a wide expanse of water that also produces some excellent fishing at the right time of year. Big barramundi are at their best in the build up to the wet season from September onwards.

Cape Domett can be accessed from the Weaber Plain Road

Fishing off the oyster encrusted rocks at Hunter Creek, Cape Leveque.

FISH FACTS

MANGROVE JACK

Mangrove jack are often found in the same locations and caught with the same tackle as barramundi, but they are more of a handful for their size around mangrove roots and rocks. 'Jacks', as they are commonly known, are a predatory species that can be found in good numbers from the Murchison River in Western Australia around the northern part of Australia and down as far as northern New South Wales on the east coast.

Mangrove jacks are very aggressive for their size, and will attack quite large minnow lures intended for bigger barramundi, however they are better targeted with smaller lures or saltwater flies. Bait fishing with strip baits or dead whole small mullet can be employed, but a hungry jack rarely refuses a live bait. Most anglers target these fish from boats that are negotiated up mangrove creeks and use a medium baitcaster loaded with 6 kg line to coax a hooked jack from the snags.

Most of the fish found in estuaries rarely exceed the 1.5 kg, and if they are bigger they are almost impossible to land amongst the mangrove roots. Bigger jacks are often caught on baits fished on the deeper reefs found offshore in many northern locations, and these fish can reach weights upwards of 6 kilograms. These large mangrove jacks can be very old, with the largest being aged up to 50 years old.

Mangrove jacks have a firm and pleasant tasting flesh that also makes them popular amongst anglers.

repeatedly extracting vehicles from seemingly impossible situations with little prospect of help.

An access fee applies and camping is available at Honeymoon Bay, Pago Mission and McGowans Beach. Pago Mission is for self-contained campers only. Fishing is good for a range of species in the ocean or in the King Edward or Drysdale rivers, with mud crabs being a particular attraction.

Best access to the areas either side of Kalumburu is via helicopter, mainly from Kununurra to many of the more remote areas. The cost is offset by the difficult driving that is avoided and the spectacular scenery and photographs that can be taken in the area.

ADMIRALTY GULF

Admiralty Gulf can be reached by 4WD along the Port Warrender Road, where anglers can launch a dinghy from the beach at Walsh Point or Crystal Head. Fishing in the Gulf or from the Lawley or Mitchell rivers is very productive for a wide range of species including the mighty barramundi, mangrove jacks and mud crabs. Mackerel, queenfish, trevally and golden snapper are often caught in the Gulf, but anglers must be extremely careful as the waters are home to numerous sharks and crocodiles and are subject to massive tides. There are no supplies available at Port Warrender but the Drysdale River Homestead does sell fuel.

From Admiralty Gulf all the way to Derby there is no access for landbased fishing. Visiting anglers must rely on boats large enough to cover long distances without having to rely on supplies of food, fuel and water.

Chartering a big mother ship that is capable of such a journey is one option as it can then provide access to remote bays, creeks and rivers via smaller dinghies. Broome is the main base for the larger charter boats. The cost might put off many anglers for such a venture, but the chance to fish some of the most wild and remote areas of the world in the Kimberley more than justifies that expense for others.

DERBY

Although shore fishing is limited at Derby, fishing from the town jetty for threadfin salmon, bream and mud crabs can be fun. The nearby creeks are a better option if you have a dinghy, as barramundi, mangrove jacks, threadfin salmon, fingermark

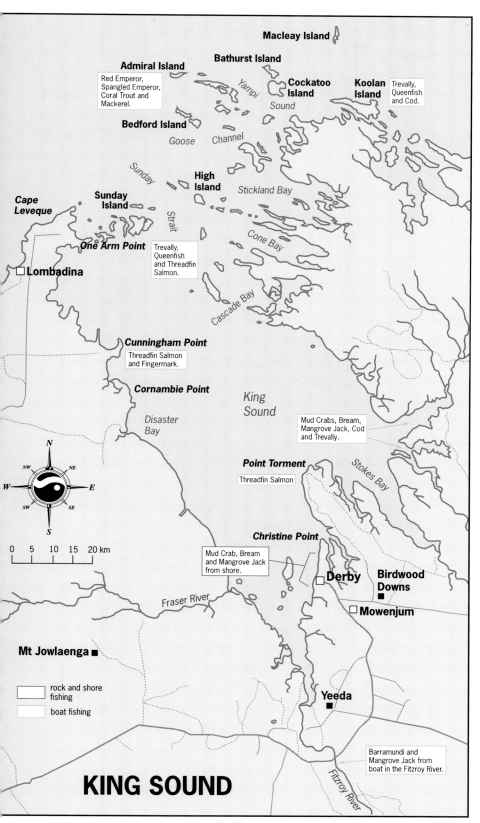

Red Emperor, Spangled Emperor, Coral Trout and Mackerel.

Trevally, Queenfish and Cod.

Trevally, Queenfish and Threadfin Salmon.

Threadfin Salmon and Fingermark.

Mud Crabs, Bream, Mangrove Jack, Cod and Trevally.

Threadfin Salmon

Mud Crab, Bream and Mangrove Jack from shore.

rock and shore fishing

boat fishing

Barramundi and Mangrove Jack from boat in the Fitzroy River.

KING SOUND

KING SOUND

Boat anglers fishing King Sound can explore several small islands, rivers and creeks along the coast to the north and west of Derby. Fraser River, Doctor's Creek and Alligator Creek are good places to fish for threadfin salmon, mangrove jack, barramundi or mud crabs. Fishing with heavy lines baited with a small live fish around any rock bars and shoals out in the Sound can result in black jewfish and golden snapper or estuary cod. Many anglers choose to target barramundi or threadfin salmon on spin tackle by casting minnow lures around the rivers and creeks.

STOKES BAY

Lying to the north of Derby, Stokes Bay provides many angling opportunities for all of the common species found in the Kimberley. Access to the area known as the Blue Holes, where black jewfish and golden snapper are often targeted by boat anglers with live bait, is from the Point Torment track and ramp. On the eastern side, the Meda and Robinson rivers are popular spots for barramundi, threadfin salmon, mangrove jacks and mud crabs. To the south the May River offers similar fishing opportunities but can also be fished and accessed from the shore.

FITZROY RIVER

Southwest of Derby, the mighty Fitzroy River enters King Sound. This river is well known for barramundi. Boat access is from Derby where good numbers of barramundi can be caught usually after the wet season. The tidal pools along the Fitzroy provide some great barramundi fishing and can be accessed by tracks leading off Yeeda Station roads. There is good camping at Yeeda Station, but fees will apply. Shore-based anglers can fish spots like 'Telegraph Pool' where a live bait is fished into the deep water for very big barramundi that will be waiting for the next high tide. After the Ord, the Fitzroy is the premier barramundi-fishing river and well worth a visit. Note that an 80 cm maximum size limit applies in the Fitzroy but commercial fishing is banned in the river.

bream and mud crabs are all about in good numbers. It can be a good run to get to blue water, but even just offshore, pelagic species like mackerel and tuna can be caught. Anglers should take care when using the two ramps in town as they are not in very good condition and can make launching a boat a major exercise.

Derby is a great place to launch a fishing trip into the Kimberley, despite the rough boat ramps, as all other supplies are available.

CAPE LEVEQUE

Northwest of Derby, the tip of Cape Leveque is a good place to stay and enjoy the local fishing possibilities. There are camping facilities, some chalets and a small store set up for tourists. The local Bardi Aboriginal community owns the whole establishment. Small boats can access the nearby reefs for good fishing for a variety of species or 4WD trip can be made to Hunter Creek for a spot of mud crabbing.

ONE ARM POINT

One Arm Point is a good place to fish from a small boat for pelagic and reef species. There are no camping facilities here and it is important to understand the tide movements to avoid getting stuck. It is a long time between tides and you may well be stranded on your boat. Beach launching at Kooljamin allows access to the Sunday Island Group where Spanish mackerel, trevally, queenfish, mangrove jacks, golden snapper and mud crabs can all be found.

MIDDLE LAGOON

The local Aboriginal community has provided facilities and accommodation for tourists who choose to visit this area. Beach-launching a small boat can be done on suitable tides to allow anglers the chance to fish the surrounding area. The offshore fishing is very good for trevally, queenfish, mackerel, bluebone, golden snapper and emperor. The small creeks contain good numbers of mangrove jacks and mud crabs and can be explored with a dinghy.

BROOME

Broome is a major holiday destination for people all around the world. Its history of pearling, combined with its very relaxed lifestyle, has made Broome a popular place for tourists. Broome caters for all budgets, with everything from a tent site to luxurious accommodation at the famous Cable Beach.

The fishing around Broome is also famous, especially for the sailfish that congregate in big numbers offshore. Most sails are caught and released after being tagged. The most popular method of hooking them is to troll a set pattern of rigged skipping garfish. These baits are usually set out at different distances from the stern of the boat, usually with the aid of outriggers. A teaser, designed to splash and flash through the water, is also a common item as it can really excite a curious sail

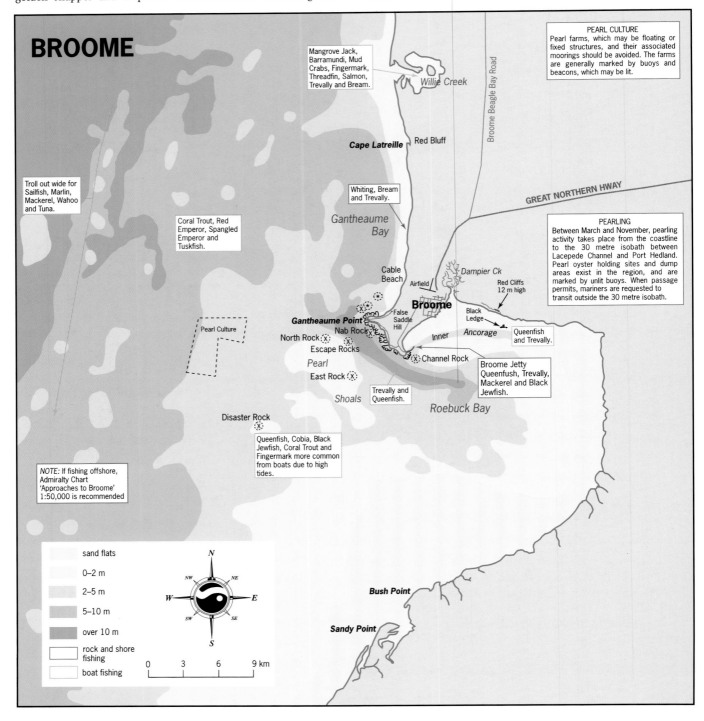

into attacking the skipping garfish baits. Once hooked, a sailfish will astound the angler with fast runs and spectacular leaps as it attempts to dislodge the hooks.

Broome's sailfish are not large, with a 25 kg fish being about standard, but their size is made up for in numbers. It is not unusual to have pods of fish move in and attack the baits all at once, resulting in multiple hookups and real chaos on the deck.

Saltwater fly anglers also have a ball targeting Broome's sailfish, luring the fish to the boat with teasers, and many anglers have boated their first billfish on fly at the sailfish grounds.

Fishing for other species around Broome is also very rewarding with barramundi, threadfin salmon, bluebone (tuskfish), trevally, queenfish, black jewfish, tuna and mud crabs being available at certain times of the year.

BROOME JETTY

Shore fishing around Broome is very limited because of the massive tides, so the local jetty has become a favourite as anglers can access the deeper water without using a boat. Many anglers use heavy hand lines from the jetty to catch black jewfish (northern mulloway), trevally and queenfish. Baits of fish or live baits will tempt these predators but once they are hooked it is a full-on battle to keep the fish away from the barnacle-encrusted pylons. Lures cast from the jetty can attract the attention of trevally, queenfish, longtail tuna and mackerel.

At night the jetty is a good place to try for bigger fish like the black jewfish, and during the warmer months it pays to fish a live bait around the end of the jetty for barramundi that take advantage of the baitfish attracted to the jetty lights.

ROEBUCK BAY

There are two ramps at Entrance Point that give boat anglers easy access to Roebuck Bay and its excellent fishing options. The main attraction is the deep canyon that is only a couple of hundred metres out from the ramps and shows depths of up to 98 m on the charts. Bottom fishing for black jewfish and using heavy lines is a very popular activity, and the famous jewfish hole that is directly out from the old ramp has produced many memorable captures of these big fish.

Other reef species also turn up in the deep water of Roebuck Bay, but the big golden snapper are high on the list of preferred targets when bottom fishing. Many use heavy hand lines rigged with a large sinker and several dropper hooks baited with either dead or live bait; others choose to use stout boat rods loaded up with gelspun line that resists stretch and water drag. Big cod and other reef fish can also test even the strongest tackle.

Retrieving boats off the beach at Cape Leveque. Watch for the huge tide variations. six hours earlier, the watermark was at the sand dunes in the background.

FISH FACTS

QUEENFISH

In the shallow coastal waters from Carnarvon northwards the queenfish is regarded by many as the ultimate sport fish. Once hooked, these fish leap high out of the water and tear off on blistering runs, and on light spin or fly tackle they will keep you entertained for the length of the fight.

Often known as 'queenies', these fish have a slim profile, large mouths and forward facing eyes that enable them to ambush baitfish efficiently. Most anglers target these fish in shallow water, and having queenfish chasing bait practically right up onto a beach is a common sight in many northern locations. Queenies respond to most lures and saltwater flies, but a surface popper skipped across the top of the water is one way to drive these fish wild. If fishing from shore, anglers should concentrate around any baitfish schools or at the mouth of creeks, especially on the rising tide when these fish move in close to shore to hunt.

From a boat you can often find queenfish hunting along drop-offs or current lines just offshore. They can also be seen when hitting baitfish, often leaping clean out of the water. Bait fishing with a live baitfish around a bait school will also attract the attention of any queenfish shadowing the school. Queenies will also take dead baits of whole pilchards at times but they respond better to live baits or lures moving quickly through the water.

Most anglers choose to enjoy the fight of a queenfish and then carefully release it once the hooks have been removed. Although they are not bad eating, the flesh is very plain and dry, and usually where they are caught there are better eating fish to take home for dinner.

Mackerel tuna schools accompanied by large numbers of terns and gulls, can often be seen breaking the surface. These little speedsters can be approached slowly and cast to with light spin tackle and small metal lures or saltwater fly gear. Other pelagic species like Spanish mackerel, cobia and longtail tuna are also taken on trolled baits and lures.

GANTHEAUME POINT

Close to the jetty, this rocky headland is a popular spot to fish for longtail tuna and mackerel that pass close to shore. Most anglers choose to cast lures or baits from the rocks to attract fish feeding in the tide. It is best fished at the top of the tide or the run out when there is sufficient water to bring the predatory species in close to the rocks. Trevally and queenfish add variety.

DAMPIER, WILLIE & CRAB CREEKS

Dampier, Willie and Crab creeks are good places to try for barramundi during the build up to the wet season, and big threadfin salmon can be found during the dry season, especially

FISH FACTS

THREADFIN SALMON

Several species of threadfin salmon are commonly targeted along the northern coast, and some of the bigger species are heavily targeted. Threadfin inhabit the shallow tidal mud flats and mangrove creeks where they hunt for small fish and prawns, usually on the incoming tide. Along the 80 Mile Beach anglers mainly chase these fish, and baits of whole pilchards fished in the muddy water can be very effective in catching a feed.

In the mangrove creeks the giant threadfin salmon can be targeted with live baits, lures and saltwater flies, and on light tackle they put up a fantastic fight made up of lightning fast runs across the shallow mud flats. These fish are highly prized amongst many anglers who rate them right up there with barramundi; in fact many believe that they are better eating than barramundi.

near the mouths of these creeks. There can also be good fishing for mangrove jack, small queenfish and estuary cod.

The dry season is a good time to chase a few mud crabs that will be about. A challenge for those who don't mind getting dirty is to find the mud crab holes at low tide and use a blunt shepherd's crook to pull out the tasty crustaceans.

Big bluebone (tuskfish) are often found on the rising tide around the mouths of the creeks and are best fished for by using small crabs for bait. By launching from the ramps at Entrance Point, anglers can travel the short distance around Roebuck Bay to the creeks.

CABLE BEACH

Most of the fishing for trevally, queenfish and threadfin salmon is done out from the beach by boat. Fishing from the beach on a rising or high tide is your best chance, especially for the highly prized threadfin salmon during the dry season. Beach launching with a 4WD vehicle is very popular and gives access to the better fishing reefs offshore.

GANTHEAUME BAY

By launching from the ramps at Entrance Point or across the sand at Cable Beach, boats can explore the waters of Gantheaume Bay. Unlike Roebuck Bay, its water depths are reasonably shallow but still produces some excellent fishing at various times of the year. Close to Gantheaume Point there are several small rocks that produce good fishing for mackerel, trevally and queenfish, whilst further out in the deeper water the reef species will respond to baits fished on the bottom.

RIGHT: Many fish are found on the reefs off Broome including this large chinaman fish which is safe to eat from Western Australian waters.

Casting lures around the wash.

ROWLEY SHOALS

These three coral atolls are one of the last frontiers of fishing and have become favourite locations for anglers. Rowley Shoals can be reached by travelling 165 nautical miles to the west of Broome. Most anglers choose to charter a large vessel from Broome for around a week to visit the Shoals, and usually in the cooler dry months from July to October.

Rowley Shoals provide fantastic fishing for gamefish or reef species. Trolling produces billfish, mackerel, wahoo and tuna with no telling what will take the lures or baits next. The sheltered waters inside the coral atolls are ideal for light line enthusiasts with large cod, emperors and even hump-headed Maori wrasse that are rare elsewhere and totally protected in Western Australia.

This can be a once-in-a-lifetime trip for even the most discerning angler.

BOAT RAMPS & TACKLE STORES

Most anglers fishing the northwest do so from a boat, whether it is a fully decked out game boat or a small dinghy carried on a trailer or car roof rack. Trailer boats are common and can be launched either from public ramps or from numerous beaches and creeks that provide 4WD access to the water.

The biggest problem with launching in this area is the huge tidal range that often prevents launching or retrieving of trailer boats on low tide. Getting stranded on a mud bank in a crocodile-infested creek happens to many anglers each year, so take the time to fully understand the water movements before setting out.

Most of the public ramps are single lane, built out of concrete with multi-level catwalks in some locations to cater for tide variations. Each year the wet season can make boating in this area hazardous with approaching storms and cyclones. It would be wise to plan a trip fishing this area during the middle of the year when conditions are better and the humidity is low.

RAMPS

Broome – Two ramps at Entrance Point Cape Keraudren
Derby – Town and Port
Wyndham – Town

TACKLE STORES

Northwest Tackle and Sport
Dampier Terrace,
Broome WA 6725
Tel: (08) 9192 1669

Workline Dive & Tackle
Short Street, China Town,
Broome WA 6725
Tel: (08) 9192 2233

C H A P T E R   2

EIGHTY MILE BEACH TO DAMPIER

EIGHTY MILE BEACH

Stretching from Cape Keraudren in the south to Broome, the Eighty Mile Beach is well known around the country. The seemingly endless beach is a well-known threadfin salmon haunt, and these fish can be caught in good numbers on the high tide in the dry season. Locate the deeper gutters along the beach at low tide to find the best spots to fish for threadfin. As the water comes in over the sand flats it is always discoloured, making lure fishing almost impossible. Instead most anglers choose to fish with pilchard baits for good results. There are numerous small sharks that come in with the tide, so a wire trace is recommended.

By using smaller hooks and the flesh of a small cockle or hermit crab you can catch a feed of delectable fresh whiting. On the low tide it is possible to walk nearly a kilometre out on the sand flats where you can inspect the many different species of shells and other creatures that have been stranded by the receding tide.

Some of the shallow estuaries of the region produce mixed bags of threadfin salmon, mangrove jacks, pikey bream, mud crabs and the occasional barramundi. Boating access is restricted to beach-launching a small dinghy, but caution in needed to prevent getting bogged or stuck by the tide. Offshore there is good reef fishing for bluebone, red emperor, coral trout and blue lined emperor. Gamefish, like Spanish mackerel, queenfish, tuna, cobia, trevally and sailfish, can be caught by trolling lures or baits behind the boat. Care is needed when fishing from small boats, as the winds in this area can blow for weeks on end, making small boats practically useless.

Access points leading to Barn Hill, Cape Villaret and Eco Beach are close to Broome and are along reasonable roads. Basic accommodation is available at Barn Hill. Further south, anglers wishing to reach Lagrange Bay can follow the track from Port Smith south to this productive fishing area. Access can also be reached through the 80 Mile Beach Caravan Park that is to the west of the Sandfire Roadhouse, but all other tracks leading through the pastoral leases in the area are closed to the public and permission should be obtained before entering.

CAPE KERAUDREN

Boat anglers take advantage of the good launching facilities here to fish for most of the common sport and bottom fish found in the northwest. The estuary system to the south of the ramp is a great place to target barramundi, golden snapper, trevally, threadfin and mud crabs.

DE GREY RIVER

Fishing at the De Grey River mouth with lures is a good place to

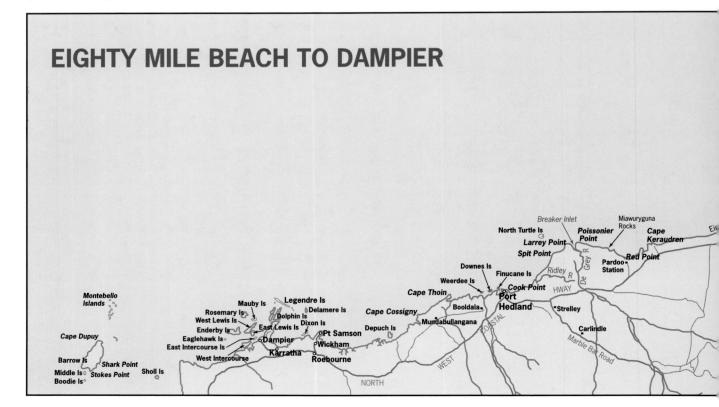

EIGHTY MILE BEACH TO DAMPIER

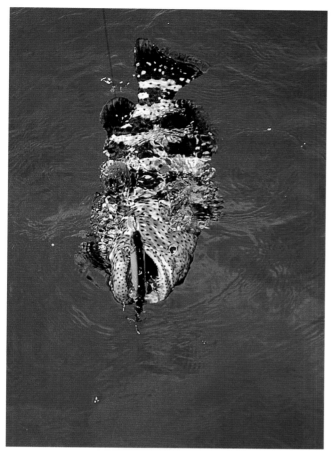

Estuary cod are a common capture on both lures and baits in the northwest.

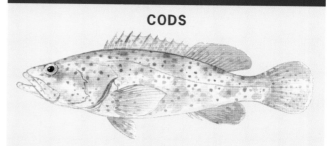

FISH FACTS

CODS

Along much of the northern coastline several species of cods frequent everything from shallow inshore waters and mangrove creeks to deeper offshore reefs. These fish are usually caught when fishing for other species and are often kept for the dinner table as they are regarded as good eating species. The larger cods often found on the deeper reefs should be released back into the water, as they are the prime breeders that are becoming increasingly scarce in many locations. It is illegal to keep any cod over 1200 mm long in Western Australia for this reason. Thankfully many anglers return fish under this size as well.

Some species like the Queensland Groper and the totally protected Potato Cod can grow to a massive size reaching several hundred kilograms in weight, and in some locations they have a bad reputation for stealing fish from anglers' lines.

Cods are easily caught on bait, lure or fly. Their large mouths and massive appetites mean that they are not too fussy about what they eat; in fact if it is alive and can fit in their mouth they will usually have a go at eating it.

In the southern regions below Geraldton two smaller species are often encountered—the breaksea cod and the harlequin fish. These are often caught whilst drifting with baits over offshore reefs and are usually kept for the table.

start, as trevally, queenfish, threadfin salmon and barramundi can be taken. Barramundi fishing can be surprisingly good and is improving as the use of recreational gill nets and commercial fishing is greatly reduced. Upstream are cod, catfish, barramundi and mangrove jacks. Reaching the river often means a boat trip from either Port Hedland or the Condon Landing, which can be reached after a rough 4WD trip. Access through the station is rarely given so anglers choosing to fish this fantastic river must be prepared to travel by boat to reach the mouth.

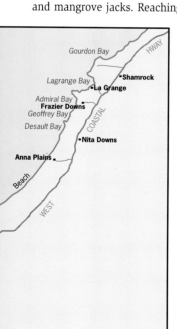

CREEKS

The numerous creeks along the coast, from the De Grey River to Finucane Island, are great places to fish with a small boat. Barramundi, threadfin salmon, queenfish, trevally, mangrove jacks, catfish, cod and bream catches are all made by fishing small lures or flies on light tackle on the incoming tide. Live bait taken in a throw net can also take good fish.

Most of these creeks are crawling with mud crabs that can be caught at low tide in the mud or picked up in drop nets from a boat.

Each dry season is a favourite time to chase threadfin salmon that run during winter. Lures, or baits like pilchards, can be cast around the creek mouths, especially in dirty water moving with the tide. Using live baits is also a good way of hooking a few salmon, and other fish like mangrove jacks and barramundi will also have a go at such offerings.

Mud crabs are a popular species that are eagerly sought by many anglers venturing into the mangroves.

PORT HEDLAND

Just under 1700 km north of Perth, the town of Port Hedland is in the heart of iron ore country and provides all modern conveniences, accommodation and some fantastic fishing opportunities. Either in town or from Finucane Island there are good launching ramps that provide boat owners with the opportunity to fish the offshore grounds or venture down into the creeks and river systems along the coast. Six metre tides should be taken into consideration when boating, especially when venturing up rivers and creeks as it is possible for the inexperienced to get-stranded without enough water to move larger boats.

PORT HEDLAND HARBOUR

Over summer, black jewfish move into the harbour and a famous spot to hook them is from the jetty. Responding well to live baits, these fish will bust you off around the pylons and it will be a lock-up battle to stop them. Boat anglers out in the harbour often catch Spanish mackerel, longtail tuna, queenfish, cobia and trevally. Local and visiting anglers eagerly seek threadfin salmon each winter, particularly at the local hot spot 'Spoil Bank' near the jetty. Trolling lures along the wharf is one way of finding out if any tackle-busting trevally are at home. Alternatively, you can fish with live baits or jigs along the pylons. Once the fish is

hooked it is important to try and pull it away from the structure, or it will break off.

SHIPPING CHANNEL AND BEACONS

The deep channel dredged to allow large iron ore tankers easy access to the harbour has become a real asset to anglers targeting a wide range of species. The channel extends some 30 km out to sea and is marked along the way with navigation beacons. These beacons are ideal fish-holding structures and produce big trevally, mackerel, cobia and queenfish. The most popular method is to cast sinking lures like jigs around the beacons and allow them to sink before briskly retrieving them to the surface, which is usually enough to draw a strike.

Trolling lures also produces the above species as well as doggy mackerel, broad barred Spanish mackerel, tuna and barracuda, whilst bottom fishing with baits can be productive for other species including black jewfish.

A few minutes with a bait jig near any of these markers will pick up enough live bait for a good day's fishing.

SPOIL BANK

The Spoil Bank is a good spot to fish for threadfin and mackerel by casting baits or lures from the shore. Access is via a vehicle

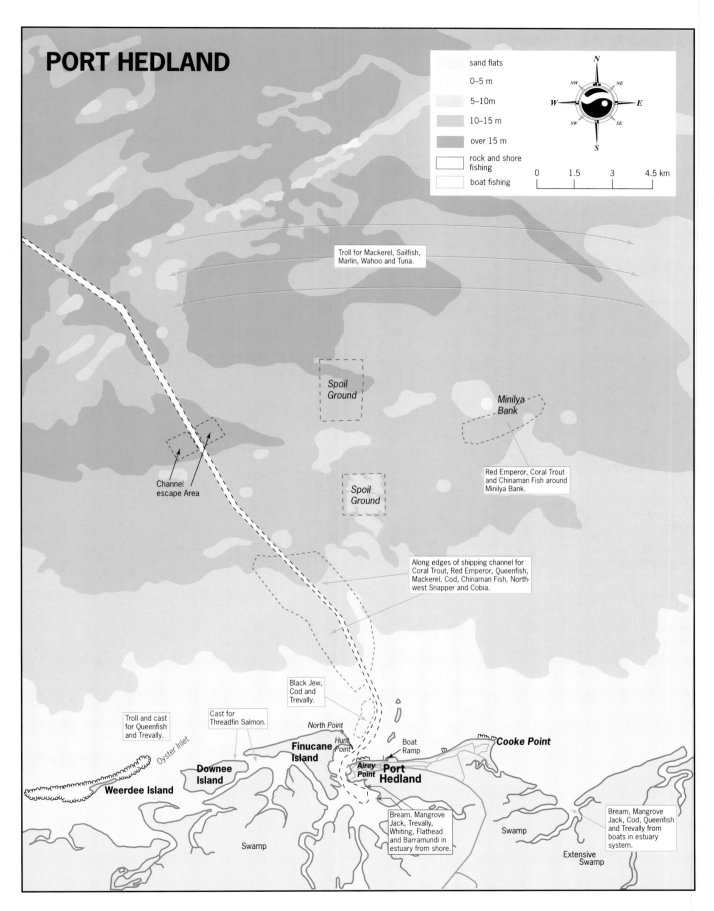

PORT HEDLAND

sand flats
0–5 m
5–10m
10–15 m
over 15 m
rock and shore fishing
boat fishing

0   1.5   3   4.5 km

Troll for Mackerel, Sailfish, Marlin, Wahoo and Tuna.

Spoil Ground

Minilya Bank

Red Emperor, Coral Trout and Chinaman Fish around Minilya Bank.

Channel escape Area

Spoil Ground

Along edges of shipping channel for Coral Trout, Red Emperor, Queenfish, Mackerel, Cod, Chinaman Fish, Northwest Snapper and Cobia.

Black Jew, Cod and Trevally.

Troll and cast for Queenfish and Trevally.

Cast for Threadfin Salmon.

Oyster Inlet

North Point

Finucane Island

Hunt Point

Boat Ramp

Cooke Point

Downee Island

Airey Point

Port Hedland

Weerdee Island

Bream. Mangrove Jack, Trevally, Whiting, Flathead and Barramundi in estuary from shore.

Swamp

Swamp

Bream, Mangrove Jack, Cod, Queenfish and Trevally from boats in estuary system.

Extensive Swamp

track. If you want to reach the end, use a four-wheel drive vehicle. The best time to fish the bank is during the cooler months when the threadfin salmon are running, but it fishes well for bream, small trevally and javelin fish near the top of the tide.

CEMETERY BEACH

A popular and close fishing spot for anglers in Port Hedland, this beach is a good place to target threadfin salmon when they run in winter. Bait fishing with whole pilchards as the tide is rising is the way to tempt these fish.

FISH FACTS

EMPEROR

Red Emperor

The sight of a big red emperor rising from the depths on the end of your line is one of the most exciting thrills an angler can experience. These fish can grow to a decent size and are usually found on the deeper offshore reefs from Shark Bay northwards.

Most anglers fish for them in depths of 40 m or more, usually over the reef and coral. The best method is to rig up with a heavy sinker on the bottom followed by a couple of dropper hooks baited with fish flesh or octopus. This is then dropped to the bottom where hopefully a big red emperor will be waiting.

These fish are regarded as prime table fare and as a result they are heavily targeted in many locations, but good numbers can still be found along much of the northern coast.

Spangled Emperor

What the pink snapper is to anglers in the south, the spangled emperor is to anglers in the north. From about Shark Bay northwards spangled emperor are heavily targeted by both boat and shore anglers.

These fish are usually found around reefy areas, and will take a wide variety of baits, especially squid, octopus or pilchards. They put up a very strong fight that is combined with short runs that will be in the direction of any reef. Often called 'North West snapper', the spangled emperor is a very common species in some areas like Ningaloo.

There is a closely related species called the blue lined emperor that is heavily targeted in Shark Bay where it is locally called the 'black snapper'. Another species 'the red throated emperor' is a common catch around the Ningaloo Reef. All of these emperors are excellent eating species and as a result most are kept for the table.

Shore anglers usually fish for spangled emperor with heavy surf rods and reels that have the grunt to pull these fish away from reefy areas. Out of boats the favourite method is to berley heavily and then drop baited lines to the bottom where the emperors are feeding. These fish will also cruise up from the depths following a berley trail almost to the back of the boat, and can be taken on baits drifted back down.

These fish will often move into shallow water after dark on a high tide, and can easily be hooked on baits. Lure and fly fishers also enjoy catching these fish in shallow water, and they will aggressively attack minnow lures, metal slices, poppers and saltwater flies cast around coral bomboras.

RIGHT: Mark Cottrell displays a serious barracuda.

DEPUCH ISLAND

Lying just to the north of the Sherlock River mouth is this big rocky island that is a popular boat-fishing spot for big mackerel, trevally, cobia and tuna. Other smaller islands in the area also produce some good fishing, whilst the nearby creeks are full of mud crabs, barramundi, threadfin, mangrove jacks and cod. Launching at Balla Balla Creek at high tide is the quickest way to reach the island that sits just out of the mouth of this creek; alternatively, the longer run from Cossack / Port Samson ramps can be chosen.

POINT SAMSON

The town of Point Samson provides accommodation, boat launching and some shore fishing from around the site of the old jetty or from the groynes at the new harbour constructed for the prawning fleet. Small-boat anglers launching at Point Samson have access to mackerel, big trevally, queenfish and longtail tuna.

The plateau due northwest of Delambre Island provides some first rate trolling for small marlin and sailfish in the blue water while the top of the plateau provides some jumbo Spanish mackerel, barracuda and tuna. Bottom fishing is also popular on the many reef patches for species such as chinaman fish (perfectly safe to eat in Western Australia), coral trout, red emperor, spangled emperor and cod, which are favoured for their table qualities.

There is a small causeway that crosses the road into Point Samson that can provide excellent fishing for mangrove jacks, trevally, long tom, queenfish and even barramundi for shore-based anglers. The small creeks are good places to chase mangrove jacks, small trevally, cod, catfish and mud crabs. Like

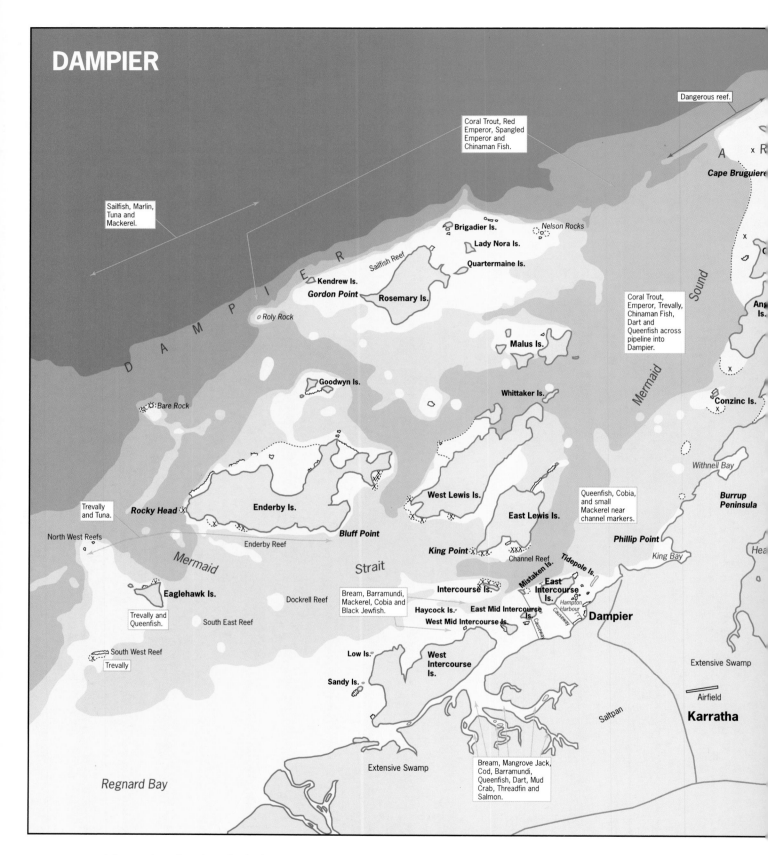

DAMPIER

Dangerous reef.

Coral Trout, Red Emperor, Spangled Emperor and Chinaman Fish.

Cape Bruguiere

Sailfish, Marlin, Tuna and Mackerel.

Brigadier Is.

Nelson Rocks

Lady Nora Is.

Quartermaine Is.

Sailfish Reef

Kendrew Is.

Gordon Point

Rosemary Is.

Roly Rock

Coral Trout, Emperor, Trevally, Chinaman Fish, Dart and Queenfish across pipeline into Dampier.

Malus Is.

Mermaid Sound

Ang Is.

Conzinc Is.

Goodwyn Is.

Bare Rock

Whittaker Is.

Withnell Bay

Burrup Peninsula

West Lewis Is.

East Lewis Is.

Queenfish, Cobia, and small Mackerel near channel markers.

Phillip Point

Trevally and Tuna.

Rocky Head

Enderby Is.

King Point

Bluff Point

Channel Reef

Tidepole Is.

King Bay

Hea

North West Reefs

Enderby Reef

Mistaken Is.

East Intercourse Is.

Mermaid

Strait

Intercourse Is.

Hampton Harbour

Dampier

Eaglehawk Is.

Dockrell Reef

Bream, Barramundi, Mackerel, Cobia and Black Jewfish.

Haycock Is.

East Mid Intercourse Is.

West Mid Intercourse Is.

Causeway

Trevally and Queenfish.

South East Reef

South West Reef

Low Is.

West Intercourse Is.

Extensive Swamp

Trevally

Sandy Is.

Airfield

Karratha

Saltpan

Extensive Swamp

Bream, Mangrove Jack, Cod, Barramundi, Queenfish, Dart, Mud Crab, Threadfin and Salmon.

Regnard Bay

most of the northern locations the high tide is usually the best time to fish the jetty and creeks, so it pays to plan ahead to prevent getting stuck launching or retrieving the boat, or finding there is not enough water to bring the fish in.

CAPE LAMBERT

Situated close to Port Samson is Cape Lambert where the long jetty is unfortunately off limits to anglers but in the past has produced some excellent catches of black jewfish, mackerel,

trevally and queenfish. All of these species are still available if the angler is prepared to make a short boat trip from Port Samson. The offshore reefs are good places to fish for coral trout, red emperor, trevally, cod, spangled emperor, mackerel and tuna.

SHERLOCK RIVER

This large river provides excellent fishing for queenfish, trevally, doggie and broad barred Spanish mackerel out at the mouth, and mangrove jacks, threadfin salmon, barramundi and catfish

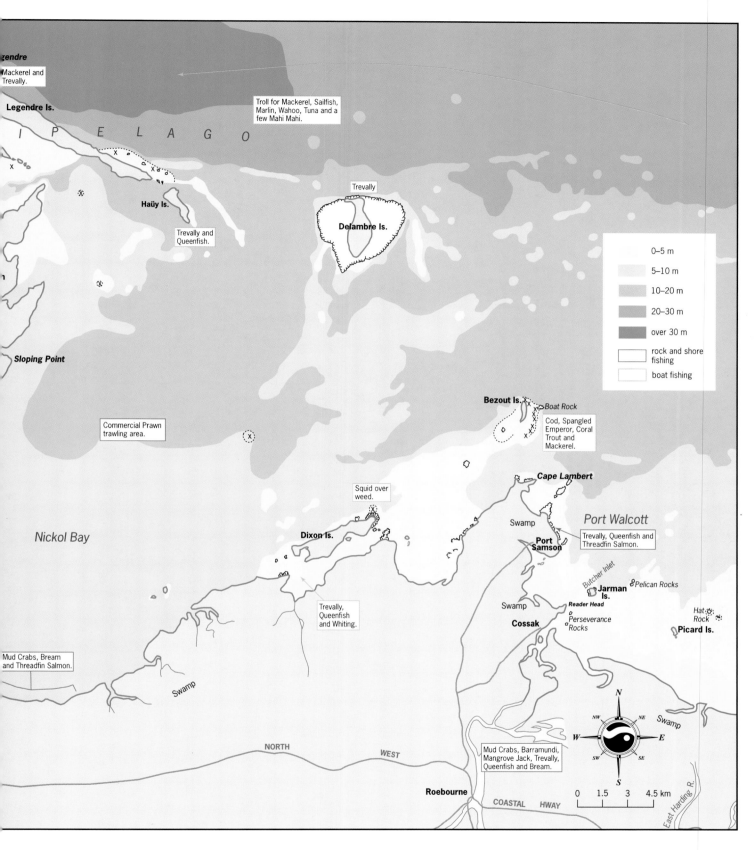

gendre

Mackerel and Trevally.

Legendre Is.

I P E L A G O

Troll for Mackerel, Sailfish, Marlin, Wahoo, Tuna and a few Mahi Mahi.

Haüy Is.

Trevally and Queenfish.

Trevally

Delambre Is.

	0–5 m
	5–10 m
	10–20 m
	20–30 m
	over 30 m
	rock and shore fishing
	boat fishing

Sloping Point

Commercial Prawn trawling area.

Bezout Is. Boat Rock

Cod, Spangled Emperor, Coral Trout and Mackerel.

Cape Lambert

Squid over weed.

Swamp

Port Walcott

Nickol Bay

Dixon Is.

Port Samson

Trevally, Queenfish and Threadfin Salmon.

Butcher Inlet

Jarman Is.   Pelican Rocks

Swamp

Reader Head

Perseverance Rocks

Trevally, Queenfish and Whiting.

Cossak

Hat Rock

Picard Is.

Mud Crabs, Bream and Threadfin Salmon.

Swamp

N

NW   NE

Swamp

W   E

SW   SE

S

NORTH   WEST

Mud Crabs, Barramundi, Mangrove Jack, Trevally, Queenfish and Bream.

Roebourne

COASTAL   HWY

0   1.5   3   4.5 km

East Harding R.

further upriver. Most boat anglers launch from Balla Balla Creek and follow the coast along until they reach the river.

COSSACK

Taking a small dinghy up the creeks between Cossack and Port Hedland gives you access to mangrove jacks, barramundi, tarpon, trevally, threadfin salmon and mud crabs. Light tackle and a few crab drop nets are all that is needed.

Quality reef species are available offshore to boat anglers with

Perseverance Rocks being a good close-in spot for trolling or bait fishing.

CLEAVERVILLE

This popular fishing area is reached by following the track from the main highway down to the coast where fishing can be done by small boat or from the shore. Trevally and threadfin salmon are the prime targets, but other species like black jewfish, northwest snapper, cod and mackerel are all possible from a boat

The boat ramp at Karratha in the build up to a cyclone.

During the Dampier 2002 junior fishing clinic run by the Nickol Bay Sportfishing club, Cody Carpenter captured and released a snub-nosed dart (permit). It took a prawn at the beach next to the Hampton Harbour Boat Club in Dampier.

which can be launched from the shore on the high tide and motored out to the deeper waters offshore. The creeks are a good place to try for mangrove jacks, bream, javelin fish and mud crabs.

KARRATHA / NICKOL BAY

Karratha lies just inland but has several good fishing spots close by that are of interest to anglers chasing smaller estuary species. Beach-launching a small dinghy is the way to go, and this can be done at Hearson Cove, which is reached from Dampier Road out on the Burrup Peninsula. There is easy access to Cowerie Creek or Airport Creek where mangrove jack, threadfin salmon, bream, whiting, trevally, queenfish, the occasional barramundi and mud crabs can be found. A good 4WD can get anglers to the end of the Burrup Peninsula for some excellent remote camping and fishing for the standard Pilbara inshore species. There are many significant aboriginal art sites in the area so treat these with the utmost respect.

Maitland Pool, which is crossed by the NW Coastal Highway to the south of Karratha, is worth a look for small barramundi, queenfish, trevally, giant herring and tarpon. A light flick rod with a few small lures should be sufficient to handle most of the fish found there.

Remember to pack plenty of insect repellent when fishing the mangrove creeks and bays in the northwest, as sandflies and mosquitoes can be a real problem in many areas. Flies will probably be a nuisance everywhere but at least they don't bite and leave you itching weeks later as sandflies do.

COWERIE CREEK

A popular little creek for local and visiting anglers, Cowerie Creek fishes very well for queenfish, trevally and threadfin salmon at the mouth, and barramundi and mangrove jacks further up the creek. A rough track makes its way to the creek but a 4WD is essential when trying to reach any of the creeks.

Other nearby creeks worth trying are Four, Six and Nine Mile creeks that all produce mixed bags of estuary species including barramundi, mangrove jacks and mud crabs.

DAMPIER

The towns of Dampier and Karratha have one of the highest boat ownership rates per capita of population in Australia, and with the Dampier Archipelago at the doorstep it is easy to see why. The main launching ramp at Hampton Harbour is where you can set out to the many islands lying offshore, and all modern conveniences can be found in both towns, including accommodation, but it pays to book in advance, especially during school holidays over the winter months.

DAMPIER ARCHIPELAGO

Made up of numerous large and small islands, this whole area provides some top rate game and bottom fishing. Numerous small shacks are spread around the Archipelago, especially at East Lewis, Malus and Rosemary islands. The Department of Conservation and Land Management (CALM) oversees them and ensures they adhere to the strict environmental guidelines. This allows boat anglers to spend several days on an island enjoying the fishing in the area at a very relaxed rate. In the warmer months there is the risk of cyclones, which can keep you from

heading out in your boat for weeks. At any time however, the winds can blow strongly and affect fishing but there is usually a lee fishing spot to be found.

Big trevally, long tom and queenfish can be tempted with lures, especially surface poppers cast over likely looking reef and drop-offs. The rocky bays and weed banks around the islands are usually home to squid that make excellent bait; even better they can be fried up for dinner.

The rocky or sandy bays are top spots to cast small lures or saltwater flies for a mixture of species that live there. Sometimes bigger trevally, cobia or longtail tuna will move into these shallow waters, so it pays to have a heavier spinning outfit ready.

Trolling with either baits or lures will turn up anything from big Spanish mackerel, longtail tuna, cobia, coral trout and trevally to sailfish. There are plenty of sailfish and a whole trolled garfish or pusher type lure is the preferred fishing method to catch them. Good numbers of sailfish are even taken on Halco Laser Pro lures put out for Spanish mackerel.

One of the best sailfish grounds is from Rosemary Island

One of the shallow coral lines off an island in the Dampier Archipelago.

through to Goodwyn Island and down to Bare Rock. The winter months are the pick of the times to target the sails as the seas are usually calm with little wind, bringing safe boating and ideal trolling conditions.

Bottom fishing attracts coral trout, red emperor, spangled emperor, Chinaman fish, cod and several species of trevally. Some of the more productive areas are Mermaid Sound and Madeleine Shoal, but with a good echo sounder and persistence, good table fish can be found in the whole area.

Big tides can make launching and navigation hazardous through some reefy country and strong currents that race through some of the passages between islands ensure anglers treat the conditions with respect. Boat handlers must be experienced and able to read charts accurately. For an area with fishing of the quality to be found in Dampier, there are no full time guides. Try and get some local knowledge if possible, as this is one way of staying out of dangerous areas and definitely improving catches.

Tony La Tosa with a black marlin beside the boat, prior to release.

Northern Dampier Archipelago

The whole of the Dampier Archipelago is fishy and worth spending days exploring new and exciting fishing opportunities.

There is some excellent fishing for large trevally and queenfish around Delambre Island that forms the northern end of the archipelago. There is also excellent cast-and-retrieve fishing with poppers or chrome lures around Huey Island and the western edge of Legendre Island. Lure casting under some of the cliffs on Legendre can provide a mind-blowing experience and some first-rate photographs.

Special care must be taken around Hammersley Shoal, which runs southeast from the southern end of Legendre Island, as at high tide it can be difficult to spot. There is some great lure casting from the sand Keast and Cohen islands for golden trevally, dart and other smaller pelagics. Turtles and even dugongs can be seen in the flats inside Legendre Island and this could well become a sanctuary zone under CALM proposals. Flying Foam Passage provides some good fishing including for large tiger sharks with large live or dead baits. A permanently fixed houseboat, which comes with its own dinghy for a special holiday, is based near Sea Ripple Passage.

The channel markers heading towards the Woodside plant all provide good fishing for trevally, cobia, mackerel and live bait on bait jigs. Many locals fish on the submerged gas pipeline for coral trout, Chinaman fish, cod and spangled emperor. There is a safety closure around the Woodside gas facility.

Southern Dampier Archipelago

There are many opportunities to fish in the southern areas. You can try around the loading jetty at Hammersley Iron (when there are no shipping movements) for pelagics and black jewfish, or the tender vessel and tug moorings where giant cobia and trevally can be found. Anglers can cast the shore breaks on any of the islands for a wide range of trevally, queenfish, long tom and doggie mackerel. All provide excellent fishing.

There is great fishing around Enderby Island, where 6 kg queenfish can be encountered. It is also an excellent picnic spot,

RIGHT: Dave Dubblboer with his first marlin, a black. In the Dampier/Karratha region many black marlin are mistaken for blues.

BELOW: A large bait school of northern pilchards that extended down to 45 metres! Marlin, sailfish and wahoo were patrolling this area north of Legendre Island.

FISH FACTS

MARLIN

A dedicated group of game fishers put in the hours chasing these magnificent fish off the Western Australian coast each year. All three species blue, black and striped marlin show up from time to time but the most common out from Perth is the striped marlin. The Rottnest Trench, which is a deep canyon sitting to the west of the island, is a favourite hunting ground for marlin, and large lures or baits trolled in this area are the way to come into contact with them.

The State's marlin hot spot is the North-West Cape region, near the town of Exmouth. Here the continental shelf is very close to land and as a result large pelagic species like marlin can be fished for without having to travel great distances.

Big seaworthy boats fitted out with quality gamefishing tackle are necessary tools if you want to chase marlin, and a skilled skipper and crew is needed once the fish is hooked. These fish have the ability to run great distances under heavy drag settings, so gear failure and angler or crew inexperience will quickly put the odds in favour of the fish. Many anglers keen to catch their first marlin would be best chartering a boat and crew that specialises in catching these great fish.

If it all holds together and you manage to bring the fish to the boat for a tag to be put in then you will understand why so many anglers pursue these massive fish and nothing else. Marlin are considered a prize game species and although there is nothing illegal about killing one, almost all anglers choose to tag and release their fish these days.

with good fishing available to those walking the beaches and using a small chrome lure. Low tide at night can produce some really large tropical rock lobsters, just by walking the exposed reefs; the more keen can snorkel for them during the day.

Northwest and southwest reefs produce well and prevailing conditions will determine which one is preferable. Bare rock is also a great spot for really big trevally and queenfish. Further offshore are the sailfish and mackerel grounds.

Bottom fishing is extremely popular, especially on the outside edge of the sailfish reef and on the cod grounds further to the south. Fishing any likely lump seen on the sounder could produce a huge variety of really big, tasty reef fish.

This area contains one of the best fishing spots on the planet, if only fishing weren't banned. The Dampier salt ponds ban fishing apparently due to concerns about the ecosystem in the area, or so a sign nearby proclaims. However, the ponds are surrounded by hectares of dead mangroves, an ecosystem that no longer survives and huge barramundi, giant herring and cod cannot be touched, even by trained guides. This is indeed a real shame.

MONTEBELLO ISLANDS

The British used these islands as atomic test areas in the 1950s and they were off limits to all but naval vessels over the next 40 years. Today there is little threat from radiation even though it can be detected at some sites

MONTEBELLO ISLANDS

Montebello Islands are the site of a nuclear test by Great Britain in the 1950s. It is very remote and should only be fished from a well fitted out charter boat or a large and reliable recreational boat.

Recreational boats should not travel alone and need to carry copious spare fuel, all safety equipment and water. Fish abound.

The Montebello Islands rank with Rowley Shoals and the remote Kimberley as a wilderness fishing experience.

Species include: Sailfish, Marlin, Mackerel, Tuna and Wahoo in deeper water. Casting to reef breaks will produce Trevally, Queenfish, Longtom, and Coral Trout. Bottom bouncing will produce Red Emperor, Northwest Snapper, Coral Trout, Chinaman Fish, Cod, Trevally, Shark and some giant Mangrove Jack.

on the islands. Most anglers fish the Montebellos from smaller boats that accompany larger mother ships chartered for fishing and diving. Private boats venturing here must carry extra fuel and all provisions, including water and safety gear.

The surrounding sand and coral waters contain a huge range of reef and pelagic species. Trolling lures or baits around the deep oceanic drop-offs out from the islands can result in numerous tuna species, including the prized and aggressive dog-tooth tuna, as well as species of

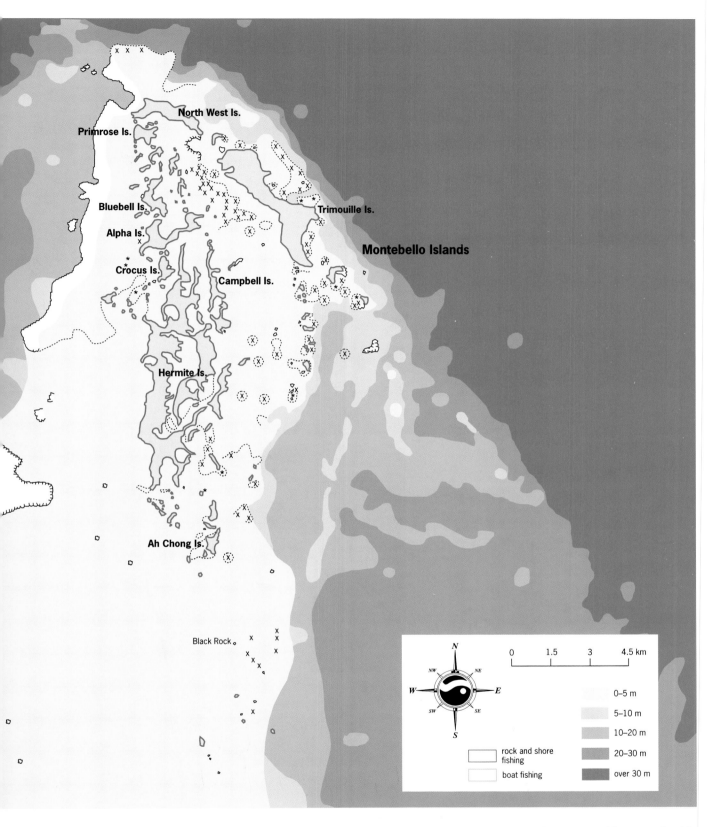

North West Is.

Primrose Is.

Bluebell Is.

Alpha Is.

Crocus Is.

Campbell Is.

Trimouille Is.

Montebello Islands

Hermite Is.

Ah Chong Is.

Black Rock

0	1.5	3	4.5 km

rock and shore fishing

boat fishing

0–5 m

5–10 m

10–20 m

20–30 m

over 30 m

mackerel, wahoo, marlin, sailfish, trevally, cobia and occasional dolphin fish. Fishing the deeper reefs can reward the angler with big red emperor, long-nosed emperor, spangled emperor, coral trout, Chinaman fish and various cod species.

Using lighter tackle from the shore or the shallows near the islands can produce spangled and long-nosed emperor, queenfish, trevally, mackerel, coral trout and cod. Large tropical rock lobsters are easily caught around the shallow coral bomboras by skin divers.

Most charters run during the cooler months of the year because of the better boating conditions and the problems with

cyclones during the warmer months. Bring a wide range of tackle on a trip to the Montebello Islands, as there are numerous species to be targeted, and many new experiences to be gained.

Maitland River

The mouth of the Maitland River is a good place to throw a few lures around for queenfish and trevally, whilst further upstream barramundi, tarpon, and trevally find the fresh water to their liking. In the hotter months, barramundi are prime targets in the area's rivers.

FORTESCUE RIVER

South of Dampier, the Fortescue River has a good reputation for producing black jewfish, threadfin salmon and barramundi. Strip baits of fish or a live mullet are good choices for bait fishers. If you prefer lures, then casting smaller minnow lures should do the trick. If you have a small dinghy or car topper you can access the river by launching from the beach at Cape Preston.

BOAT RAMPS & TACKLE STORES

Big tides still play an important part in this area when it comes to safe and enjoyable boating. The majority of anglers fish this area by boats that have been launched from the concrete public ramps provided. Alternatively there are numerous other launch sites that require a 4WD vehicle.

Like the Kimberley, this area is prone to storms and cyclones in the wet season months—November to March—so be prepared to move out of the area should a big cyclone be approaching and don't risk extended trips to offshore islands.

RAMPS
Point Samson – Town
Cossack – Town
Port Hedland – Public ramp on Finucane Island
Dampier – Harbour

TACKLE STORES

Smirkey's Sports
Shop 21A,
South Hedland
Tel: (08) 9172 2145

Hedland Emporium
1 The Esplanade,
Port Hedland
Tel: (08) 9173 4033

Tackle Time
Karratha WA 6714
Tel: (08) 9144 2288

LEFT: The ultimate reward—hooked up to a black marlin.

C H A P T E R   3

ONSLOW TO THE QUOBBA COAST

O N S L O W

About 1300 km north of Perth the town of Onslow offers accommodation and launching facilities. The fishing from shore is limited, however in Beadon Creek anglers can cast lures or baits from the rocks at the mouth for trevally and queenfish. There are also good numbers of mangrove jacks, small threadfin salmon, javelin fish, estuary cod, bream and mud crabs in this creek, so a small dinghy is an advantage.

Lures and saltwater flies will work on many of the species in the creek but a small live bait fished on a medium outfit will bring excellent results. Offshore there are trevally, queenfish, mackerel, tuna and mixed reef species waiting for the keen boating angler.

At Beadon Creek there is a good ramp that permits most vehicles to launch easily at any tide. The boating angler has the choice of fishing the creek or venturing the short distance out through the mouth to the ocean. The preferred times for visiting Onslow or the Mackerel Islands offshore are the cooler months of the year because of the lower daytime temperatures and better boating conditions. The possible chance of a cyclone during the warmer months—November to March—may disrupt many travel plans, but the fishing is still very productive during these months.

MACKEREL ISLANDS

This small group of islands has become a very popular holiday destination for many southern anglers, and anglers can book to stay on Thevenard Island to enjoy the fantastic fishing. Large boats can be driven across or you can fish from one of the smaller tinnies provided, although having the ability to travel further out from the island to the less-fished waters is a big advantage these days.

Thevenard Island is well known for its excellent bottom fishing with red emperor, coral trout, spangled emperor and cods available. Pelagic species like mackerel, tuna and sailfish attack trolled lures and baits, and trevally and queenfish are about in good numbers. When boat fishing close to the island use berley of crushed pilchards to attract big golden trevally, spangled emperor and the occasional cobia. Sharks are very common at times and can prove to be a problem stealing hooked fish from your line.

Walking along the shore of the island is a popular pastime for many anglers, and casting small lures or saltwater flies is often a successful way of catching a wide range of species. From the sandy beach, predatory fish like trevally, mackerel, barracuda and queenfish often prowl quite close to shore and a small metal slice lure, popper or saltwater fly is rarely refused.

On the Mackerel Islands there are several holiday shacks that can be booked for extended stays during the cooler months of the year, but bookings should definitely be made in advance as this is, for good reason, a very popular holiday destination for anglers.

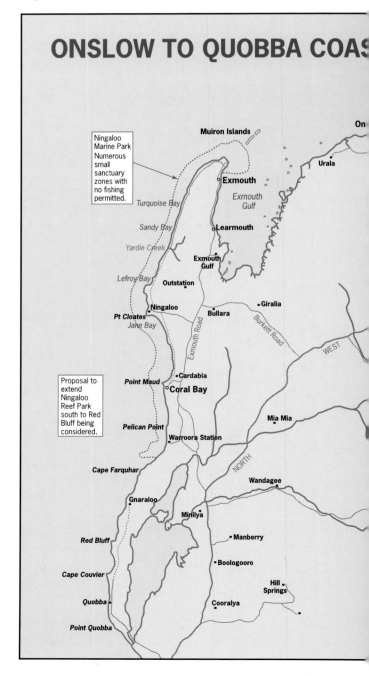

NORTH WEST CAPE

The North West Cape is one of the favourite fishing destinations in the State. Situated 1300 km north of Perth, the town of Exmouth was originally built to service the US base until it was scaled down and handed over to the Australian navy in the 1990s. Now the town survives on the massive tourist interest, which includes Cape Range National Park and Ningaloo Reef, as well as the fantastic fishing. By taking the turn off the North West Coastal Highway just north of Minilya Roadhouse, the road then leads out towards the Cape to the popular fishing locations of Coral Bay and Exmouth. The fishing and environment at Ningaloo Reef is considered by many to be superior to the Great Barrier Reef.

MUIRON ISLANDS

The Muiron Islands sit out from the tip of the Cape and are easily reached by medium to large boats from the ramp at Bundegi. The fishing around the islands is fantastic for both pelagic species

The North West Cape at Exmouth is well known for its mega giant trevally like this specimen taken from the shore by Kurt Blanksby.

Taken from shore at Exmouth, this big barracuda was caught on a popper.

and bottom species. Big spangled emperor, Chinaman cod, coral trout and Chinaman fish are common from the coral lumps around the islands. Locals believe that bottom fishing in an area where the many sea snakes are spotted will bring good results. There is a small sanctuary zone at the cod hole on the southwest part of South Muiron Island.

OYSTER REEF

From the oyster reefs at the tip of the Cape, near the wreck of the Mildura, anglers can target queenfish and big giant trevally that can be in the unstoppable size range. The most popular method is to stand on the oysters as the tide is falling and cast lures like metal slices or poppers and retrieve them back quickly to attract these fish. Big golden trevally, queenfish, and shark mackerel are all taken using this method. Late in the afternoon put on a very big surface popper and bloop it back to attract the attention of the massive giant trevally that hang out here. Very heavy tackle is required to even stand a chance of winning a battle with one of these fish, so use 30–50lb braided line on a big spinning reel and a heavy spin rod. If you do manage to land a fish it will usually be upwards of 20 kilograms.

EXMOUTH

The Cape stretches northwards providing the shallow and warm gulf waters to the east that are home to a wide range of species. They also support a large king prawn fishery during the season. On the western side the coast is protected by the Ningaloo coral reef that stretches south past Coral Bay. The inside of the reef is a fantastic place to target many tropical species of fish from the low rock ledges or sandy beaches. There are numerous access points to some really great fishing spots all the way down to Yardie Creek. A small dinghy is one way to really enjoy the great fishing inside the reef, however the shallow coral lumps make it very dangerous for bigger boats.

The most popular species taken inside the reef are spangled emperor, various species of trevally, queenfish, bluebone and several species of cod. The coral lumps are also home to some massive tropical crayfish and squid are also a common sight. The clarity of the water makes it an ideal skin-diving area, and big turtles, dugongs and sharks of all sizes are common. A small dinghy can be launched from several beach locations down in the National Park; the boat ramp at Tantabiddi provides access for bigger boats.

Outside the reef the water depth drops off rapidly and the warm blue water is home to many great game and reef fish. Trolling lures or garfish on the outside of the reef is very popular, and catches of mackerel, trevally, tuna, wahoo, cobia, sailfish, barracuda and dolphin fish are common. Further out anglers with the right tackle can target some really big marlin.

By fishing the reef lumps on the western side of the reef you can expect to catch spangled emperor, red emperor, coral trout, trevally and several species

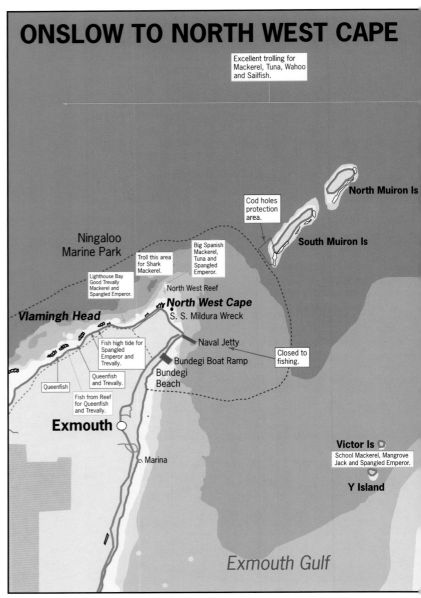

ONSLOW TO NORTH WEST CAPE

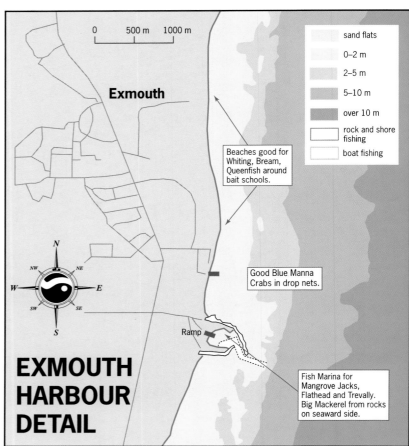

EXMOUTH HARBOUR DETAIL

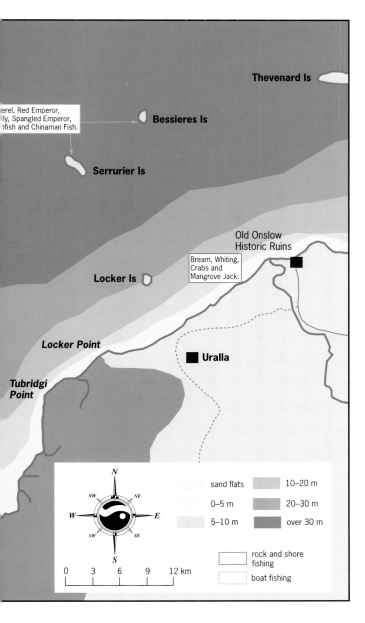

Thevenard Is

erel, Red Emperor,
ly, Spangled Emperor,
fish and Chinaman Fish.

Bessieres Is

Serrurier Is

Old Onslow
Historic Ruins

Bream, Whiting,
Crabs and
Mangrove Jack.

Locker Is

Locker Point

Uralla

Tubridgi
Point

sand flats | 10–20 m
0–5 m | 20–30 m
5–10 m | over 30 m

rock and shore fishing
boat fishing

0 3 6 9 12 km

BELOW: Wapet Creek near Learmonth Airport at Exmouth is a popular fishing and crabbing spot.

FISH FACTS
CORAL TROUT

From Geraldton northwards a coral trout is a prized catch amongst anglers fishing the offshore reefs. The eating qualities of this species are rated very highly and as a result these fish are heavily targeted.

Coral trout are usually caught in better numbers and size from the deeper offshore reefs, but in some locations the shallow coral bomboras (or bommies) close to shore hold good numbers. In the deeper waters most are caught on heavily weighted lines baited with strips of fish, whilst in shallower waters they can be taken on cast or trolled lures. A surface popper cast around a coral bombora will usually attract the attention of any coral trout living there, but the angler must be forceful and quick to keep the fish from diving back into cover once it is hooked.

These fish vary in colour from location to location and it is not unusual to see colours ranging from a dull brown to a bright red, with either blue or black spots. Most coral trout in WA are bar-cheek coral trout. These fish have big mouths full of sharp, holding teeth that enable them to catch small fish. Although a wire trace is not necessary, a good shock leader of heavy monofilament will hopefully prevent these fish cutting the line on the coral.

Fish should be quickly released back into the water or put in a cool Esky as soon as possible if they are intended for the table.

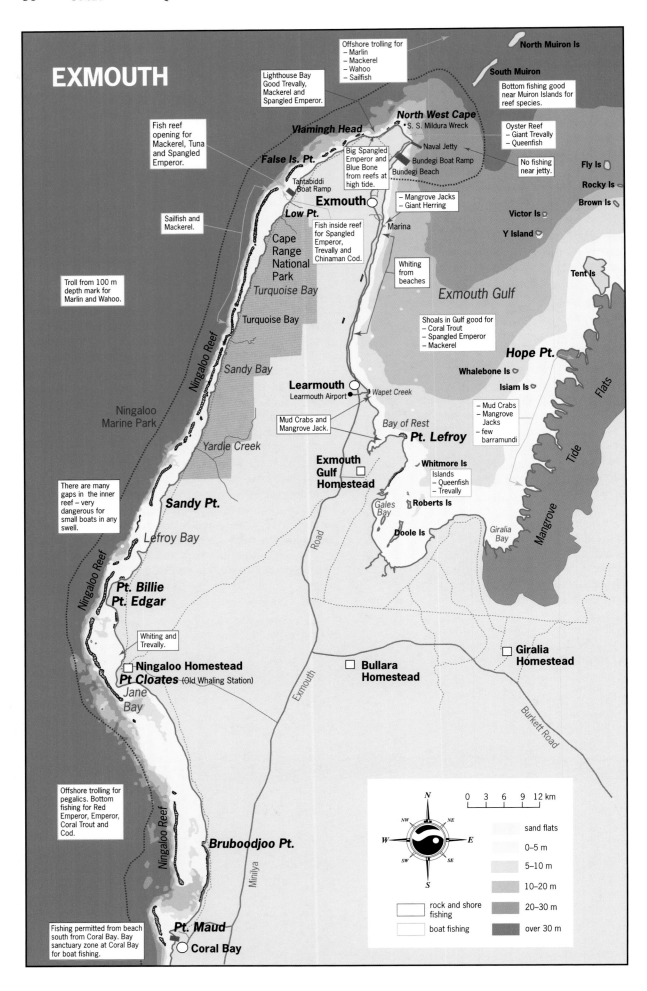

of cod. Tough tackle is needed to prevent many of these species from burying themselves in the coral, so lock-up-and-hang-on tactics by anglers are commonplace once a fish is hooked.

From the shore there are numerous access points where anglers can fish with bait or lures for many different species. A rising tide just after dark is a good time to fish with whole pilchards around the western side for big spangled emperor—a highly prized table fish. The beach and area around the boat ramp at Bundegi are well-known haunts of queenfish, trevally and mackerel that harass the big schools of hardyheads that hug the beach there. A live hardyhead cast out on the edge of the bait school does not last long at high tide in this area, and lure and fly fishers also have plenty of opportunities at predatory fish moving in to crash the bait.

The boat marina in town is a great location for shore-based anglers to fish for queenfish, mackerel, longtail tuna, trevally and cobia from the rocks. Big mangrove jacks live under the moored boats and pylons and will respond to fish baits both live and dead, but pulling them out can be a real effort. Boat anglers can launch with ease, at any tide, to access Exmouth Gulf or head around the Cape towards the Ningaloo Reef, North West Reef or the Murion Islands.

CAPE RANGE NATIONAL PARK

Following the Cape down on the western side the Cape Range National Park starts just south of the boat ramp at Tantibiddi. From here a bitumen road takes you down to Yardi Creek where a 4WD is required to keep heading south to the southern park boundary and Coral Bay. Along the way the road passes numerous access points to the coast where anglers can camp at designated points, or just spend day trips fishing the area. Dinghies can be beach-launched at Pilgramuna or to the south at Yardi Creek. The Ningaloo Reef that sits a short distance out from shore, fringes the protected lagoon that follows the Cape down.

Inside the lagoon, boat anglers cast or troll lures for trevally, queenfish, mackerel and cobia. Baits fished around the coral bomboras will often result in spangled emperor, trevally, various cods, coral trout and bluebone. On a calm day small dinghies can venture out through the gaps in the reef to fish for game species like big mackerel, wahoo, tuna, sailfish and dolphin fish. Dropping baited lines down outside the reef is a popular way to score numerous reef species that can often be difficult to stop once they are hooked.

EXMOUTH GULF

Boat anglers travelling down into the sheltered Gulf waters can make their trip from Bundegi or launch from the marina in the town of Exmouth. The most common species taken in the Gulf are trevally, mackerel and queenfish, but there are several shoals found further out that produce some good catches of spangled emperor and coral trout. Keep an eye out for feeding birds as these usually give away the location of tuna schools feeding on baitfish. Many big Spanish mackerel and sailfish have been caught in the Gulf. If you spot any big manta rays give them some attention as they usually have some big cobia swimming with them. Try casting lures, flies or an unweighted mulie as close to the manta as you can without foul-hooking it. Any big cobia swimming with the ray should cruise out and take your offering.

From the shore in the Gulf many anglers take advantage of the large numbers of whiting and bream that are common across the shallow flats. Behind the prawn processing plant it can be almost too easy to catch a feed of these fish. Big bluebone and small sharks can also be found on an incoming tide, whilst those prepared to put up with the sandflies can target mangrove jacks and mud crabs in the mangroves at the bottom of the Gulf. The old jetty at Learmonth is a popular spot to fish for the queenfish, mackerel and trevally that move in to feed on the baitfish taking refuge under the pylons. The same thing happens further up the coast at Bundegi, and fishing a small live bait or throwing a lure can be great fun if the fish are raiding the bait schools.

The massive naval jetty is off limits to the public, and boats are not permitted to anchor near the structure. However, from the shore it is a great place to throw big poppers for giant trevally and barracuda.

Strict bag and size limits apply to this entire Ningaloo area, so get hold of a brochure from the Fisheries Department or tourist bureau before wetting a line.

There are excellent modern facilities and numerous caravan parks in Coral Bay and Exmouth, and safe, sealed roads and a large airport at Learmonth means that this stretch of the WA coastline is available to anyone.

YARDI CREEK

This small creek is a popular tourist spot, and during the season buses deliver thousands of tourists to this spot to venture up the creek to sightsee. The creek allows beach launching of dinghies

Many species of trevally are found in WA waters, as was this golden trevally.

A big queenfish on a popper is what sportfishing in the northwest is all about.

This brassy trevally took a lure cast from a northern beach.

FISH FACTS

SAILFISH

These fish are reported to be the fastest fish in the ocean. Sailfish are a tropical species that is found from about Shark Bay northwards, but seem to be found in the best numbers at Coral Bay, Dampier, Exmouth and Broome.

Considered purely a game species, these fish are rarely killed these days, with many anglers content to just tag and release them as they are brought to the boat. Most sailfish are attracted to the back of a boat as it trolls a teaser—a bright object that reflects light and splashes about near the surface. Near this, a spread of rigged garfish or lures is used to tempt the sailfish that has cruised up to investigate. Many anglers now also target these fish with saltwater fly tackle, casting at the fish as it moves in behind the teaser and fishing the fly once the teaser is quickly removed from the water.

Tackle for sailfish depends on the size fish encountered, as smaller fish around the 30 –40 kg range can easily be knocked over on 6–10 kg tackle or 10–12 weight fly rods. Bigger fish often require heavier tackle, and although they can still be stopped on lighter gear the chance of the fish recovering after a lengthy battle on light gear is minimal.

Sailfish have been hooked from the shore at places like Steep Point and Quobba, usually on ballooned baits of garfish. The only problem with catching one of these fish from the shore is landing it, and once it has been hauled up a high cliff face the chance of releasing it alive is not good. Some anglers have been known to break the line once the fish is brought close to the rocks, allowing it to swim away before hungry sharks move in on it.

The gold spot trevally is one of the most common species caught in Ningaloo waters.

that can be used to fish the creek itself or to venture out into the coral waters of the lagoon.

During the summer months the creek is usually landlocked with a large sandbar, and only when big tides and heavy rain occur does the creek break through to the ocean. The creek itself supports a wide range of smaller species like cods, mangrove jacks and trevally, but each year some surprisingly big fish are taken inside the creek. Most anglers choose to fish with light outfits, casting small lures or baits around the deeper holes.

The 4WD track leading to the south of the creek can only be reached during the warmer months when the creek can be crossed safely. The fishing locations to the south are often very productive for anglers fishing from the shore, with big trevally, queenfish, spangled emperor and the occasional mackerel and cobia showing up to make things interesting.

Most use heavy spin or beach fishing rods to cast metal lures, poppers or baits like pilchards on ganged hooks into likely looking water. Use 8–10 kg breaking strain line or gelspun, as the chance of hooking a big fish from the shore is very good in this area. A lighter spin outfit with 4 kg line and a few small lures and jigs is a good way to have fun with the numerous small dart, trevally and emperor that abound in the shallows. Saltwater fly anglers can often wade big sand flats or cast into deep drop-offs for a huge list of species including the highly prized bonefish and permit.

CORAL BAY

Many anglers travel no further north than Coral Bay as it offers all modern conveniences and excellent fishing but book accommodation well in advance, as in holiday times this whole area is completely packed with tourists. The Coral Bay turn-off is passed on the Minilya Road as you travel towards Exmouth.

From the shore around Coral Bay there are plenty of opportunities to target northern gamefish like queenfish and trevally. Keep an eye out for bait schools hugging the shallows, as these will be targets of predators especially on a rising tide. Cast lures like poppers around the bait schools to tempt any hunting fish, or bait up a small live bait that has been caught from the bait school, and cast it out close by. Any trevally or queenfish seeing the struggling baitfish will not think twice before devouring it.

There are also plenty of smaller species like dart, threadfin salmon and whiting to tackle with light gear. Fishing at night with bigger baits and heavy surf tackle is often productive for

spangled emperor, small sharks and big trevally.

Coral Bay is visited mostly by boating anglers who take advantage of the very productive waters that lie offshore, and most visit this area in the cooler months—May to August—to take advantage of the calmer conditions. Launching is easy for most trailer boats but very low tides can cause a few problems with the shallow sand and coral waters. It is important to follow the markers out through the north or south passages to the deeper waters outside the reefs; otherwise the risk of hitting the reef is high.

Offshore from Coral Bay the big, clear lagoons are home to a wide range of marine life, and once the South Passage is reached the chance of hooking big pelagic species is very good. This gap in the reef is a top spot to float out a balloon with a live bait for really big Spanish mackerel. Trolling lures and baits usually produces trevally, Spanish and shark mackerel, wahoo, tuna, barracuda, dolphin fish and sailfish. Bottom fishing is world class with plenty of big spangled emperor, red emperor, trevally and several species of cod to keep your arms stretched. Most anglers use either heavy hand lines or stout boat rods with dropper rigs to fish the deeper reefs. An octopus makes a sturdy and reliable bait but pilchards, squid or fish baits will also produce results in these waters.

WARROORA

Warroora has excellent beach fishing for spangled emperor and trevally. The shallow waters should not be overlooked as during a rising tide, especially after dark, some good fish can be taken on baits fished with surf gear. From here to the north is where the Ningaloo Reef begins. Warroora is a great place for anglers who do not like the crowds just to the north at Coral Bay.

GNARALOO

Reasonable accommodation can be obtained here and beach launching for boats is the norm. Small-boat anglers target spangled emperor, red emperor and mackerel, whilst beach fishing can be productive for trevally, tailor and spangled emperor.

QUOBBA COASTLINE

This coastline is well known for having some of the best rock fishing in Australia. Unfortunately it is also extremely dangerous, having claimed many lives over the years. The high cliffs stretch north along the coast where anglers can fish from several platforms into deep blue water at their feet. This section of the coast should only be fished in calm conditions, as each year people are washed off the rocks and getting back out of the water is almost impossible. Your only hope is that a boat can find you

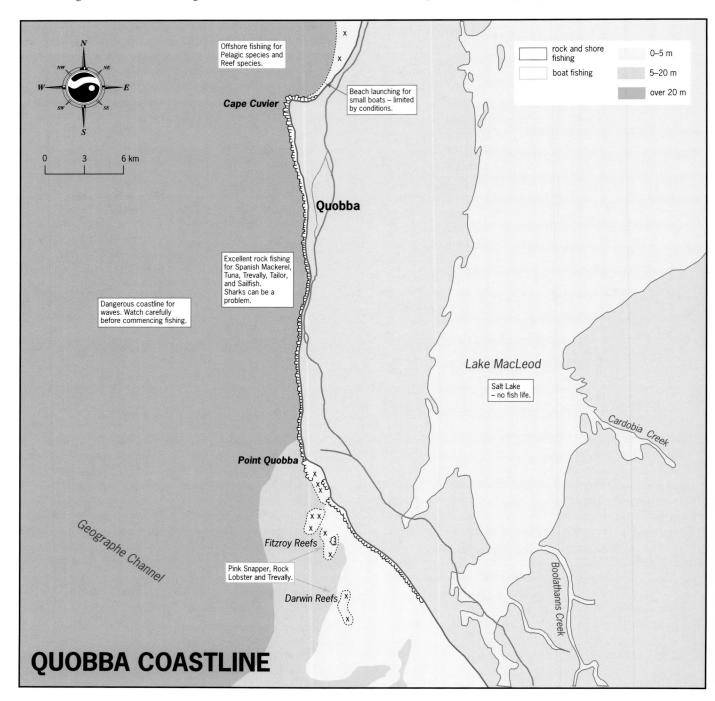

N
NW   NE
W   E
SW   SE
S

0   3   6 km

Offshore fishiing for Pelagic species and Reef species.

Cape Cuvier

Beach launching for small boats – limited by conditions.

rock and shore fishing
boat fishing
0–5 m
5–20 m
over 20 m

Quobba

Excellent rock fishing for Spanish Mackerel, Tuna, Trevally, Tailor, and Sailfish. Sharks can be a problem.

Dangerous coastline for waves. Watch carefully before commencing fishing.

Lake MacLeod

Salt Lake – no fish life.

Cardobia Creek

Geographe Channel

Point Quobba

Fitzroy Reefs

Pink Snapper, Rock Lobster and Trevally.

Darwin Reefs

Boolathanns Creek

QUOBBA COASTLINE

FISH FACTS

TUNA

Several species of tuna inhabit Western Australian waters and they are usually targeted by boat anglers, apart from some of the deeper rock-fishing locations.

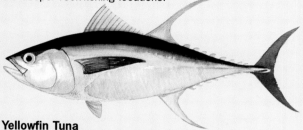

Yellowfin Tuna

The prize species is the yellowfin tuna, a big powerful tuna with plenty of stamina that will quickly wear out angler and tackle if not up to the job. Big yellowfin can be found all around the WA coast but several areas are well known for producing fish in the 30 kg plus bracket, and hearing of fish over the old 100 pound mark is not uncommon.

Most big yellowfin tuna are hooked whilst trolling lures in deep water for gamefish, so the tackle used is normally up to the job. Long powerful runs and plenty of stamina are the trademarks of a big tuna's fight. Being able to keep the fish from sounding to the depths is important; otherwise the angler will be in for a lengthy battle that will stretch the line to its limit. In shallow water a big yellowfin will go on a long run and if the reel's line capacity is not great, being spooled will be inevitable.

Most choose to target big yellowfin with heavy game outfits that have large overhead reels with drag systems and line capacity capable of tackling big tuna. Smaller fish can be knocked over on lighter gear but the angler must still be prepared for a tough fight. Recently anglers have been targeting big yellowfin tuna with heavy saltwater fly tackle, resulting in several world record captures on these tough fish.

Longtail Tuna

Longtail tuna, or northern bluefin, would be the next most popular species chased by anglers, and these fish are also well known for their strength and stamina. Found mostly in northern waters from Geraldton upwards, longtails often frequent shallower waters. Although they don't reach the same bragging size of the yellowfin, a big longtail can exceed 30 kilograms. Most of them are in the 8–15 kg range and at this size they can be great fun on medium spin or fly tackle.

Longtail tuna are often taken from the shore as they venture into shallow water to chase baitfish, but by far the best way to chase them is by boat as they crash bait schools.

Striped, mackerel and southern bluefin tuna

Smaller species of tuna like striped tuna, mackerel tuna and southern bluefin (in WA waters), provide plenty of thrills for anglers with lighter spin gear or fly tackle. These species of tuna are easily spotted as they break the surface chasing baitfish, and birds diving over them can be seen from some distance. The trick is to position the boat up-current of the breaking fish, with the motor cut so that you don't spook them. When they are close enough small metal slices or saltwater flies can be cast at the fish.

Apart from yellowfin and southern bluefin, most tunas don't make very good eating with their very red and oily flesh that does not keep well. They are better used as strip baits or released shortly after capture.

Bonito

Bonito are a popular small species that also move inshore in big schools and can be targeted from rocky headlands or rock groynes or by boat. These aggressive little tuna possess very sharp teeth that make short work of smaller baitfish so a minnow lure or live bait is a top way to tempt them.

Most anglers choose to cast minnow lures into deep water from rocky headlands along the south coast or from rock groynes like North Mole in Fremantle. When the bonito are on, the action is fast and furious as many anglers vie for spots and hooked fish dart about close to the rocks testing anglers' tackle.

Anglers will need to check on current Fisheries Regulations for daily bag limits and minimum legal sizes—website: www.fish.wa.gov.au/rec or telephone (08) 9482 7333.

---

several hours later, once the alarm is raised. Why do so many risk their lives to fish this stretch of coast? The depth of the water and the huge range of fish species available make the area irresistible to anglers.

Quobba Station provides reasonable accommodation, but booking in advance is advised. In holiday seasons it can almost be impossible to get a spot on some of the more famous ledges, as they can only comfortably fish a certain number of anglers at any time.

RED BLUFF

Attracting surfers from all over the world, this spot also attracts anglers with its excellent fishing, so it can become very crowded. The camping facilities are basic. The fishing is mostly done with baits from the low ledges where snapper, baldchin groper, spangled emperor and trevally are taken. Big mackerel and cobia have been hooked by ballooning larger baits out into the bay when the wind co-operates.

Red Bluff also provides a sheltered beach where small dinghies can be launched from the beach to access some top fishing just off the coast. Big mackerel and tuna are regular captures on trolled lures and baits, and fishing the bottom will produce pink snapper, spangled emperor, red emperor and several species of cod.

THE CAVES

This popular landbased gamefishing spot can be reached via the track leading north from the Homestead at Quobba. To reach The Caves, you must descend down a steep goat track so physical fitness is a major consideration for anglers who want to fish this spot. There are many opportunities to target large pelagic species like mackerel, tuna, cobia and trevally from the ledges there. Extreme caution is needed again as this area can be very hazardous in a big sea.

CAMP ROCK

Camp Rock which can be reached by car, lies next to the wreck of the Korean Star. The spin angler has plenty of opportunities to

RIGHT: Fishing from Garth's Rock for mackerel and cobia with the wreck of the *Korean Star* in the distance.

This cobia, taken from the famous Garth's Rock, was caught on pilchard bait.

chase mackerel, and casting a white leadhead jig from this rock and retrieving it back flat out, is one way to have some fun. This ledge is closer to the water so landing fish is a bit easier, but keep an eye on the ocean at all times.

GARTH'S ROCK

The most popular ledge is Garth's Rock, named after Max Garth who, back in the 1970s, helped pioneer fishing in this area. Garth's is reached by scaling down a steep goat track from the top of the cliffs, or running the gauntlet of the low ledges at water level from Camp Rock just to the north. Either way, the weather and sea conditions must be very calm and you must be a very fit person as there is no easy way to get you out.

Once on the rock you look out into the bay with the Cape Cuvier salt works to the south and deep blue water all around you. Big fish are the norm from Garth's so you need to bring serious tackle such as 10 kg spin gear and a range of metal lures or leadhead jigs. If you like bait fishing, a strong surf rod with a deep-spool Alvey reel spooled up with a minimum of 15 kg line is the go. Balloon fishing from the rock when the winds are correct can be a very productive way to target big mackerel and tuna, however the large number of sharks means that you will spend plenty of time battling unstoppable noahs between decent macks. If you do hook a big mackerel or tuna it is a real game of cat and mouse to get it out of the water before the sharks 'tax' it.

Spinning off the rock for shark mackerel and Spanish mackerel is great sport, especially in November and December when big schools of sharkies move in close to the coast. Saltwater fly anglers can have an absolute ball from the rock on numerous species, but use at least a 10-weight outfit with plenty

The November run of shark mackerel from the Quobba coastline attracts hundreds of anglers each year.

of backing to be in with a chance. Big tiger sharks patrol the front of the rock and many an angler has hooked big cobia that seem to swim with them. In fact this is the number one place in Australia to hook a cobia from the shore and fish averaging 15–30 kg are pretty common.

Bottom fishing produces big pink snapper and baldchin groper and some huge tailor can be taken from the white water close to the rocks. Massive Queensland gropers that live in the reefy ledges below the rock are almost as bad as the sharks for stealing hooked fish, so it can be a real effort to be successful at Garth's. A rope gaff is essential to get fish up onto the rock, and just remember that what you catch and keep you must carry back up the cliff to your car—very hard work indeed!

WHISTLING ROCK

This is a very dangerous place to fish due to the fact that you must negotiate a short section at waterline to reach the main rock. Once there, anglers use spin and bait tackle for most of the common species. Ballooning from this high rock has been very popular over the years, however it is probably far too risky to fish unless the sea is very calm.

HIGH ROCK

Even though this spot is pretty high out of the water, there have been several people washed off to their deaths over the years. The big swells rolling in across the deep water out in front of high rock, crash up and over the top with ease so it is a place to avoid unless the sea is very calm. The fishing out from High Rock is as good as it gets anywhere, with big Spanish mackerel, shark mackerel, cobia, tuna, snapper, spangled emperor and trevally being hooked regularly.

A rope gaff is needed to reach hooked fish at the base of the cliff, but once again extreme care must be taken as it is just not worth falling or being washed in from this spot as there is no way back out. This is another popular spot for helium ballooning, where 20 kg-plus Spanish mackerel are a common capture in autumn when the winds are favourable.

THE BLOWHOLES

To the south of Quobba Station, The Blowholes are found where the beach ends and the cliffs start. Fishing from the beach is popular and big tailor, spangled emperor, small sharks and trevally are common catches. Small-boat anglers can launch from the beach and gain access to the excellent fishing just off shore. Trolling produces big mackerel, tuna and cobia, whilst bottom fishing is very productive for most reef species. Balloon fishing with helium is a very popular method from here north.

To attract very big Spanish mackerel and tuna, large baits are floated out under helium-filled party balloons. Very heavy tackle is needed for this type of fishing—powerful rods and reels with big line capacities. Most anglers use deep-spooled Alvey reels or big overhead game reels that hold a minimum of 1000 m of 15 kg line.

BOAT RAMPS & TACKLE STORES

From Onslow south the tides can still have enough variation in them to create some problems with launching and retrieving larger trailer craft, but dinghy anglers don't seem to have too many problems. Many smaller craft can be bank-launched from the Ashburton River, but from here south, access to the coast is very limited until you head out on the North West Cape towards Exmouth.

Around the Quobba area there are no public ramps but beach launching by 4WD at Red Bluff Beach or the Blowholes allows access to offshore waters. The sea conditions play a big part in whether or not you can launch from these spots.

The summer months are often prone to approaching cyclones and extreme care is needed at this time of year. Many visiting anglers from Perth choose to escape the winter chill during the middle of the year in this area. Generally the calm boating conditions in winter make this coastal area very popular with boat anglers.

RAMPS
Onslow – Beadon Creek
Exmouth – Bundegi and Marina near Town or Tantibiddi on western side of cape.
Coral Bay – Town

TACKLE STORES

Bettsy's Seafood & Tackle
Pellew Street,
Exmouth WA 6707
Tel: (08) 9949 1410

Bluewater Tackle
3 Maley Street,
Exmouth WA 6707
Tel: (08) 9949 1315

Exmouth Tackle & Hardware
Lot 134 Maidstone Crescent,
Exmouth WA 6707
Tel: (08) 9949 1179

Coral Bay Tackle
Shop 4, Coral Bay Arcade,
Robinson Street,
Coral Bay WA
Tel: (08) 9942 5873

C H A P T E R   4

CARNARVON TO TAMALA

CARNARVON

With a pleasant temperate climate, Carnarvon is famous for its fruit and vegetables. The town has the appearance of an oasis with massive banana plantations of green contrasting to the dry red dirt. Carnarvon is just over 900 km north of Perth and boasts some of the best fishing right at its doorstep. It provides all modern facilities and every type of accommodation.

MYABOOLYA BEACH

To the north of Carnarvon is the popular and productive Myaboolya Beach, which is a fantastic place to fish for big mulloway, sharks and tailor. Fishing with heavy surf gear is the way to go here, as the chances of hooking into a decent fish are good. Whole pilchards or mullet fillets as dead baits should do the trick, but if you can put out a live bait then you are bound to attract mulloway or sharks. There are smaller species to be taken from the beach if you are not interested in fighting something big and with a 4WD vehicle you can travel some distance looking for a likely spot to cast a line.

CARNARVON JETTY

Famous for the runs of big mulloway, the long town jetty at the opening of the Gascoyne River is a must to fish. When the mulloway are schooling the jetty becomes a hectic fishing platform with anglers using heavy hand lines, and rods set out and baited with live baits or whole dead fish. Fifty or more mulloway have been landed on a good night, but most nights see at least a couple of fish hooked. A rope gaff is needed to haul the fish to the top of the jetty and strong line is needed as many large fish free themselves on the pylons below.

Other good fish regularly taken from the jetty include mackerel, queenfish, trevally and tailor on lures and baits. Smaller sharks can be landed on baits but many 'an unstoppable' has been hooked on setlines intended for mulloway. Fish the shallows for smaller species like bream.

The town has many beaches that anglers can fish for bream and whiting, while the small creeks have a few mangrove jacks hiding in them, especially Oyster Creek to the south of the town.

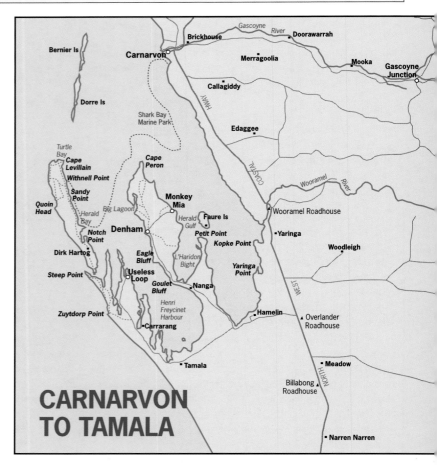

CARNARVON TO TAMALA

Big tailor are common around the coastline from Carnarvon to Shark Bay.

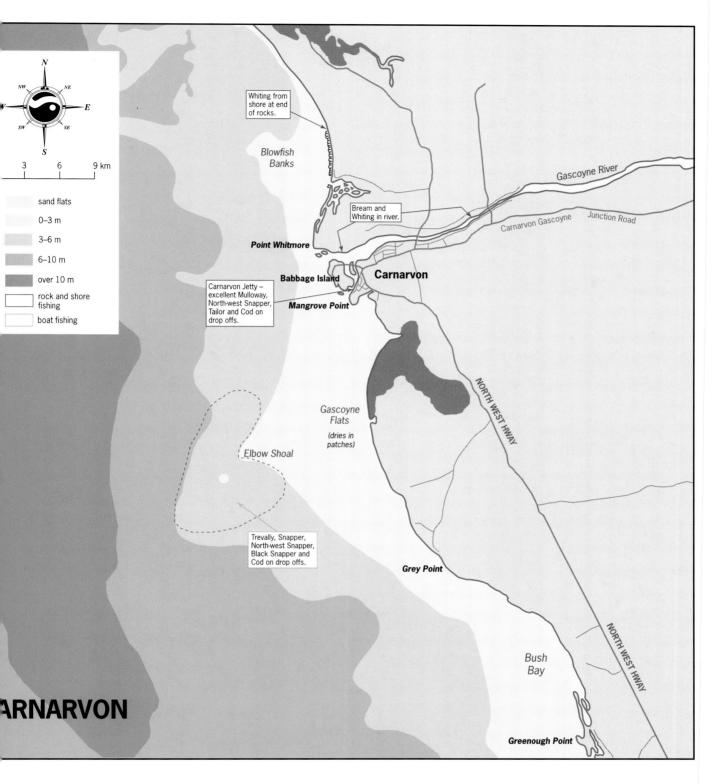

N

NW · N · NE
W · · E
SW · S · SE

3   6   9 km

sand flats
0–3 m
3–6 m
6–10 m
over 10 m
rock and shore fishing
boat fishing

Whiting from shore at end of rocks.

Blowfish Banks

Gascoyne River

Bream and Whiting in river.

Carnarvon Gascoyne Junction Road

Point Whitmore

Babbage Island   **Carnarvon**

Carnarvon Jetty – excellent Mulloway, North-west Snapper, Tailor and Cod on drop offs.

Mangrove Point

NORTH WEST HWY

Gascoyne Flats

(dries in patches)

Elbow Shoal

Trevally, Snapper, North-west Snapper, Black Snapper and Cod on drop offs.

Grey Point

ARNARVON

Bush Bay

NORTH WEST HWY

Greenough Point

OFFSHORE CARNARVON

Boat fishers can launch in the harbour and fish the productive waters out from Carnarvon, including Bernier and Dorre islands where massive Spanish mackerel are often taken. You will need a decent boat and plenty of fuel to reach the islands, otherwise, just fish the excellent waters closer in for spangled emperor, pink snapper, mackerel, cobia and cods which will respond to a variety of baits or lures.

RIGHT: Fishing for tailor from the rocks is a popular pastime for many visiting anglers.

CARNARVON

Shark Bay, situated 800 km north of Perth, is probably one of the most important recreational fishing locations in Western Australia, as anglers can target a wide range of species either from shore or boat. The bay has several long peninsulas that shelter the western and eastern gulfs. On the seaward side the Zuytdorp Cliffs follow the coast from Steep Point south to Kalbarri.

Many tropical species of fish mix with temperate species in Shark Bay, providing a rich selection of species for anglers to target. Special regulations help to manage certain fish stocks. Dugongs, turtles and dolphins are common in the shallow bays, and massive seagrass beds provide safe nurseries for many species of marine life.

There are sealed roads into the main town of Denham and out to Monkey Mia; elsewhere a 4WD vehicle is needed to reach many of the other productive fishing spots, especially on the western side along the Zuytdorp Cliffs. There are several caravan parks throughout the bay, as well as designated camping spots that are controlled by rangers from CALM.

Most anglers visit in winter to escape the colder conditions further south and this is also the time when the pink snapper are at their best. Severe over-fishing of pink snapper in the western and eastern gulfs has forced Fisheries WA to bring in strict new rules to conserve breeding stocks. Closures of big areas to all snapper fishing, strict size and bag limits elsewhere are hopefully reversing some of the damage done by over-fishing in the past.

CAPE PERON

This is a 4WD destination only, and a long, rough, dirt track takes you up the peninsula to the cape. Camping is permitted and this whole area north is National Park so strict rules apply. Shore fishing from the many locations close to the cape will produce many species from snapper, tailor and mulloway to sharks, whiting and flathead. Occasionally tropical species of trevally and queenfish will show up and mackerel are always a possibility. Most anglers fish with large beach rods from the shore and a whole pilchard on ganged hooks usually accounts for any tailor, mulloway, snapper and sharks. Smaller rigs on lighter outfits will usually snare you a feed of whiting and bream from the beaches and bays of the area.

BIG LAGOON

To the north of Denham a rough track leads you past Little Lagoon to a very productive mini-estuary called 'Big Lagoon'. This is a very popular fishing spot, which can be accessed by land or dinghy. Big whiting, bream and flathead are commonly caught and good-sized tailor are numerous. By trolling

Longtail tuna are fast and powerful fish that will take lures, bait and saltwater flies.

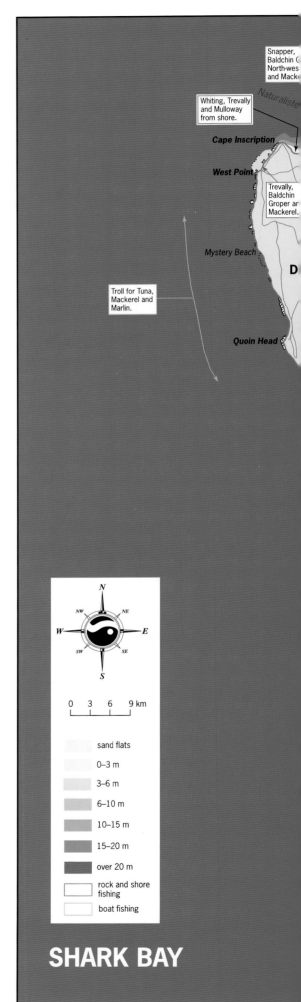

Snapper, Baldchin G North-wes and Mack

Whiting, Trevally and Mulloway from shore.

Naturaliste

Cape Inscription

West Point

Trevally, Baldchin Groper ar Mackerel.

Mystery Beach

D

Troll for Tuna, Mackerel and Marlin.

Quoin Head

N
NW   NE
W   E
SW   SE
S

0   3   6   9 km

sand flats

0–3 m

3–6 m

6–10 m

10–15 m

15–20 m

over 20 m

rock and shore fishing

boat fishing

SHARK BAY

SHARK BAY

Snapper

Mulloway, Mackerel, Shark and Tailor.

Long Point

COASTAL HWY

Cape Peron North

Broadhurst Bight

Herald Bight

Whiting, Tailor Pike, Squid, Garfish and Trevally.

Denham Sound

Guichenault Point

Herald Bluff

Hopeless Reach

Disappointment Reach

Troll for Tuna and Mackerel.

Crab and Whiting.

Cape Lesueur

Big Lagoon

Whiting

Cape Rose

Boat ramp

Snapper, Black Snapper and Mulloway.

Snapper

Peron

Monkey Mia

Whiting and Flathead.

Faure I.

Middle Bluff

Baldchin Groper and Black Snapper.

Snapper

Dubaut Point

Little Lagoon

Peninsula

Lagoon Point

Beware — numerous Stonefish.

Petit Point

Kopke Point

d Bay

Denham boat ramp.

oden

Notch Point

Denham Channel

Tailor from shore at Eagle Bluff.

Tailor and Whiting from shore at Kopke Point.

Cape Bellefin

Cape Heirisson

Snapper, Whiting and Tailor.

Lharidon Bight

Hutchison Is.

ailor and Mackerel.

Slope Is.

Eagle Is. **Eagle Bluff**

Hamelin Pool

Nature Reserve

oint

Useless Inlet

Bellefin Prong

Whiting, Tailor and Mulloway from shore.

Yaringa Point

Cape Ransonnet

Wilson Is.

Carbia Homestead

Lafebre Is.

Goulet Bluff

Nanga Station

Salt

Whiting from shore.

Nanga Bay

Boat ramp

Pan

Crayfish Bay

Edel   **Land**

Henri Freycinet Harbour

Dulverton Bay

Zuytdorp Point

Charlie Is.

Garden Point

Freycinet Is.
Double Is.

White Is.

Brown Inlet

Snapper

Depuch Loop

Baudin Is.

Salutation Is.

Whiting from shore.

Three Bays Is.

Smith Is.

Tailor

Fording Point

Disappointment Loop

Baba Point

Tamala Station

This small threadfin salmon was taken at dusk from a beach in Shark Bay.

Swallowtail dart inhabit the warm, shallow waters along northern beaches.

lures behind a dinghy you will soon locate any tailor in the area, otherwise fish with light outfits and small hooks on the bottom for the whiting, bream and flathead. Once again a rising tide seems to be the best time, particularly early in the morning or at last light, especially for the big tailor.

LITTLE LAGOON

Just 3 km north of the town this little inlet is a great place to spend a few hours fishing for whiting in its sheltered waters. It can be reached easily in 2WD vehicles and fishes the best on the rising tide. Use a light flick rod with 3 kg line and a small hook and ball sinker rig with small pieces of prawn threaded onto the hook to tempt the big yellowfin whiting that feed here in big schools. Flathead and small tailor are also caught here at times. Beware the large population of stonefish.

DENHAM

This is the largest town in the Shark Bay region and provides services to thousands of tourists each year. It has caravan and

ABOVE: The calm, sheltered beaches of Shark Bay are ideal spots to fish for many different species including whiting, bream, flathead and tailor.

camping grounds, boat ramps, shops and all other modern luxuries for the travelling angler. Fishing by boat out into the bay is by far the most popular method with snapper, mulloway and mackerel being the main targets for most. The deeper channels (which can easily be seen during the day) running through the shallow sand and sea grass beds are the prime locations to fish for larger species. Anchoring up and setting out a steady berley trail behind the boat is the trick to fishing these deeper channels. Fish whole pilchards on ganged hooks or whiting heads on single hooks back down the berley trail, and try to use as little or no weight on the rig as possible. It pays to avoid wire traces unless you spot mackerel behind the boat; otherwise you will waste too much time fighting sharks that often plague the area. From the shore in front of the town big whiting can be caught during the day. From the jetty anglers can also target tailor, whiting, mulloway, black snapper (blue lined emperor), pink snapper and squid. Most of the pink snapper taken from the shore around Denham and the Bluffs are well undersize and should be returned carefully to the water as soon as possible after capture.

EAGLE BLUFF

The fishing at Eagle Bluff is productive from the shore. It is a very good spot for big tailor and mulloway after dark, and it fishes best on a rising tide with a reasonable sea breeze blowing.

GOULET BLUFF

This is a very productive shore-fishing spot that can be reached easily by travelling north from Nanga and taking the track down to the Bluff. During the day, catches of whiting and small pink snapper are common. However, it is after dark this place really fires with snapper, mulloway, tailor and sharks making up the bulk of the catches. Use a heavy surf rod with 10 kg line and cast out a whole pilchard on a set of ganged hooks with the aid of a suitable spoon or star sinker. If you pick an afternoon when there is a good sea breeze blowing and the tide is rising then you will

This big flowery cod was returned to the water soon after capture as cod are protected in WA once they exceed 120 cm in length.

Highly prized from reef areas, the baldchin groper (one of the group of tuskfish known as bluebone) is a tough customer to land when hooked.

encounter plenty of tailor. As darkness falls, bigger predators like sharks, mulloway and pink snapper will move into the shallow areas to feed. A wire trace is often used to prevent tailor up to 4.5 kg and small sharks from biting through the line.

MONKEY MIA

Well known for the friendly dolphins that attract thousands of tourists from all around the world, Monkey Mia is a very popular and productive place to fish. Most anglers fish out in the eastern gulf for snapper and mulloway from boats. There are charter boats available and caravan and camping facilities as well.

Fishing from shore after dark will produce tailor, whiting, flathead and mulloway. Until recently the eastern gulf has been closed to fishing for pink snapper due to overfishing of spawning fish especially near Faure Island. Limited fishing is now permitted but check with fisharies and limit your take of snapper which can be found in the 8–12 kg size range.

DIRK HARTOG ISLAND

This massive island, which stretches north from Steep Point, is only now becoming a popular fishing destination. The island is run by the Wardle family who previously used it for sheep farming but who now work with CALM to run Eco-tourism on the island.

The fishing potential from the shore is endless with its numerous rock and beach locations. The western side has rugged

cliffs that drop into deep blue ocean, and anglers must be extremely careful when fishing as rough seas and a big swell make most ledges very dangerous. On the right day though big mackerel, pink snapper, baldchin groper, massive tailor, trevally and sharks are regular visitors.

Heavy spin and baitfishing tackle is needed to fish here and tackle losses will be very high but the results usually make it well worthwhile. Balloon fishing from several of the ledges can produce very large Spanish mackerel, tuna, sharks and sailfish. Spinning with leadhead jigs, metal slices or poppers will do the trick for many pelagics, while bait fishing with pilchards or rock crabs will see hookups from snapper and baldchin groper. A rope gaff is essential for landing fish from nearly all of the western rock locations, as anglers will be fishing from several metres above the water.

RIGHT: The rugged coastline of Dirk Hartog Island's western side.

BELOW: The western side of Dirk Hartog Island provides some exceptional fishing for tailor, snapper and mackerel from the safer platforms.

On the sheltered eastern side, the shallow sand flats and bays are ideal for whiting and flathead fishing from the shore. Fishing with light tackle and small pieces of bait or tiny lures is the way to get results for many species. There have been plenty of surprise bonefish captures by anglers fishing for whiting and flathead on Dirk Hartog, so a concerted effort with a fly rod might be very rewarding. Other species that are common on the eastern side are giant herring, tailor, trevally, dart and sharks.

The accommodation available on the island is mostly camping at designated sites or you can stay at the homestead for a few more dollars. Your 4WD can be transported to the island on a barge that ferries across to the island or you can rely on the island's vehicles for transport.

Boat fishing around Dirk Hartog is nothing short of fantastic. Trolling along the cliffs on the western side is a very popular method for targeting big Spanish mackerel and tuna. Fishing baits on the bottom over the reef and coral will usually result in catches of pink snapper, emperor and baldchin groper. Smaller boats fishing the safer, shallower waters can have a ball on big tailor, whiting, pink snapper and mulloway.

STEEP POINT

Without doubt the most famous landbased fishing location in Australia, is the westernmost point of the mainland. The fishing spots are situated high up on the cliffs that follow the coastline and from here spinning or bait fishing the deep blue water out in front is almost always productive. At the Point, anglers mostly cast bibbed minnow lures on 8–10 kg spin tackle to target the big Spanish mackerel.

In the 1970s, anglers began experimenting with gas ballooning large baits out off the cliffs, resulting in some awesome captures of big mackerel, cobia, sailfish, sharks and tuna. This form of fishing is still very popular today from the point, and it can be mesmerising just sitting back and watching the bright balloons dancing across the water waiting for a strike. Heavy tackle, comprising custom-built ballooning rods mounted with big overhead reels or Alveys, is needed to handle many of the fish hooked from the Point on balloon rigs.

Bait fishing the bottom for big pink snapper, spangled emperor and mulloway, especially after dark, is very popular. Big yellowtail kingfish patrol the base of the cliffs but can be very hard to hook as they inspect every bait. When one is hooked, the 25 kg-plus king usually wins the battle around the rocks within seconds. There have been numerous sailfish caught from the rocks and several marlin have been hooked on light spin tackle over the years, although rarely landed.

South of the Point there are several rough tracks heading south where other locations can be found with a bit of effort. These southern ledges produce fantastic catches of baldchin groper and pink snapper however reaching many of these spots requires rope ladders and plenty of courage. This is a very dangerous part of the coast and if the swell is up it is best to avoid these exposed ledges and fish them another day when the sea is calm.

Camping is permitted out at the Point and a ranger has been stationed there to keep an eye on things and collect the reasonable fees that are charged. You must be self sufficient when fishing Steep Point, and bring in all of your supplies including fuel and water to last your stay. However there is a pay phone in place to keep everyone back at home up-to-date on who is catching the biggest fish!

The road out to the Point is 4WD only, though there are rumours that a sealed road might be put there in the future. Many anglers are not in favour of this but the demand for tourists to visit the westernmost point might see it go ahead.

CRAYFISH BAY

Situated about 25 km down the coast from Steep Point is Epineux Bay, which is better known as Crayfish Bay. A beautiful but rugged surf beach extends for a couple of kilometres around to a rocky headland that provides several interesting fishing locations. This is jumbo tailor country, and lures cast through the white water and surf will usually attract the attention of these trophy-size fish. Tailor in excess of 10 kg are there for the taking and plenty of smaller fish, averaging 4–6 kg, make for very exciting fishing.

From the rocky point at the south occasional mackerel can be hooked, while the bottom fishing with bait is very productive for big baldchin grouper and pink snapper. Smaller species like tarwhine and whiting can be caught from the surf and sand patches amongst the reef, whilst at night the odd mulloway and sharks make for interesting fishing.

Turtle Bay on the northern tip of Dirk Hartog Island is well known for its good fishing.

Barges are used to transport vehicles and supplies to Dirk Hartog Island.

FISH FACTS

MACKEREL

Spanish Mackerel

Spanish Mackerel

Western Australia has a reputation for producing some of the best fishing for Spanish mackerel in Australia, either from the shore or boat. These fish spend their days hunting baitfish, and often hunt in packs, harassing their prey with lightning speed and razor sharp teeth.

Spanish mackerel are found mostly in the deeper water along the back of reefs or deep drop-offs, but at times they will be found hunting the shallows, searching for food. Their range starts at about Perth and heads northwards all the way around the top of Australia where their numbers vary with water temperatures and the availability of baitfish.

Some of the best shore-based fishing for Spanish mackerel is from the high cliffs along the Quobba coastline. Here anglers spin with lures or float out baits of whole tailor or garfish under balloons for these fish. When hooked, a Spaniard will usually tear off on a long, line burning run, almost in a straight line. If you manage to survive the first few long runs the fish are usually beaten and can easily be brought in for gaffing. Out in boats trolling lures is a very popular method of catching these fish, and by concentrating your efforts around diving terns hovering above feeding fish or along ridges and drop-offs, you stand a good chance of hooking them.

Bait fishing from a boat is usually done by floating out a whole pilchard or garfish under a balloon or by slowly drifting one of these baits without any weight back down a berley trail. Wire is a necessity as a mackerel will make short work of monofilament line with their teeth. Really big mackerel are often hooked around openings in reefs with live baits fished under balloons. This method has accounted for fish over 40 kg from the Coral Bay and Exmouth areas. Prized for their eating qualities, these fish are heavily targeted by many anglers.

Shark Mackerel (or Sharkies)

This is a smaller species of mackerel that spend their time feeding on baitfish, like the Spanish mackerel. The name shark mackerel comes from the ammonia smell that arises when these fish are cleaned, much the same as for sharks, but the taste of the flesh is white and delicious.

'Sharkies', as they are more commonly known, are nearly always found in big schools, and in November they can be found in huge numbers along the stretch of coast from Carnarvon to Exmouth. From the rocks at Quobba many shore-based anglers cast lead-head jigs at schools of shark mackerel, resulting in many fish being hooked. Unfortunately the schools of fish attract large numbers of sharks that can be a real problem stealing hooked fish from lines.

From a boat, anglers trolling lures along the back of reefs can usually find sharkies, and their fight is very similar to that of a Spanish mackerel, comprising several fast runs that usually tire the fish quickly.

Bait fishing for sharkies is usually done with pilchards on ganged hooks, complete with a short wire trace to give protection from their sharp teeth. This rig is usually fished up near the surface or allowed to slowly drift down a berley trail where the sharkies will be feeding.

Spotted Mackerel

Spotted, School and Broad-barred Mackerel

There are a couple of smaller species of mackerel that turn up in the same areas as shark and Spanish mackerel, these are spotted and school mackerel.

Spotted mackerel are easy to identify as they have numerous small spots instead of stripes like on a Spanish mackerel. School mackerel often look like juvenile Spanish mackerel but lack the heavy banding along the sides; instead they seem to only have a few bands or large blotches. Broad-barred mackerel are another species that also turns up in northern locations and like all mackerels they respond to the same type of fishing methods.

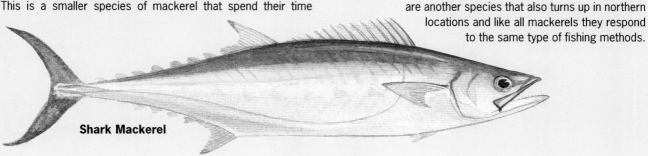

Shark Mackerel

FALSE ENTRANCE

Just a short way south of Crayfish Bay is Dulverton Bay or as it is better known 'False Entrance' and Zuytdorp Point. Like Crayfish Bay this area is prime big tailor country with wild surf and reef extending south until the cliffs once again take over. Casting metal slices or surface poppers through the broken water is best to find these jumbo-sized tailor. A good reliable 4WD is necessary to access these areas, as many of the tracks are very rough.

NANGA

This popular holiday spot lies at the base of the Peron Peninsula and can be reached by following the Shark Bay Road heading towards Denham. Camping and caravan facilities are available as well as some accommodation. There is a boat ramp at Nanga where most anglers travel out into the bay to target snapper and mulloway. The best method is to venture out just on dusk when the tide is rising and find a deep hole with your sounder and GPS, then berley up with fish scraps. A heavy rod with 10–15 kg line or gelspun is used to cast lightly weighted baits of pilchards or whiting heads back into the berley trail where the big mulloway and pink snapper will be feeding. From the shore, whiting, flathead and tailor are common catches and can be caught using a light flick rod.

The snapper stocks in the Freycinet area have been depleted and special rules have been put in place, including special tags for snapper that need to be purchased from the Fisheries Department before landing any snapper anywhere in Freycinet Estuary.

TAMALA

Situated at the bottom of the Freycinet Estuary is the small tourist camping spot of Tamala where visiting anglers in small dinghies fish the shallow, calm waters of the estuary for whiting and bream during the day and big mulloway and pink snapper after dark. Fishing from the shore is very productive for whiting and flathead in the warm, shallow water. Camping is permitted at Tamala and small boats such as dinghies can be launched from the beach.

USELESS LOOP

The massive salt-mining operations are run out of the little settlement of Useless Loop, and unfortunately access is restricted. There are some good shore-fishing locations for snapper, mulloway, tailor, whiting and flathead all along Useless Inlet. The salt evaporators and the causeway crossing the main evaporator pond are fantastic fishing spots for a wide range of species, including jumbo tailor, but sadly much of this area including the causeway itself, is off limits to the public.

BOAT RAMPS & TACKLE STORES

There are good public launch facilities at Carnarvon, Denham and Monkey Mia, allowing trailer boats easy access to the surrounding waters and offshore islands. Launching smaller trailer craft from the beaches in Shark Bay is very popular with many anglers, especially around the holiday spots like Nanga, Tamala and Steep Point. The cooler months of the year seem to be the best for boating in this area until the winter cold fronts set in from the south. Occasionally cyclones during the summer months reach far enough south to cause concern if fishing in this area, so keep a close eye on the weather forecasts.

RAMPS
Carnarvon – Harbour
Denham – Town
Monkey Mia – Town

TACKLE STORES

Carnarvon Sports
Carnarvon WA 6701
Tel: (08) 9941 2627

Freeman's Fibreglass & Boating
Carnarvon WA 6701
Tel: (08) 9941 4161

Bait and limited tackle is available at many service stations in the region.

C H A P T E R   5

KALBARRI TO GERALDTON

KALBARRI

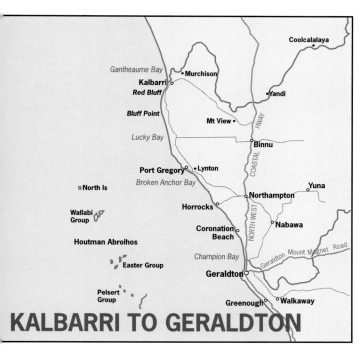

KALBARRI TO GERALDTON

At the mouth of the Murchison River is the popular fishing and tourist town of Kalbarri. With a coast made up of spectacular cliffs providing some excellent rockfishing platforms and the sheltered and safe Murchison River that winds its way upstream for some distance, Kalbarri is a haven for many recreational anglers. There are plenty of choices in accommodation and boat-launching facilities in the town.

Fishing from the cliffs to the south of Kalbarri can be very rewarding but anglers must be extremely careful when fishing this area because of the danger of being washed off the rocks by big waves. If the seas are up and waves are regularly crashing against the cliffs don't attempt to fish this area, and never fish it alone.

FRUSTRATION REEF

The keen angler, on foot, can embark on a journey northwards to fish many productive reef holes leading up to Frustration Reef, an area made up of rock and beach locations with deep gutters and plenty of white water to fish. Big mulloway are the most

Yellowfin whiting are a popular catch from the Murchison River at Kalbarri.

popular species targeted, and fishing with a whole fillet of mullet on ganged hooks is very successful. Big tailor can also be caught with heavy surf-fishing tackle and bring plenty of spare rigs as the reefy country is sure to tax a few.

OYSTER REEF

Many anglers cross the Murchison with a small dinghy and then leave it on the shore to fish the northern reef spots on foot. Oyster Reef, which makes up the northern river mouth, is a popular place for big tailor, and baitcasting whole garfish, mulies or throwing poppers from here is a very reliable method to take tailor from 2–6 kilograms.

MURCHISON RIVER

From the mouth of the river some excellent catches of big mulloway have been made, usually after a fair bit of rain, which will push the dirty water down to the mouth and attract the fish. Black bream, whiting and chopper tailor are all common catches in the lower reaches, and crabbing with baited drop nets for blue swimmer crabs and mud crabs can be very productive at times. Further upriver black bream are the main target for most anglers who fish rockbars, snags and deep holes with prawns.

CHINAMAN REEF

Heading south from Kalbarri along the coast the shore anglers have many places to try their luck, starting at the river mouth at Chinaman Rock where mulloway and big tailor are regular catches. Fish with a long surf rod and 10 kg line and use a ganged hook rig baited with a whole pilchard or garfish.

BLUE HOLES

Further south are the Blue Holes where

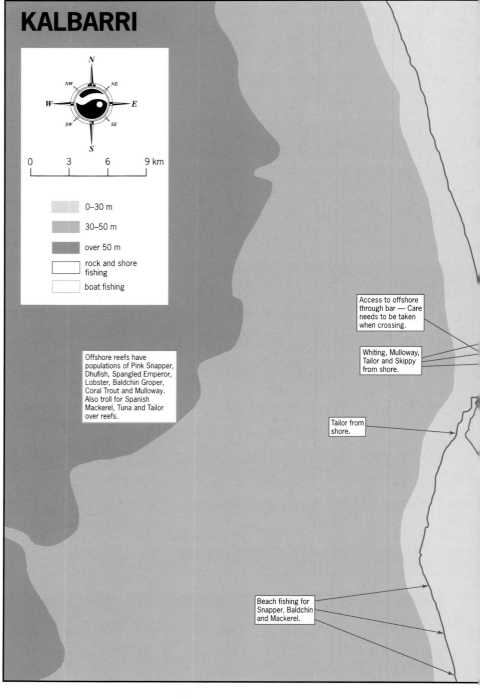

KALBARRI

0   3   6   9 km

0–30 m

30–50 m

over 50 m

rock and shore fishing

boat fishing

Access to offshore through bar — Care needs to be taken when crossing.

Whiting, Mulloway, Tailor and Skippy from shore.

Tailor from shore.

Offshore reefs have populations of Pink Snapper, Dhufish, Spangled Emperor, Lobster, Baldchin Groper, Coral Trout and Mulloway. Also troll for Spanish Mackerel, Tuna and Tailor over reefs.

Beach fishing for Snapper, Baldchin and Mackerel.

anglers casting poppers across the white water and deep holes hook into big tailor up to 6 kilograms. Another popular method for these big tailor is to cast an unweighted whole garfish out on ganged hooks and then slowly retrieve it—the large tailor will soon respond with a savage strike. You can catch your gardies for bait from Jakes just to the north of Red Bluff. Fish the area north of the car park. There is a proposal to restrict fishing in the area to the south of the car park so check with locals before fishing the area.

RED BLUFF

This rock-fishing location is favoured by many because it produces big tailor, mulloway, sharks, Samson fish and pink snapper from the shore. The best method is bait fishing using heavy surf-fishing tackle comprising a ganged hook rig baited with mulies, a short trace of heavy mono, or wire if you intend landing smaller sharks, weighted down with a spoon or star

sinker to suit the conditions.

WITTECARRA

Another productive shore spot for tailor, mulloway and sharks.

The Gorges: Rainbow Valley, Pot Alley, Eagle, Goat Gulch, Shell Cake and Layer Cake

These higher rock platforms extend southwards and put the angler in a position to fish deeper water right at their feet. Big tailor, mulloway, pink snapper, dhufish, sharks, Samson fish and cod are all possibilities from these ledges.

Extreme care must be taken as in big seas these platforms are all swamped by big swells, and their height from the water means that you need a long pole gaff or a rope gaff to land fish. Balloon fishing, when the easterly winds allow, can put anglers in with the chance of landing Spanish mackerel or tuna from the rocks.

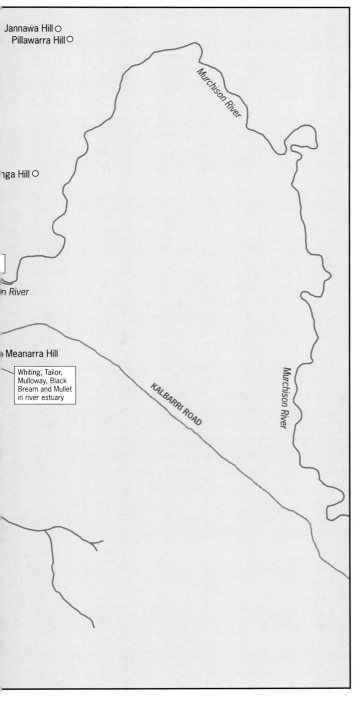

Jannawa Hill ○
Pillawarra Hill ○

ıga Hill ○

n River

Meanarra Hill

Whiting, Tailor, Mulloway, Black Bream and Mullet in river estuary

Murchison River

Murchison River

KALBARRI ROAD

FISH FACTS

PRAWNS

Both king and school prawns are targeted by anglers in Western Australia, mostly for food but sometimes for bait. The estuaries like the Swan and Peel are home to good numbers of king prawns that are scooped from the river at night during autumn as they run out with the tide. On a good night several hundred big king prawns can be caught. The river around East Fremantle also takes on the image of a crowded car park as boats and light go in all directions chasing prawns. Others choose to scuba dive at night with a torch and butterfly net to snare a feed along the bottom of the river. Both methods are hard work but well worth the effort when it comes time to eat.

The river prawns are usually caught at night by dragging a net between two anglers through the shallows of an estuary. Catches vary from year to year and the warmer months are generally better both for wading in the water and for the numbers of prawns caught.

Like the king prawns, the river prawns make great eating or can be used as bait for a wide range of species.

At Kalbarri, big tailor are often hooked from the shore by anglers fishing with baits and lures.

KALBARRI OFFSHORE FISHING

Many visiting anglers tow boats up to Kalbarri to fish, be they small dinghies to explore the river or bigger craft capable of serious offshore work. The only problem with the Murchison River is the tricky negotiation of the river mouth to gain access to the open ocean. It is important to sit back and watch for a while and then time your crossing when it is safe. The big commercial cray boats with plenty of horsepower make it look far too easy. Don't forget that the skippers are very well qualified and make this crossing hundreds of times in a year. If you are unsure, then take your time. If the cray boats are refusing to go out in rough weather then stay on shore.

Once you are safely out past the river mouth then you can fish the very productive waters of Kalbarri. Trolling lures along the cliffs can catch big tailor, Spanish mackerel, Samson fish and tuna. Out further, in deeper water, the bottom fishing can be fantastic and produce pink snapper, dhufish, mulloway, baldchin

groper and various cods. When the river is flowing and pushing dirty brown water out into the ocean then trolling along the colour change with lures or whole garfish and mullet is very productive for really big Spanish mackerel. A number of charter boats are also available at Kalbarri

Beach fishing can be full of surprises. Here a little whaler shark is lifted for a picture before being released.

WAGOE BEACH

A very popular beach-fishing location, Wagoe Beach has accommodation that must be booked well in advance. A 4WD vehicle is needed to move up and down the beach to fish into the sand holes between the reef. Wagoe is where the beach ends and the cliffs start to the north and it is famous for really big tailor, sharks and mulloway from the shore. Heavy surf means anglers use big sinkers and bait rigs on surf-fishing tackle. Along with the tailor and mulloway there are plenty of pink snapper, flathead, trevally, Samson fish, dart and the occasional cobia, or dhufish

are taken from the beach. If the wind is an easterly then it is well worth sending out a balloon as this method works really well from Wagoe when targeting big Spanish mackerel and tuna.

The beach stretches all the way south to Lucky Bay and anywhere along this stretch the fishing can be great.

PORT GREGORY

Port Gregory has safe, small-boat fishing inside the reef and a small jetty in town that is great to fish for smaller species on light tackle. To the south of town there is 4WD access to the mouth of the Hutt River where big tailor, mulloway, sharks and whiting can be targeted. Use surf-fishing tackle and fish late in the afternoon for best results, or if the river is flooding and pushing brown water out into the ocean, be prepared to find mulloway feeding in the dirty water.

HORROCKS

A small crayfishing town that has a caravan park, Horrocks attracts plenty of keen anglers every year. They bring up small dinghies to fish the sheltered waters inside the reef for tailor, whiting, Samson fish, silver trevally and squid. The small jetty in town is also a favourite spot for smaller species and a top place for squid after dark.

Access along the beaches is good for 4WDs, giving beach anglers the chance to fish for big tailor, mulloway and sharks from numerous surf spots. Small boats can be launched with ease to access the offshore grounds, and many choose to fish this area in autumn when the sea and wind conditions are at their best. Mackerel can be caught during summer but strong sea breezes can make it very uncomfortable in smaller boats.

Trolling lures along the back of the reefs can produce Samson fish, mackerel and big tailor. Bait fishing with dropper rigs over reefy ground is a popular method for producing big WA dhufish, pink snapper and baldchin groper. Boats working to the south towards Wagoe catch big tuna and mackerel, usually on trolled lures or baits.

GERALDTON

Geraldton is the next major city north of Perth and has some excellent local fishing opportunities available to boat and shore anglers. There are all modern conveniences and plenty of accommodation from caravan parks to up-market hotels.

CORONATION BEACH

This popular fishing beach is just to the north of the city and is heavily fished for tailor, whiting and herring during the day. At night the beach is a great spot to catch mulloway, big tailor and small whaler sharks. It fishes best when the sea breeze is in, however after a period of rough weather, weed can be a real problem fouling your line. Most anglers use surf rods and whole pilchards on ganged hook rigs cast out with a suitable star or spoon sinker.

SUNSET BEACH

One of the closest beaches to Geraldton to fish, Sunset Beach is a great place to catch herring and big sand whiting during the day, and when the sea breeze comes in there are usually plenty of chopper tailor and occasional small whaler sharks caught.

THE HARBOUR AND BREAKWATER

The harbour and breakwater are popular spots with the locals

who target everything from herring, tailor, gardies and whiting to big mulloway and sharks at night. Occasionally Spanish mackerel are taken from the breakwater and some big black bream are caught in the harbour by anglers using half a mulie for bait.

DRUMMONDS COVE

Drummonds Cove is another popular beach-fishing site which is located just south of Coronation. It produces tailor, whiting, herring, mulloway and small sharks from the surf and is best fished late in the afternoon or at night when the larger fish move in close to feed. For best results, use surf fishing tackle with a rig comprising ganged 5/0 hooks baited with a mulie, then a short mono or wire trace up to a swivel and a star sinker. During the day try fishing lighter with ganged whitebait on #2 hooks for herring and whiting.

POINT MOORE/SEPARATION POINT

Good for herring and whiting, Point Moore/Separation Point is better known for tailor, and is heavily fished in the summer months for chopper sized tailor. Trolling small metal slice lures behind a boat between Point Moore and Drummonds Cove is usually a good way to pick up a feed of tailor.

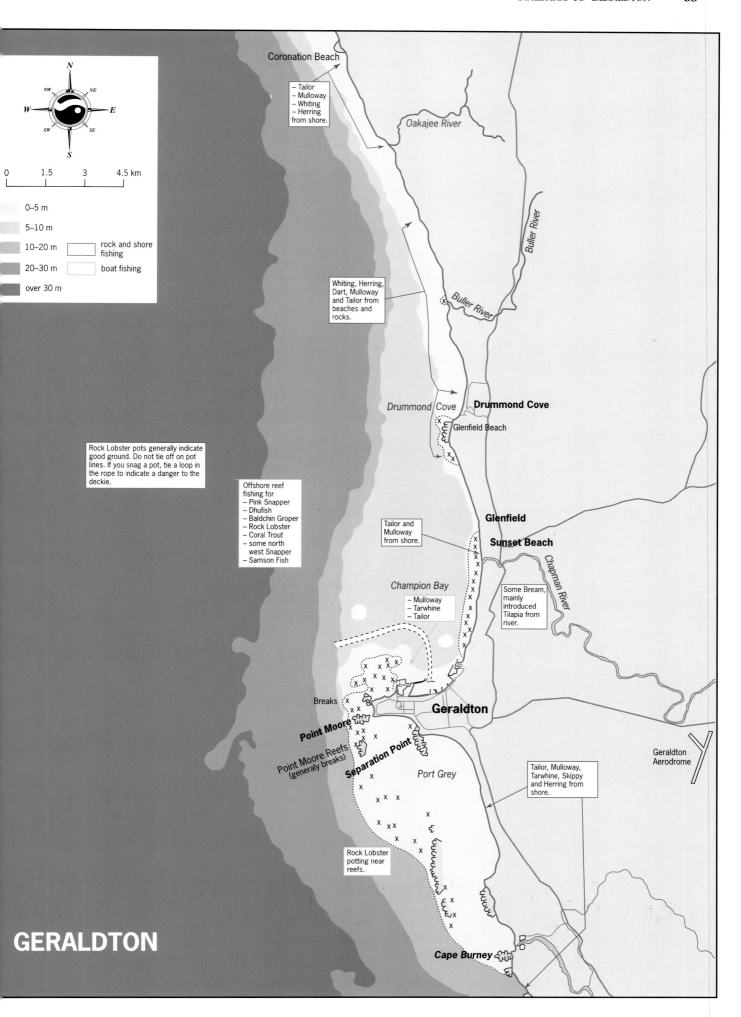

Coronation Beach

– Tailor
– Mulloway
– Whiting
– Herring
from shore.

Oakajee River

Buller River

Buller River

Whiting, Herring,
Dart, Mulloway
and Tailor from
beaches and
rocks.

0   1.5   3   4.5 km

0–5 m
5–10 m
10–20 m   rock and shore
                 fishing
20–30 m   boat fishing
over 30 m

Drummond Cove   **Drummond Cove**

Glenfield Beach

Rock Lobster pots generally indicate
good ground. Do not tie off on pot
lines. If you snag a pot, tie a loop in
the rope to indicate a danger to the
deckie.

Offshore reef
fishing for
– Pink Snapper
– Dhufish
– Baldchin Groper
– Rock Lobster
– Coral Trout
– some north
  west Snapper
– Samson Fish

Glenfield

Tailor and
Mulloway
from shore.

Sunset Beach

Chapman River

Champion Bay

– Mulloway
– Tarwhine
– Tailor

Some Bream,
mainly
introduced
Tilapia from
river.

Breaks

Geraldton

Point Moore

Point Moore Reefs
(generaly breaks)

Separation Point

Port Grey

Geraldton
Aerodrome

Tailor, Mulloway,
Tarwhine, Skippy
and Herring from
shore.

Rock Lobster
potting near
reefs.

GERALDTON

Cape Burney

FISH FACTS

SNAPPER

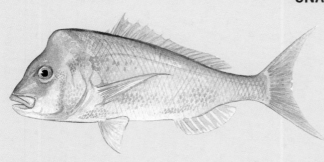

Pink Snapper

Like the dhufish, the pink snapper is high up on the list of popular species that anglers love to catch. The eating qualities of pink snapper are highly regarded and as a result these fish are targeted heavily from Carnarvon all the way south to Esperance. However severe over-fishing of pink snapper in the western and eastern gulfs of Shark Bay has forced Fisheries WA to bring in strict rules to conserve breeding stocks. Closures of big areas to all snapper fishing, strict size and bag limits have been imposed to help reverse some of the damage done by over-fishing in the past.

Pink snapper are usually targeted from boats and this allows anglers to effectively search for areas that attract snapper—usually reefy areas or deep channels. Most use baits of pilchards, octopus or squid, but a whole whiting head is considered by many to be the number one snapper bait. From the deeper offshore reefs anglers drop baited rigs to the bottom with the aid of large sinkers and the quick bites from pink snapper are easily felt with gelspun lines even in 50 m or more of water.

In shallow waters where big schools of pink snapper aggregate, many anglers have in the past chosen to anchor and berley to attract the fish. Then they fish with whole pilchards or other small baitfish like slimy mackerel that are allowed to drift down the berley trail with little or no weight. Snapper will put up a strong fight with plenty of head shaking and short runs;

providing the fish can be kept away from any reef there is little chance of losing it.

In the shallow waters a medium rod and reel loaded with 10 kg line is all that is needed to catch snapper, but if you are fishing close to a reef or wreck then you might like to up the stakes a little. From the shore, snapper are usually taken from the high cliff areas where anglers will require a strong rod and line to pull the fish up from the bottom where it will try and cut the line. Most snapper are kept for the dinner table as their firm, white flesh makes them a big favourite amongst those of us who enjoy a meal of fish.

If you intend fishing for pink snapper check with the Fisheries Department on the up-to-date regulations.

Queen Snapper

Otherwise known as a 'blue morwong', queen snapper is often taken by bottom fishing the deeper reefs of the southwest corner. These fish are usually found in the same areas as dhufish and pink snapper, and although not targeted they are a welcome catch because of their good eating qualities.

Queen snapper have small mouths and as a result a smaller hook on a dropper rig baited with squid or octopus is usually an effective method of hooking them. They are rarely caught from the shore but some of the rock headlands that jut out into deep water along the south coast are known to produce queen snapper at times.

Mulloway are a prize catch from the beaches and shore reefs from Kalbarri to Geraldton.

Although not often targeted, Samson fish are about in good numbers along the west coast and they will test most anglers and their tackle to the limits.

SOUTHGATES/TARCOOLA

From here south, the coast is made up of some excellent beach/reef with deep gutters and holes that extend down towards Flatrocks. This is the place to target big fish from the beach, and mulloway, Samson fish, sharks and large tailor are taken from the surf and reef holes. Heavy surf tackle should be used with large baits like mullet fillet or whole pilchards on ganged hooks. There are also plenty of herring, whiting and chopper tailor throughout this stretch of coast to keep most people happy, but if it is the bigger fish you want then put the hours in after dark, preferably on a rising tide.

GERALDTON OFFSHORE

With excellent launching facilities, Geraldton offers some top boat-fishing options, from small dinghies catching herring, gardies and squid in close, to larger boats taking advantage of the offshore reefs for big Samson fish, dhufish, pink snapper, coral trout, baldchin groper and cod. Trolling is often successful for various tuna species and mackerel, especially during the summer months. Bottom fishing with a heavy boat rod or hand line is still a very popular method for dhufish and snapper; many boats fish with dropper rigs baited with octopus, squid or pilchards.

ABROLHOS ISLANDS

The Abrolhos Islands not only support the richest commercial rock lobster grounds in Australia, they offer the recreational angler a huge range of fish species and fishing experiences. Lying 50 km offshore you need a decent-sized and reliable boat to reach the islands, but once there the bottom fishing, diving and trolling is world class. Warm currents from the north have surrounded the islands with live coral, making them ideal diving or fishing sites. Big baldchin groper, pink snapper, dhufish, coral trout, cods, yellowtail kingfish, amberjacks and Samson fish are all common catches. Trolling lures account for mackerel, tuna,

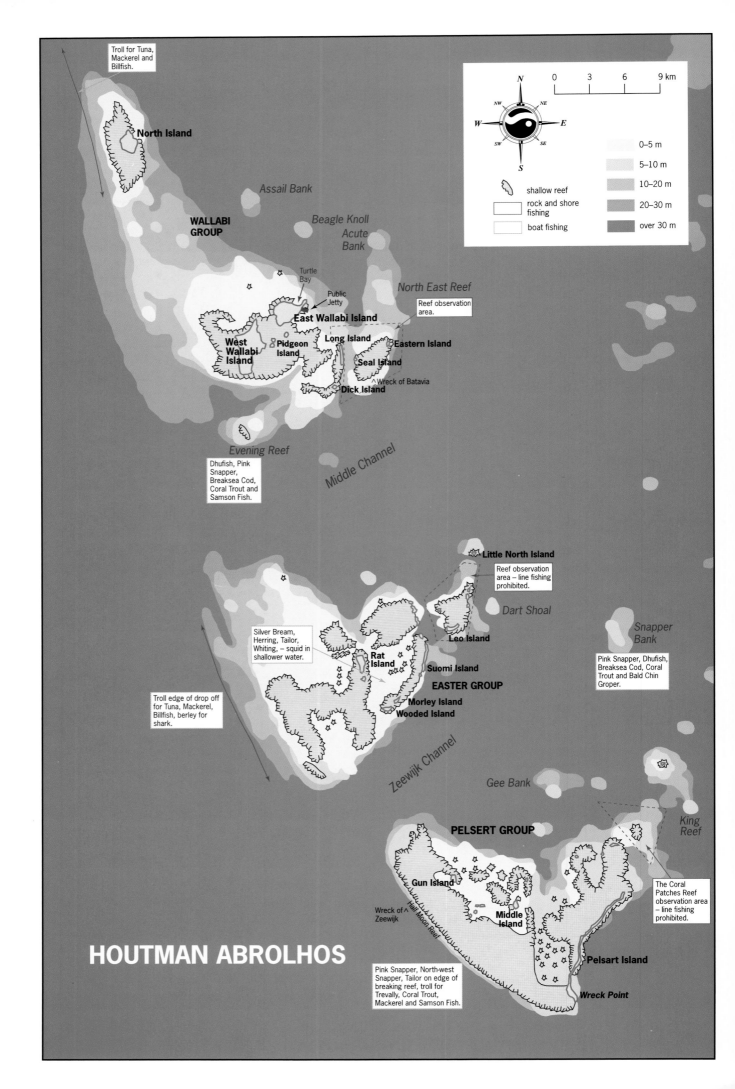

Troll for Tuna, Mackerel and Billfish.

North Island

Assail Bank

WALLABI GROUP

Beagle Knoll

Acute Bank

Turtle Bay

Public Jetty

North East Reef

Reef observation area.

East Wallabi Island

Long Island   **Eastern Island**

West Wallabi Island   **Pidgeon Island**

Seal Island

Dick Island   ^ Wreck of Batavia

Evening Reef

Middle Channel

Dhufish, Pink Snapper, Breaksea Cod, Coral Trout and Samson Fish.

☆ **Little North Island**

Reef observation area – line fishing prohibited.

Dart Shoal

Silver Bream, Herring, Tailor, Whiting, – squid in shallower water.

Leo Island

Snapper Bank

Rat Island

Suomi Island   **EASTER GROUP**

Pink Snapper, Dhufish, Breaksea Cod, Coral Trout and Bald Chin Groper.

Morley Island

Wooded Island

Troll edge of drop off for Tuna, Mackerel, Billfish, berley for shark.

Zeewijk Channel   *Gee Bank*

King Reef

PELSERT GROUP

The Coral Patches Reef observation area – line fishing prohibited.

Gun Island

Wreck of ^ Zeewijk

Half Moon Reef

Middle Island

Pelsart Island

Wreck Point

HOUTMAN ABROLHOS

Pink Snapper, North-west Snapper, Tailor on edge of breaking reef, troll for Trevally, Coral Trout, Mackerel and Samson Fish.

N
NW   *NE*
W   *E*
SW   *SE*
S

0   3   6   9 km

0–5 m
5–10 m
10–20 m
20–30 m
over 30 m

shallow reef
rock and shore fishing
boat fishing

FISH FACTS

MULLOWAY

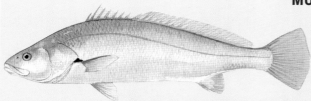

For most anglers the mulloway is the biggest fish they stand a chance of hooking from the shore along the southern Western Australian coastline. From about Carnarvon southwards to the Great Australian Bight, the mulloway is the king of the surf and estuaries. These are predatory fish that are often found in shallow water along beaches and reef areas, often entering estuaries and rivers where they will often stay, providing there is enough food and habitat to keep them there.

Mulloway are often caught in excess of 25 kg, and a fish of this size is considered a real prize from the shore, however most seem to show up in the 6–18 kg size range. Small mulloway up to around 3 kg are referred to as 'soapies', due to the taste of their flesh at this age, and it is not until they reach a bigger size that the eating qualities improve.

Most mulloway are taken after dark, as this seems to be the time when these big fish move into the shallows to feed under the cover of darkness. A rising tide is usually the preferred time to chase them, especially from the beach or rocks but in the estuaries the slack water at the change of the tide usually triggers them to feed.

Most anglers target mulloway with heavy surf gear comprising a 3 m rod fitted with a reel capable of holding 200–300 m of 10 kg line. This is usually more than enough to stop even a big mulloway, as after a few long runs these fish usually come in easily. If there is shelter in the form of a reef or bridge pylon close by then anglers must use all of their skill to prevent the fish from wrapping the line around the structure and gaining its freedom.

Baits of whole or filleted fish like mullet or tailor are ideal for mulloway, but the humble pilchard probably accounts for more mulloway in WA than any other bait. A small live bait in the form of a fish or squid can be absolutely dynamite on these predators and will often produce the goods when dead baits are being ignored.

In the Swan River many keen anglers are now casting minnow lures or saltwater flies around bridge pylons after dark for excellent results. The predatory nature of the mulloway means that it will respond to a wiggling lure or darting fly if spotted, and the thrill of catching one of these fish on an artificial is well worth the effort put into continually casting.

Large numbers of these fish sometimes show up at certain locations along the coast, and the famous runs of mulloway from the Carnarvon Jetty are eagerly anticipated each year. Many target these fish from boats either in the ocean or estuaries, allowing the anglers to fish the deeper holes or locations around bridges that are out of shore range.

In the north of the State another species, the black jew, is found. This is a close relative of the southern mulloway and attracts plenty of fishing effort around places like Broome. Anglers usually target these tough fish from a boat that is anchored over a deep hole or wreck, and a heavy line baited with fish fillets or squid, is dropped down. When hooked, a black jew is a tough customer and it will do its best to wrap the line around any structure it can find. Many anglers use heavy monofilament on a hand line so that they can try and reef the fish up off the bottom as soon as possible. Occasionally these fish are taken on lures being fished for other species. The black jew is considered good eating.

---

dolphin fish, sailfish and marlin. Access to the islands themselves is strictly controlled and only the commercial rock lobster fishers are allowed to stay on them, making up a small community with a school during the island's rock lobster season which runs from 15 March to 30 June.

A number of charter boats work the Abrolhos Islands from Geraldton or Dongara. A trip to the Abrolhos Islands can be a once in a lifetime experience but sea conditions can be quite rough.

S-Bend

Just to the south of Geraldton is the S-Bend, an area named after a huge sweeping bend in the North West Coastal Highway at this point. The comfortable caravan park here provides a great place to stay while you experience the fantastic beach fishing of this area. The famous flat rocks are just a couple of kilometres south of here, and this is the one place in WA where dhufish are consistently taken from the shore. Each year dozens of big dhufish that range from little 4 kg specimens up to 15 kg monsters please and surprise beach anglers fishing into the deep reef holes, usually with weighted mulies to target tailor. Along with tailor and dhufish there are plenty of big mulloway, Samson fish and sharks to keep your arms stretched. Herring, whiting and flathead are also taken from the beach on lighter tackle.

BOAT RAMPS & TACKLE STORES

The massive rock lobster industry has been a real bonus for many recreational boating anglers because of the need for safe harbours and facilities for the commercial lobster fleet. As a result many of the smaller centres from Kalbarri to Jurien Bay have good boat launching facilities and harbours. The best boating conditions are in the autumn months when the winds are not too strong. During the summer months the sea breezes often prevent safe offshore boating for all but the larger craft.

RAMPS

Kalbarri – Grey Street and Fishermans Jetty
Geraldton – Batavia Coast Marina and Town Beach

TACKLE STORES

Kalbarri Marine & Hardware
465 Grey Street,
Kalbarri, 6536
Tel: (08) 9937 1175

Kalbarri Sports & Dive
Shop 3, Kalbarri Arcade
44 Grey Street, Kalbarri 6536
Tel: (08) 9937 1126

Barlo Firearms & Tackle
20 Anzac Terrace,
Geraldton WA 6530
Tel: (08) 9921 6822

Geraldton Sports Centre
208 Marine Terrace,
Geraldton WA 6530
Tel: (08) 9921 3664

CHAPTER 6

DONGARA TO GUILDERTON/ MOORE RIVER

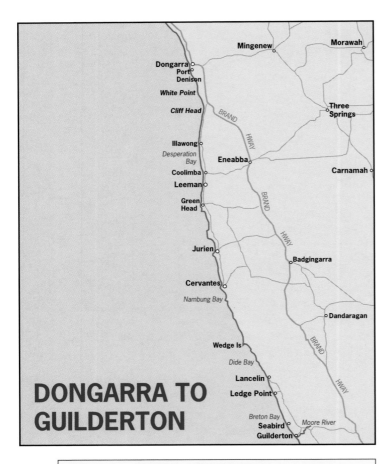

DONGARRA TO GUILDERTON

DONGARA

Another major rock lobster fishing town with all modern facilities and plenty of accommodation, Dongara is a very popular fishing spot. The beach fishing to the north of town is accessed by 4WD tracks up through the dunes, leading to numerous spots to try for tailor and mulloway. The south beach is flatter and shallower but still requires a 4WD to travel along it, and is great for chopper tailor, herring and whiting.

The breakwalls in town are popular at night with mulloway anglers who fish with heavy surf gear baited with whole mulies or small live baits, and on some nights the action can be hectic when the mulloway move in. The breakwall is a top tailor spot as well and also produces plenty of herring, whiting and squid.

Boat fishing out from Dongara is excellent for big dhufish, pink snapper and big Samson fish. Most of these species can be found around the numerous bomboras and reefs that lie out from Dongara. Trolling during the summer months is usually productive for tuna and Spanish mackerel.

FISH FACTS

DHUFISH

In Western Australia the prize fish on the list of many boat anglers living from Kalbarri to the Great Australian Bight, is dhufish. Often called Jewfish, jewie or dhu, these fish are no relation to mulloway that are also called Jewfish at times.

The dhufish is a large fish that inhabits the offshore reefs and has earned the reputation and price tag for having the most delicious tasting flesh of any species. As a result these fish are very heavily targeted and they no longer inhabit many of the inshore reefs. Strict bag and size limits have eased the pain a little for this species but the availability of GPS and colour sounders has exposed them to just about every boat angler in the State.

The dhufish is a predatory species with a large mouth that will feed opportunistically on a wide range of foods often favouring octopus, squid, crayfish and reef fish that it sucks in with a rapid opening of its mouth. Most dhufish taken along the west coast range from just legal to about 12 kg, and each year a handful of fish topping the 20 kg mark turn up much to the delight of the lucky angler. Male dhufish have a long filament on the soft dorsel fin.

Most anglers fish for the dhufish around reefy lumps with bottom-bouncing tackle that consists of a stout boat rod and reel loaded with gelspun line. The rig is usually a heavy sinker on the bottom with several dropper hooks up from that. Baits of squid, octopus, pilchards or other fish are bounced along the reef as the boat slowly drifts. When a dhufish is felt taking the bait many experienced anglers give them a bit of slack line to swallow before setting the hook. Striking too early will often result in the bait being pulled from the dhufish's mouth.

In shallow locations dhufish can be attracted to an anchored boat with a good berley trail, and baits allowed to drift down without too much weight are usually taken without hesitation. In shallow water a big dhufish will put up a very powerful fight, often dragging the angler's line into a cave where it can be a waiting game to try and get the fish out.

Other anglers have also had success bouncing white lead-head jigs, either plain or sweetened with a bit of bait, along the bottom for good results. Dhufish don't normally turn up on lures but occasionally a trolled lure that reaches the right depth has accounted for one.

From deeper reefs many undersize dhufish come up with expanded air bladders that need to be carefully deflated with the aid of a sterilised syringe, or the fish need to be dropped back to the depths on another line with a specially designed weight fitted with a barbless hook available from tackle stores.

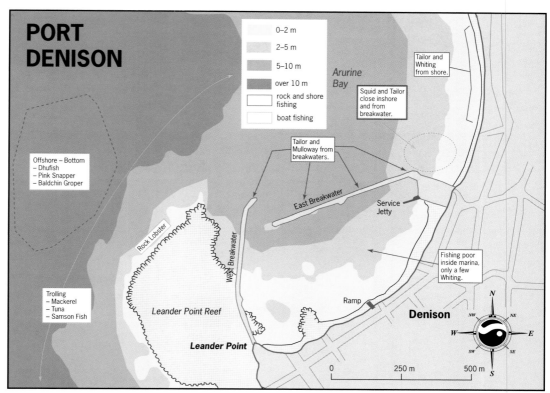

PORT DENISON

Legend:
- 0–2 m
- 2–5 m
- 5–10 m
- over 10 m
- rock and shore fishing
- boat fishing

Arurine Bay

Tailor and Whiting from shore.

Squid and Tailor close inshore and from breakwater.

Tailor and Mulloway from breakwaters.

East Breakwater

Service Jetty

Offshore – Bottom
– Dhufish
– Pink Snapper
– Baldchin Groper

West Breakwater

Rock Lobster

Fishing poor inside marina, only a few Whiting.

Trolling
– Mackerel
– Tuna
– Samson Fish

Leander Point Reef

Ramp

Denison

Leander Point

```
0        250 m      500 m
```

N NW NE W E SW SE S

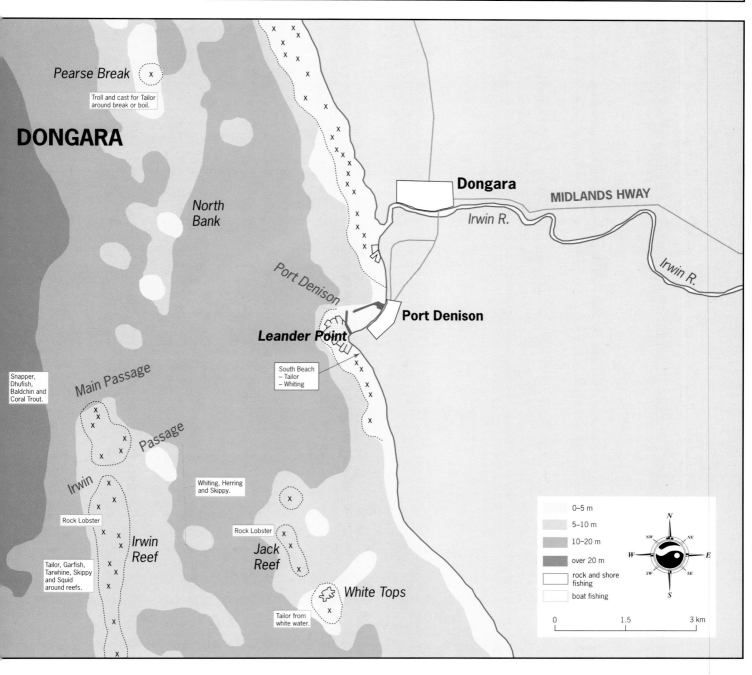

Pearse Break   x

Troll and cast for Tailor around break or boil.

DONGARA

North Bank

Dongara

MIDLANDS HWY

Irwin R.

Irwin R.

Port Denison

Port Denison

Leander Point

South Beach
– Tailor
– Whiting

Snapper, Dhufish, Baldchin and Coral Trout.

Main Passage

Passage

Irwin

Whiting, Herring and Skippy.

Rock Lobster

Rock Lobster

Irwin Reef

Jack Reef

Tailor, Garfish, Tarwhine, Skippy and Squid around reefs.

White Tops

Tailor from white water.

Legend:
- 0–5 m
- 5–10 m
- 10–20 m
- over 20 m
- rock and shore fishing
- boat fishing

N NW NE W E SW SE S

```
0           1.5          3 km
```

GREEN HEAD & LEEMAN

These little settlements were originally set up to service commercial rock lobster boats but have fast become holiday destinations for many recreational anglers. Easy boat launching is available at these destinations, and the majority of visiting anglers tow boats in to experience the fantastic offshore fishing.

The beach fishing is not as productive as that further north around Dongara because the water is much shallower and weedy, however some good catches of tailor, whiting, herring and silver trevally can be made.

By boat is the way to fully enjoy this area, as even with a small dinghy anglers can make great catches of big dhufish, baldchin groper and Samson fish from the reefs not too far from shore. Closer in, the shallower water is a great place to target silver trevally, herring, tailor, whiting and squid. Dropping a couple of cray pots around the reefs during the season is usually pretty rewarding and the diving is also very impressive.

JURIEN

Jurien is a popular boat holiday spot allowing access to close inshore reefs that produce good catches of the much-prized dhufish. Excellent boat ramps cater for boats of all sizes that flock to this area during autumn when the conditions are at their best. Bigger boats fishing the deeper reefs find the fishing much better with some really big dhufish, pink snapper, baldchin groper and Samson fish making up the bulk of their catches. In summer, Spanish mackerel can be found along the back of the reefs and drop-offs. Troll a lure behind the boat when heading out to bottom fishing spots can often result in catches of mackerel, tuna or Samson fish.

There is a marina at Jurien providing safe boat-launching facilities along with caravan parks for accommodation. The shore fishing is mostly done from the town jetty and the marina where small species like herring, whiting, silver trevally and chopper tailor can be found. At night, squid, mulloway, big tailor and small sharks can be taken, and the beaches close to town are well worth trying in the dark. The area from Green Head to Wedge Island has now been declared a Marina Park. Controversially line fishing is now banned from 21% of this area but rock lobster fishing is prohibited from only 3% in sanctuary zones. Check with local authorities for official boundaries.

Western rock lobsters support a massive fishing industry, both commercial and recreational.

WA dhufish are heavily fished for along the central west. Here a small specimen has been tagged for research. Garry Lillee the designer of the depth release device holds this fish.

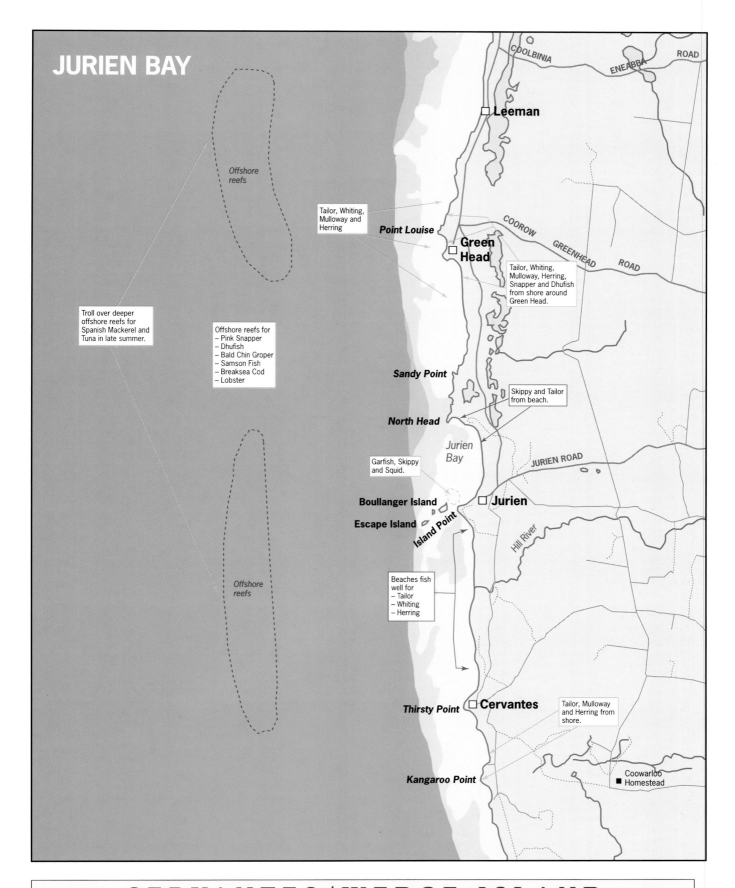

JURIEN BAY

Leeman

COOLBINIA

ENEABBA ROAD

Offshore reefs

Tailor, Whiting, Mulloway and Herring

Point Louise

COOROW GREENHEAD ROAD

Green Head

Tailor, Whiting, Mulloway, Herring, Snapper and Dhufish from shore around Green Head.

Troll over deeper offshore reefs for Spanish Mackerel and Tuna in late summer.

Offshore reefs for
– Pink Snapper
– Dhufish
– Bald Chin Groper
– Samson Fish
– Breaksea Cod
– Lobster

Sandy Point

Skippy and Tailor from beach.

North Head

Jurien Bay

JURIEN ROAD

Garfish, Skippy and Squid.

Boullanger Island

Escape Island

Island Point

□ **Jurien**

Hill River

Beaches fish well for
– Tailor
– Whiting
– Herring

Offshore reefs

Thirsty Point □ **Cervantes**

Tailor, Mulloway and Herring from shore.

Kangaroo Point

Coowarloo Homestead

CERVANTES / WEDGE ISLAND

A maze of 4WD tracks leads to numerous beaches along this stretch of coast. Beach fishing is usually done during the warmer months, as the amount of weed washed in during winter storms makes the beaches almost unfishable. Most anglers fish this area with ganged hooks and mulies weighed down with a big star sinker. This method usually results in tailor being caught, which seem to be the most common species taken from here.

Occasional big mulloway and whaler sharks come from the surf at night, and during the day there are plenty of whiting and herring in the shallows with some skippy and Tarwhine. Offshore is reasonably productive for dhufish, pink snapper and Samson fish, however you need to be able to launch from the beach and have good weather on your side.

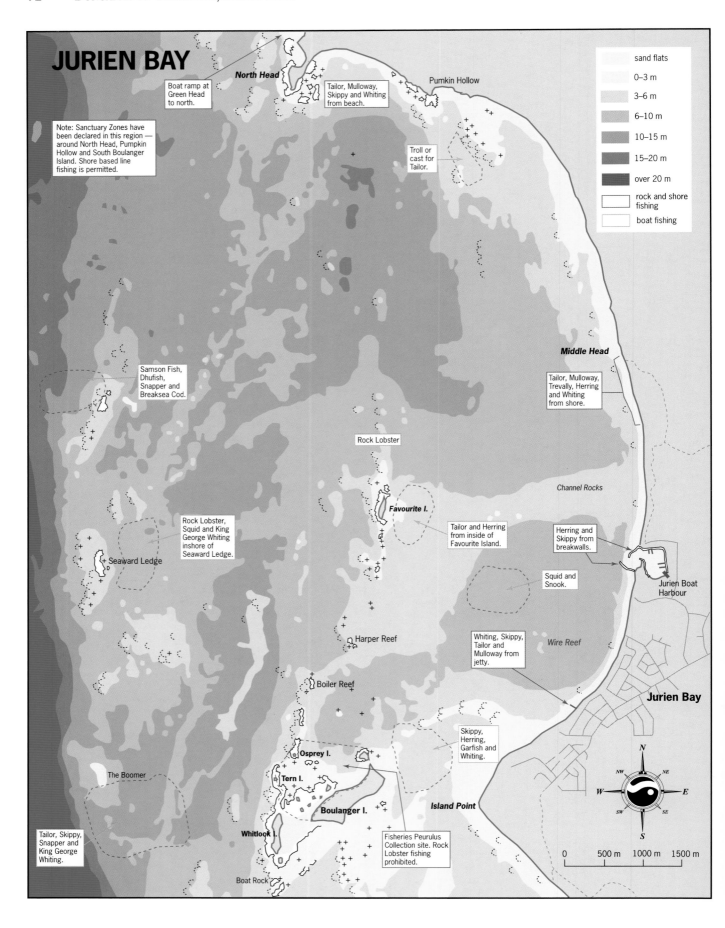

JURIEN BAY

North Head

Boat ramp at Green Head to north.

Tailor, Mulloway, Skippy and Whiting from beach.

Pumkin Hollow

Note: Sanctuary Zones have been declared in this region — around North Head, Pumpkin Hollow and South Boulanger Island. Shore based line fishing is permitted.

Troll or cast for Tailor.

Middle Head

Samson Fish, Dhufish, Snapper and Breaksea Cod.

Tailor, Mulloway, Trevally, Herring and Whiting from shore.

Rock Lobster

Channel Rocks

Favourite I.

Rock Lobster, Squid and King George Whiting inshore of Seaward Ledge.

Tailor and Herring from inside of Favourite Island.

Herring and Skippy from breakwalls.

+ Seaward Ledge

Squid and Snook.

Jurien Boat Harbour

Whiting, Skippy, Tailor and Mulloway from jetty.

Wire Reef

Harper Reef

Jurien Bay

Boiler Reef

Skippy, Herring, Garfish and Whiting.

The Boomer

Osprey I.

Tern I.

Island Point

Boulanger I.

Whitlock I.

Fisheries Peurulus Collection site. Rock Lobster fishing prohibited.

Tailor, Skippy, Snapper and King George Whiting.

Boat Rock

	sand flats
	0–3 m
	3–6 m
	6–10 m
	10–15 m
	15–20 m
	over 20 m
	rock and shore fishing
	boat fishing

N
NW NE
W   E
SW SE
S

0   500 m   1000 m   1500 m

LANCELIN

The long, white, sandy beaches of this area are popular weekend fishing spots for many Perth anglers. During the day whiting seem to be the most commonly caught fish from the beach and although mostly small they make up for lack of size in numbers. Herring are another regular catch during the day. These beaches are best fished once the sea breeze blows in from the southwest. In the warmer months big catches of tailor are made in the choppy conditions, and after dark there is always a chance of hooking mulloway and sharks in the surf.

LEDGE POINT

South of Lancelin is a great place to beach-launch a small dinghy and fish close to the reefs just offshore for herring, gardies and big silver trevally (skippy). On calmer days small boats can venture further out to where dhufish, pink snapper and Samson fish can be found around the reef lumps. A popular method is to anchor up and start a berley trail over the reef, then fish unweighted pilchards back down the trail. Be prepared to lose a few fish in the shallow water as they dive for cover in the reef. Samsons are very good at this.

SEABIRD

Seabird is a small rock lobster fishing settlement that has some great shore reefs that can be fantastic tailor spots. However, after a heavy storm the copious amount of weed washed in makes fishing very difficult indeed.

It is well worth fishing this area for mulloway. The best fishing method for tailor is to cast whole mulies from the shore in the morning when the easterly wind allows some distance to be achieved with the lightly weighted bait.

THREE MILE REEF

A couple of kilometres to the north of the river mouth is the famous Three Mile Reef, a flat section of shore reef that has a deep gutter running along its face. Early summer mornings are very popular at the Three Mile, where a mulie can be cast well out and retrieved slowly or left to wash around in the surf for big tailor. There are also plenty of smaller mulloway taken by fishing this method from the reef, and even the occasional small Spanish mackerel. Late afternoon or even after dark the Three Mile should be fished with heavy surf tackle, with whole mulies on ganged hooks weighed down with a star sinker to hold the bottom. You will snag some rigs on the bottom but there have been some big mulloway, small sharks and plenty of decent tailor taken fishing this way.

The Three Mile can be a bit dangerous to fish in rough conditions so take care. The 4WD access along the beach should only be attempted by experienced off-road drivers. Soft sand and a high tide could cause you to have a very expensive fishing trip if you end up bogged within reach of the waves.

Boat anglers target many species along this stretch of coast, and pink snapper are one of the favourites.

LEFT: Fishermen's shacks nestle in the sand dunes near Guilderton.

GUILDERTON/MOORE RIVER

At the mouth of the Moore River is the pleasant town of Guilderton, a sleepy little place that caters for tourists with a caravan park and small shop.

Moore River itself is a pretty little estuary system that is isolated from the ocean by a sandbar for much of the year. The river is almost like a fish nursery, and it can be a problem to catch fish of legal size at times, especially with the black bream. There are some thumping big black bream in Moore River but getting bait past the thousands of little ones can be very difficult. The best thing to do is to fish further upstream away from the mouth where the smaller fish seem to congregate. By small dinghy or from the bank you can fish whole river prawns around the snags or cast tiny lures to tempt the bigger, smarter bream.

The river is also home to many mullet, yellowtail grunter and whiting, however every year a few soapy mulloway to 3 kg are caught and a few mud crabs have been taken over the years. When the winter rains wash the sandbar away the river gets its

ABOVE: A black bream (bottom) and a tarwhine or silver bream (top) are often found in the same rivers and estuaries. Black bream are a popular catch in the Moore River near Guilderton.

FISH FACTS

TAILOR

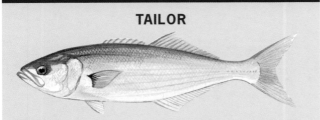

Each summer thousands of beach anglers target tailor from the surf, usually casting whole pilchards on ganged hooks into a stiff sea breeze and waiting for the sharp bites from a hungry tailor. Tailor are found in good numbers from Carnarvon southwards to Augusta; from here they thin out along the south coast where only occasional big fish are reported.

Tailor's aggressive habit of carving up baitfish has given them a fierce reputation and small fish under 30 cm are often referred to as 'choppers'. Most anglers fish for tailor from the shore with bait, usually from the surf beaches or rock headlands and groynes along the coast. Beach tailor range in size from 25–35 cm, depending on the area you are fishing. Bigger fish topping the 60 cm mark and weighing between 3–6 kg are caught around shore reefs, usually on whole garfish or a surface popper worked through the whitewater.

Kalbarri is a favourite location for targeting big tailor, especially around the mouth of the Murchison River where deep reef holes attract these fish. The biggest tailor in Australia come from the Shark Bay area, and fish of 4–8 kg are readily taken from many locations in the Bay and at Dirk Hartog Island.

In the estuaries smaller chopper tailor thrive on the abundance of baitfish, and can easily be caught on smaller lures or baits fished on light lines. The offshore reefs are where boat anglers can cast un-weighted pilchards, garfish, metal lures or poppers for bigger fish that hold up at these locations.

Because tailor have very sharp teeth use a short length of wire to prevent getting bitten off. A medium to light rod and reel is perfect for all but the biggest tailor. Many anglers enjoy a fresh feed of tailor straight from the ocean, so many are kept for the table, although research shows very high survival for released fish.

flush of new life. This is the time to be fishing the beach, chasing mulloway that move in to feed in the dirty water that is washing out plenty of small fish.

The beaches close by are great places to fish for big tailor and mulloway, especially after dark when a whole mulie or fillet of mullet is fished into the deeper holes in the surf. A small rock groyne to the north of the mouth is a good place to fish; it produces herring and whiting during the day and big tailor, mulloway and small sharks at night. Next to this groyne is a boggy beach-launching facility but a 4WD is required to successfully launch. Offshore fishing is pretty good with dhufish, pink snapper, breaksea cod and Samson fish all found around the nearby reefs.

The beaches to the south of the river are hard to access unless you know the maze of boggy tracks through the scrub and sand dunes, however once you reach the ocean there are plenty of reefy gutters and surf spots to target mulloway and tailor.

BOAT RAMPS & TACKLE STORES

This stretch of coast supports the commercial rock lobster fishing industry, and provides safe boat launching from good ramps at many of the centres down the coast. Beach-launching smaller trailer craft with 4WD vehicles is still possible at many other spots, but larger boats are best sticking to the concrete ramps provided. The tides are not a problem this far south but care is needed when boating in this area because of the numerous reefs that stretch along the coast.

The best boating weather is in the autumn months through to early winter before cold fronts bring in storms from the ocean. During summer the strong easterly winds in the mornings that quickly switch to equally strong sea breezes by noon often make boating uncomfortable and hazardous in this area.

RAMPS
Dongara/Port Denison – Boat harbour
Green Head – South Bay
Horrocks Beach
Jurien Bay – Boat harbour
Leeman – Sea Rescue and Jetty
Moore River – Town near mouth of river

TACKLE STORES
Sea Sport & Tackle
3 Roberts Arcade,
Jurien Bay WA 6516
Tel: (08) 9652 1242

CHAPTER 7

PERTH AND SURROUNDS

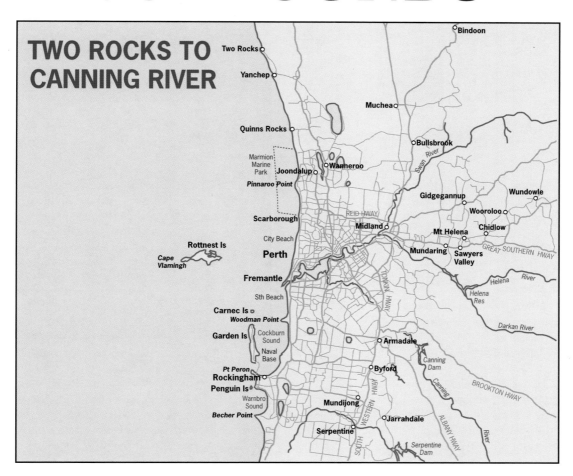

PERTH

The city of Perth is situated on the Swan River that flows westwards towards Fremantle. There are numerous beaches, reefs and islands as well as the Swan and Canning rivers to offer anglers a wide range of places to fish and species to target. With numerous boat ramps, caravan parks, hotels and motels, Perth is never short of accommodation for visiting and local anglers.

TWO ROCKS

To the north of the city is the suburb of Two Rocks where there is a safe launching marina for boat anglers and numerous beach-fishing options for shore anglers. To the north a series of boggy tracks lead anglers through the dunes to famous reef platforms such as Loonies and Dwyers, where big tailor and mulloway are common catches. Access is becoming more difficult as more tracks are closed off to 4WDs so it is uncertain how long this northern stretch will remain open.

From the rocks at the marina, tailor, herring, silver trevally (skippy), garfish and whiting can all be taken. Larger baits set out at night usually result in stingrays, however enough decent mulloway and small sharks make it worth the effort.

South of Two Rocks there are numerous shore reefs where big tailor are often taken by anglers fishing whole gardies or mullet or throwing lures like metal slices or poppers around the reef holes. This is usually done at first light or just on dark when the big tailor move into the reef holes to feed.

By boat there are numerous inshore and offshore reefs that are home to the prized dhufish, as well as pink snapper, breaksea cod and big Samson fish. Bottom bouncing from a drifting boat is the most popular method with a heavy boat rod and reel or hand line. Rigs, comprising a big sinker on the bottom with a couple of dropper hooks baited with octopus, squid or fish, are dropped to the bottom and bounced along the reef.

YANCHEP

This is a very popular shore reef where anglers wade out to fish the gutter running along the reef for big tailor. Five kilogram

To the north of Perth there are some great tailor fishing spots like Yanchep and Club Capricorn.

tailor are taken from this reef each year, usually in winter, by anglers braving the cold weather and seas, and for this reason it should be fished with extreme care. From the beach, anglers fishing into the lagoon that is formed by the outside reef, can catch tailor and occasional mulloway—this is a much safer option than wading out onto the reef.

PIPIDINNY

This popular beach was once reached by the 4WD tracks through the scrub, however local councils are restricting access to them. Pipidinny is a top tailor and mulloway beach, with good fish being regularly taken from the surf.

MINDARI KEYS

There is a safe boat marina built at Mindari, and fishing from the rock groynes is popular for tailor, herring, silver bream and whiting. From the shore reef to the north of the marina is big tailor country in winter. Good blue manna crabs are also taken inside the marina.

BURNS BEACH

This is probably the prime big-tailor country close to Perth, with limestone cliffs fronting shore reefs with deep holes. Casting poppers or metal lures over these reef holes when there is some white water can result in hooked tailor in the 2–5 kg range. From the beach there are also herring, skippy and silver bream taken by anglers using smaller baits, and some nice yellowfin whiting can also be found.

OCEAN REEF MARINA

This marina provides safe launching facilities for boats intent on fishing the productive reef grounds not far out. Dhufish, pink snapper, breaksea cod and Samson fish are regular captures from the broken ground. There are some excellent deeper offshore reefs that bigger boats can access for the same species. Closer in there is some good reef that produces tailor, silver trevally (skippy), garfish, herring and sand and King George whiting over the sand patches. Ocean Reef is extremely popular for recreational rock lobster fishers with the 'whites' run in late November to early January being the best time.

One of many good northern rock groynes to fish from is Mindari Keys.

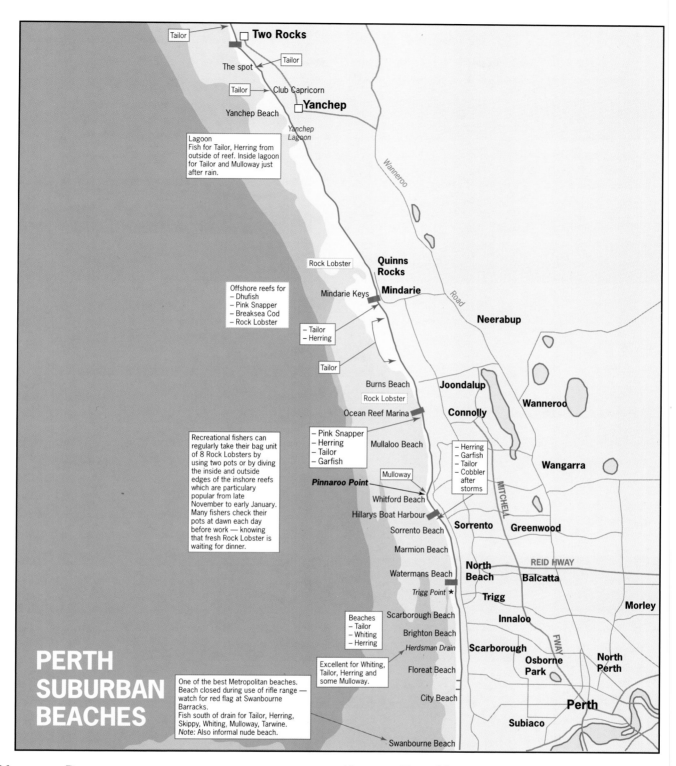

Tailor → **Two Rocks**

Tailor

The spot

Tailor → Club Capricorn

Yanchep

Yanchep Beach

Yanchep Lagoon

Lagoon
Fish for Tailor, Herring from outside of reef. Inside lagoon for Tailor and Mulloway just after rain.

Wanneroo

Quinns Rocks

Rock Lobster

Offshore reefs for
– Dhufish
– Pink Snapper
– Breaksea Cod
– Rock Lobster

Mindarie Keys **Mindarie**

Road

Neerabup

– Tailor
– Herring

Tailor

Burns Beach   **Joondalup**

Rock Lobster

Ocean Reef Marina   **Connolly**

Wanneroo

Recreational fishers can regularly take their bag unit of 8 Rock Lobsters by using two pots or by diving the inside and outside edges of the inshore reefs which are particulary popular from late November to early January. Many fishers check their pots at dawn each day before work — knowing that fresh Rock Lobster is waiting for dinner.

– Pink Snapper
– Herring
– Tailor
– Garfish

Mullaloo Beach

– Herring
– Garfish
– Tailor
– Cobbler after storms

Wangarra

Mulloway

Pinnaroo Point

Whitford Beach

MITCHELL

Hillarys Boat Harbour

Sorrento **Greenwood**

Sorrento Beach

Marmion Beach

REID HWAY

Watermans Beach

North Beach **Balcatta**

Trigg Point ★

Trigg

Morley

Beaches
– Tailor
– Whiting
– Herring

Scarborough Beach

Innaloo

Brighton Beach

Herdsman Drain   **Scarborough**

PERTH SUBURBAN BEACHES

Floreat Beach

Osborne Park

North Perth

One of the best Metropolitan beaches. Beach closed during use of rifle range — watch for red flag at Swanbourne Barracks.
Fish south of drain for Tailor, Herring, Skippy, Whiting, Mulloway, Tarwine.
Note: Also informal nude beach.

Excellent for Whiting, Tailor, Herring and some Mulloway.

City Beach

Perth

Subiaco

Swanbourne Beach

MULLALOO BEACH

This is a popular northern beach that has a good reputation for big tailor in the surf. Herring, whiting and silver bream are also taken in good numbers.

PINNAROO POINT

This is a nice sand spit that allows anglers to fish deeper water for tailor and herring.

LITTLE ISLAND

Reached by dinghy just to the north of Hillarys Boat Harbour, this is a top spot for anglers chasing herring, garfish, silver trevally and pike. Usually a few squid hang around over the weed so it pays to have a squid jig handy at all times.

HILLARYS BOAT HARBOUR

The rock walls of this marina receive a fair bit of angling pressure, and catches of tailor, herring, garfish, silver trevally, whiting and cobbler are common. The cobbler seem to turn up in the weed washed close to the rocks in winter and can be caught in big numbers on pieces of prawn. Big baits fished at night from the seaward side of the rock groynes account for plenty of stingrays but also mulloway and sharks.

Out from Hillarys by boat, there are good reef areas for dhufish, pink snapper, breaksea cod, queen snapper and Samson fish. In the rock lobster season the boat ramp is busy as recreational fishers head out each morning to check their pots. A rock lobster licence is required and recreationally caught lobsters must have the tail's central fan clipped or punched immediately after capture.

SORRENTO BEACH

Anglers usually fish from the small rock groynes for herring and tailor; at night there is a chance for mulloway and small sharks. The beach fishes well for tailor, herring, whiting and silver bream.

MARMION BEACH

This is another good beach spot to target whiting, tailor, herring and silver bream. The offshore reefs are great places to fish for bigger species and during summer, trolling or bait fishing will bring the occasional Spanish mackerel near these reefs. These reefs are better known as the Three Mile Reefs, and lying only a short distance from shore, they are easily accessed by most boats.

WATERMANS

There is plenty of shore reef along this stretch, and fishing the reefs next to the research centre is popular with big tailor chasers. The reef holes often hold herring, big whiting and some massive silver bream (tarwhine). The area immediately adjacent to the Fisheries Research Laboratories is a sanctuary zone.

NORTH BEACH

The focal point of this area is the small jetty that has a reputation as one of the best herring fishing spots around Perth. Herring and garfish are a common catch with anglers using berley cages and small hooks baited with cut prawn pieces or live maggots.

TRIGG BEACH

The Trigg Blue Holes are famous around Perth's fishing community as a great tailor spot. Big tailor are a common catch along with silver trevally, silver bream and herring. During the autumn salmon runs it is not uncommon to get large numbers of salmon holding up in the holes. From the sand patches between the reefs there are usually a few good sand and yellowfin whiting

along with some big silver bream. A small number of dedicated locals still use a special tripod as a platform—a uniquely Western Australian way to fish.

SCARBOROUGH BEACH

This is a good sand beach to target tailor in the summer months, and after dark a mulloway is a possibility. Try for sand whiting and herring from the surf during the day.

FLOREAT BEACH

A sand beach with plenty of deep gutters running along the shore makes Floreat Beach a good place to catch tailor and mulloway. Herring, silver bream and whiting are also caught during the day, but from dusk, use heavier surf tackle and whole mulies on ganged hooks for the tailor and mulloway.

CITY BEACH

Most of the fishing is done from the rock groyne where tailor, herring, garfish and whiting are caught. In summer good runs of chopper tailor move along the surf and can be caught most afternoons once the sea breeze comes in.

SWANBOURNE BEACH

Not only is it the nudist beach of Perth, Swanbourne is also a top fishing spot with tailor, herring and whiting making up the bulk of the catch. In autumn a salmon is a real possibility and after dark, mulloway and small sharks. Fishing is best to the south of where the drain enters the water. The beach is behind the rifle range and when a large red flag flies at Swanbourne Barracks, the beach is closed.

GRANT STREET

Grant Street is another of Perth's favourite herring and garfish spots and is best fished with berley and maggots using light rods.

Fishing the deeper reefs for dhufish and pink snapper is very popular out from Perth.

FISH FACTS

DOLPHIN FISH

Otherwise known as Mahi Mahi, the dolphin fish is one of the prettiest fish in the ocean with its electric blue and gold colouring. They are usually found in deeper offshore waters where they school up under floating objects like floating weed or man-made fish attracting devices (FADs).

They are aggressive fish that can reach over 20 kg but average 2–8 kilograms. Out from Perth many boats venture west of Rottnest Island where numerous fish attracting devices have been moored to the ocean floor with rope and chain by the Gamefishing Association. These large floats attract gamefish and large numbers of dolphin fish take up residence under them each year.

Dolphin fish will take lures and saltwater flies cast around and at the FADs, whilst others can be picked up by trolling the area. Bait fishers often cast pilchards or live herring for excellent results, and once hooked, the fish must be steered away from the FAD where it will try and hide. In the north of the State many dolphin fish are taken by boats trolling for other species like mackerel, and some of the biggest specimens caught each year are taken out from places like Exmouth and Coral Bay.

Dolphin fish flesh is white and tasty especially when fresh, and so are still rated pretty highly as table fish amongst anglers. Many game anglers choose to release these fish, being interested only in their spirited fight that usually involves plenty of jumping and tailwalking.

COTTESLOE GROYNE

Cottesloe rock groyne receives a fair bit of pressure all year round as it has a reputation for producing big tailor. Lures cast out towards the reef have accounted for some really big tailor each year, usually early in the mornings. During the day it is a good spot for herring and garfish from the rocks. Small boats often troll around the reef where they pick up the big tailor and herring. At night, mulie baits pick up big tailor, mulloway, small sharks and stingrays.

LEIGHTON BEACH

Fish in the surf during the day for whiting, small silver bream and herring; late afternoon and at night it is a good spot for tailor over summer.

CABLE STATION REEF

This reef is a popular surfing spot that also has a reputation for producing really big tailor. Fishing early morning with lures like metal slices, which can be cast a long way, has accounted for some really big tailor from this spot each year.

PORT BEACH

During summer Port Beach is a favourite swimming beach for many, and late in the afternoons chopper tailor run along the surf line, providing anglers with the thrill of catching a few fish for dinner. During the day there are mostly small whiting and a few herring in the surf.

NORTH AND SOUTH MOLE

These two massive rock walls protect the mouth of the Swan River, and both are very popular fishing spots for a huge range of species. The North Mole is the longer of the two. Extending westward it allows anglers to fish the deeper water flowing in and out of the Swan. Both moles are ideal places to target big fish, especially at night when mulloway, snapper, sharks and rays can be hooked on large baits fished on heavy tackle on the bottom. During the day spinning with lures or baitcasting pilchards are popular ways to catch bonito and salmon during the season, and tailor almost all year round. Every now and then an angler gets a real shock from the tip of North Mole when a Spanish mackerel takes a lure or bait intended for something else. The rocks of these moles are well established reefs that attract a huge number of species such as rock lobster, squid and cuttlefish, and big silver trevally (skippy) are a popular catch close to the rocks. Other species like tarwhine, whiting, herring, garfish, yellowtail, blue mackerel, flounder and flathead are all common catches, on lighter tackle, from the rocks. The use of a berley cage rig is one of the best ways to catch fish from the

FISH FACTS

SAMSON FISH

Despised by some boat fishers and targeted by many rock fishers along the south coast, the Samson fish is one of Western Australia's most respected fighting fish. Samsons are very common all along the coast from Shark Bay to Esperance. They are usually found not far from land and can be easily attracted to your fishing location with a berley trail.

Most Samson fish caught average around the 10–25 kg, and at these sizes they will stretch the anglers' arms and tackle to the limit. Big Samsons over 30 kg are taken each year but many more are lost because of the awesome strength of the species. Samson fish are as strong as, but not as dirty as yellowtail kingfish.

Although many anglers will keep a Samson fish for food, their average table qualities have protected them from heavy recreational and commercial fishing pressure. As a result big numbers can be found at some offshore reefs or rocky headlands along the south coast.

Boat anglers drifting for snapper and dhufish despise Samson fish because of the effort needed to land one and often the resulting loss of a rig and precious fishing time. For landbased anglers a tussle with a big Samson is looked forward to, and many fish live herring under balloons from the south coast rocks in an attempt to catch them. Heavy tackle is generally necessary, as they will usually make short work of anything light. Most anglers fish with bait for them, usually pilchards or fish fillets but a live herring or skippy is rarely refused once a big Samson fish spots it.

At times Samson fish can be caught on trolled lures or on poppers cast around reefs, but dropping jigs down in deep water is a very effective way to hook them. The recent discovery of aggregations of Samson fish to 55 kg near Rottnest Island is attracting world wide attention and from November to March provides world class deep water jigging.

rocks—pollard and oil are mixed and crushed into the berley cage above a small hook on a leader and baited with cut prawn or maggots.

There is plenty of parking out on the Moles, and they can become very crowded when the bonito or tailor are running. Several hundred anglers, sometimes shoulder-to-shoulder, then take to the rocks.

THE SWAN RIVER

FREMANTLE HARBOUR

Access to the wharves is allowed on the southern side where anglers can fish from the high wharf into the harbour itself. Most anglers target yellowtail, slimy mackerel, silver trevally (skippy), tarwhine and herring by using a berley mixture of pollard and fish oil to attract the fish. At times good tailor and bonito can be taken from the wharf, and on autumn nights runs of big mulloway are eagerly awaited by dedicated anglers who are prepared to fish all night.

FREMANTLE TRAFFIC BRIDGE

Over the years many anglers have been rewarded for the effort needed to climb down from the catwalk onto the concrete platform of the old traffic bridge. Fishing from this spot is limited to a few anglers at a time but catches of big tailor, tarwhine, skippy and herring are often made. Big baits fished after dark account for some really large mulloway each year, and occasionally small Samson fish and pink snapper show up to add variety. During the king prawn run each autumn, some lucky scoopers manage to catch a decent feed of these tasty crustaceans as they run out with the tide and big blue manna crabs are also caught.

STIRLING BRIDGE

Most of the fishing from this bridge is by boat anglers fishing near the pylons or trolling baits and lures for tailor. Shore fishing under the bridge itself is reasonable during summer with flathead, flounder, tailor, herring and skippy being caught on bait, lure and fly tackle.

EAST FREMANTLE

Out from the Leeuwin boat ramp is a narrow stretch of the river that is the favourite spot to scoop king prawns each autumn. On good nights when the big kings are running out with the tide it is possible, from your boat, to scoop several hundred with the aid of a good light and long scoop net. This has become so popular over the years that it is not uncommon during prawn runs to have over a hundred boats in this small area all trying to get a spot and a feed of prawns.

Fishing for big yellowfin whiting from the shore in this area is a must: you need to fish after dark when the whiting move into the shallows and the annoying blowfish depart, and you require fresh

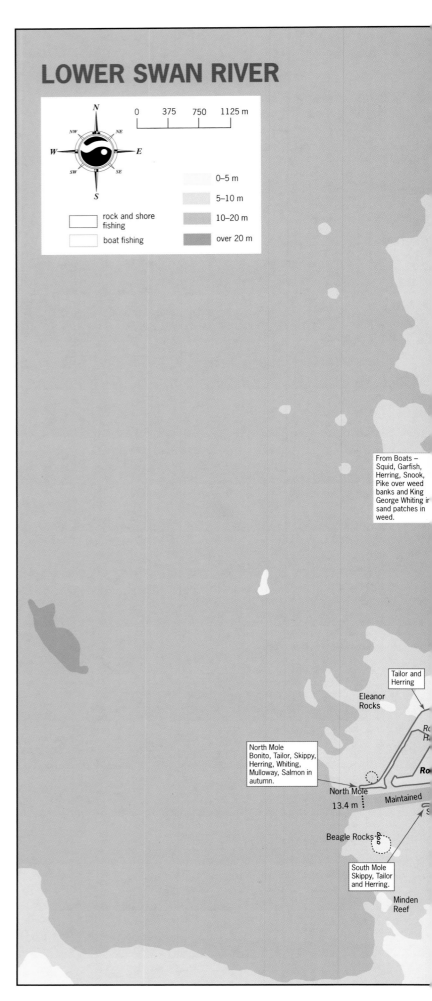

LOWER SWAN RIVER

0   375   750   1125 m

rock and shore fishing

boat fishing

0–5 m
5–10 m
10–20 m
over 20 m

From Boats – Squid, Garfish, Herring, Snook, Pike over weed banks and King George Whiting in sand patches in weed.

Tailor and Herring

Eleanor Rocks

North Mole
Bonito, Tailor, Skippy, Herring, Whiting, Mulloway, Salmon in autumn.

North Mole
13.4 m

Maintained

Beagle Rocks

South Mole
Skippy, Tailor and Herring.

Minden Reef

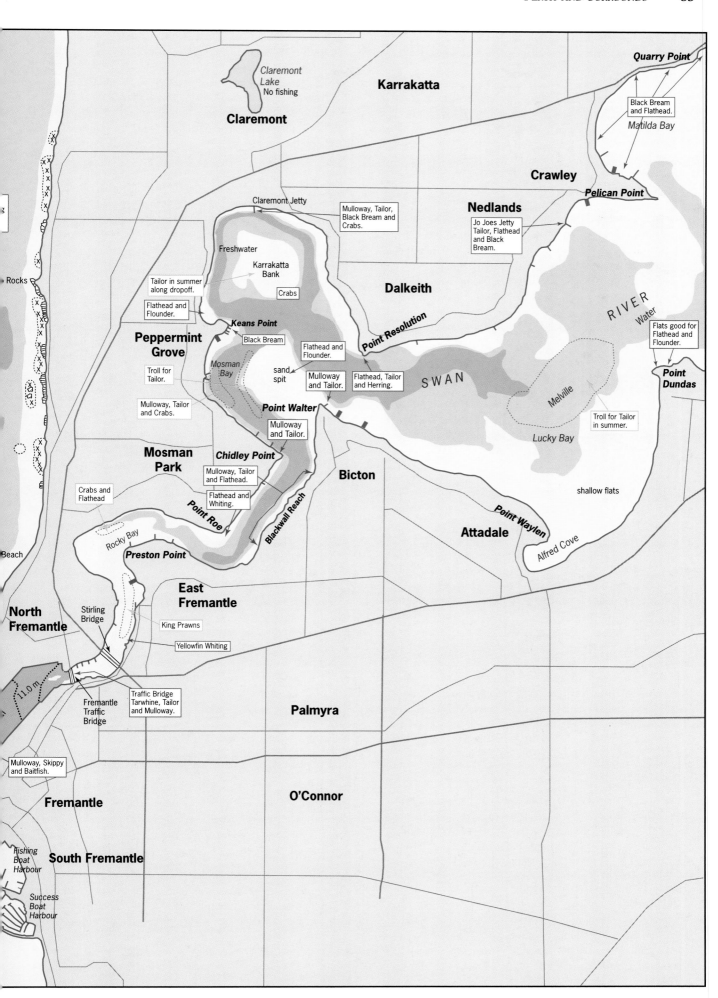

Claremont
Lake
No fishing

Karrakatta

Claremont

Quarry Point

Black Bream
and Flathead.

Matilda Bay

Crawley

Claremont Jetty

Mulloway, Tailor,
Black Bream and
Crabs.

Nedlands

Jo Joes Jetty
Tailor, Flathead
and Black
Bream.

Pelican Point

Freshwater

Karrakatta
Bank

Dalkeith

Crabs

Tailor in summer
along dropoff.

Flathead and
Flounder.

Point Resolution

R I V E R

Water

Flats good for
Flathead and
Flounder.

Keans Point

Black Bream

Flathead and
Flounder.

**Peppermint
Grove**

*Mosman
Bay*

sand
spit

Mulloway
and Tailor.

Flathead, Tailor
and Herring.

S W A N

*Point
Dundas*

Troll for
Tailor.

Mulloway, Tailor
and Crabs.

Point Walter

Mulloway
and Tailor.

Melville

Troll for Tailor
in summer.

Lucky Bay

**Mosman
Park**

Chidley Point

Mulloway, Tailor
and Flathead.

Bicton

shallow flats

Crabs and
Flathead

Flathead and
Whiting.

Point Roe

Blackwall Reach

Attadale

Point Waylen

Rocks

Beach

Rocky Bay

Preston Point

**East
Fremantle**

Alfred Cove

**North
Fremantle**

Stirling
Bridge

King Prawns

Yellowfin Whiting

110 m

Fremantle
Traffic
Bridge

Traffic Bridge
Tarwhine, Tailor
and Mulloway.

Palmyra

Mulloway, Skippy
and Baitfish.

Fremantle

O'Connor

*Fishing
Boat
Harbour*

South Fremantle

*Success
Boat
Harbour*

Swan River blood worms dug from the river to get results. These whiting are well worth all the effort and will hit the bait hard.

ROCKY BAY

Steep limestone cliffs shadow the deep channel that runs close to shore along Rocky Bay. Access is via a rough track to the water where shore anglers can fish for big flathead, flounder, tailor, skippy and herring. Boat anglers also catch the same species and in summer can drop a few crab nets down for a bonus feed of big blue mannas.

BLACKWALL REACH

Set in a bush park, the high cliffs of Blackwall Reach make popular fishing spots especially in summer. Tailor, herring, flathead and flounder are all taken from the cliffs, whilst at night some big mulloway can be hooked on live baits or whole pilchards. Stopping them amongst all of the boat moorings can prove to be difficult. Crabbing is excellent but the depth of the water requires you to use long ropes on your crab nets.

CHIDLEY POINT

A small beach allows anglers to fish the sand spit and deep channel running close to Chidley Point. In summer this is a prime tailor spot, and casting small lures, flies or bait fishing with whitebait or mulies is usually very successful. Big mulloway can be caught here on large baits cast out into the deep water, and some nice flathead are often caught close to the drop-off.

MOSMAN BAY

This deep, curving bay is the number one mulloway spot for boat anglers, as large numbers of fish school up in the deep water usually close to the sunken wrecks and boat moorings. Berley of chopped pilchards is often used to bring the fish under your boat, then lightly weighted pilchards or live baits are fished back down. During summer Mosman Bay also produces plenty of tailor and fishing closer to shore you can usually find a few flathead and flounder. Crabbing in the deep water is well worth the effort, as some of the biggest crabs in the Swan come from here.

POINT WALTER

Fish from the small jetty where chopper tailor, flathead, flounder and whiting can be caught. Big mulloway can be hooked at night from the jetty, whilst crab nets should turn up a feed. The big sand spit leading out into the river can be waded in summer for flathead and flounder; these are usually taken on jigs, small lures or with saltwater fly tackle. Blowies make bait fishing during the day impossible on the spit. The deep channel right out at the end is a good spot to pick up chopper tailor and herring.

FRESHWATER BAY

A pleasant, shallow bay, Freshwater Bay is popular in summer with flathead and flounder anglers who wade close to shore, casting lures or flies. The jetty at Keanes Point is heavily fished for tailor, herring, whiting and the occasional mulloway in summer and black bream and cobbler in winter. This is also a good area to throw in a few crab nets.

CLAREMONT JETTY

Claremont has a long public jetty that allows access over sand flats to the deep channel that is some distance from shore. This jetty is another good mulloway spot at night, along with tailor, herring, silver and black bream, flathead, flounder and crabs. The shallow bay around from here is a good spot to target

flathead and flounder on spin and fly tackle and in summer giant herring can be hooked on the same tackle.

KARRAKATTA BANK

This bank is well known to many boat anglers as the best place to troll small lures and whole whitebait or mulies for tailor. The fish hold up around here and schools can be found by watching the birds diving over them. Fishing the bottom or trolling the drop-offs can turn up a few flathead and flounder.

POINT RESOLUTION

There is a deep channel running close to shore past the sandbar, which provides excellent fishing for tailor, herring, flathead and flounder in summer. Big mulloway can be hooked from the shore, and fly and lure anglers sometimes tangle with giant herring. The rocky shore attracts some decent black bream especially in winter, and crabbing by boat is usually pretty good.

MELVILLE WATER

Dinghy anglers favour this area in spring and summer when the chopper tailor are about in big numbers. Trolling this big area is a very relaxing and enjoyable way to catch a feed of tailor.

PRIVATE YACHT CLUBS

Gone are the days when access to these private jetties was tolerated, and sadly you can only fish from the shore and cast out alongside the jetties these days. This is still a very effective way to catch big black bream that just love these clubs especially during winter. Whole river prawns fished on the bottom are bound to attract the breams' interest—just be prepared to lock up and try and drag the hooked fish out of the pylons. If you do intend fishing inside the clubs just remember to take all of your rubbish with you; don't leave bait or fish offal there and don't clean any fish in the club. You are allowed to fish from the shore, as they can't prevent access to the foreshore of the river, but don't trespass onto the jetties.

APPLECROSS

There is a small public jetty at Applecross that receives plenty of fishing pressure from anglers chasing tailor, flathead, flounder and mulloway. The shallow flats either side of the jetty are a better option, and by wading you can catch flathead and flounder on small lures or flies. By boat, the water out from here is good for trolling up a few tailor or dropping in a few crab nets.

MATILDA BAY

This bay leads around from the Royal Perth Yacht Club towards the Narrows Bridge. Many spots along this stretch are popular fishing locations for anglers chasing black bream, cobbler, tailor and mulloway from the shore. At various times of the year tailor, mulloway and black bream can be fished for by boat. The jetty at the old Swan Brewery site produces good bream during the cooler months.

NARROWS BRIDGE

Right at the city's doorstep the Narrows is situated at a bottleneck in the river, and produces some excellent catches of tailor, big mulloway and black bream. Fishing mostly from shore, anglers cast out to the closest pylons with baits. Big black bream are taken using whole river prawns or lures while each year some massive mulloway are taken on mulies or live bony herring fished on heavy tackle. Boat anglers also target big mulloway and black bream and usually fish close to or climb onto the deeper pylons.

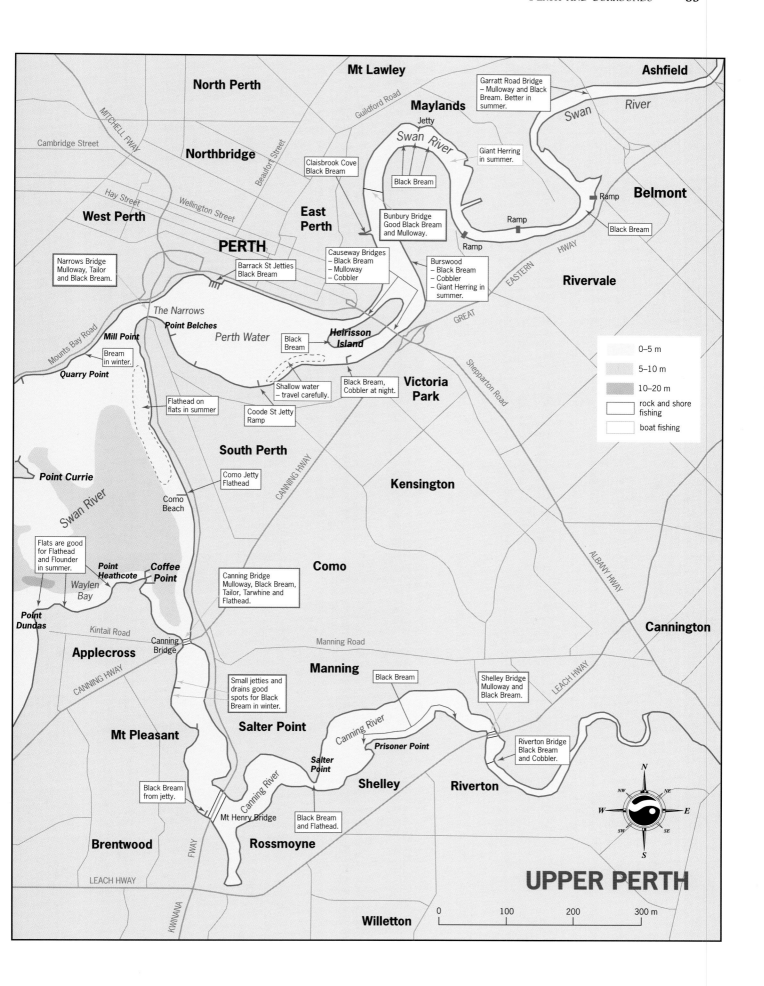

UPPER PERTH

PERTH WATER

Angler access to the jetties at Barrack Street is not permitted. Water along Riverside Drive is lightly fished from shore for black bream and cobbler. By boat there are some good spots for black bream close to the jetty pylons.

SOUTH PERTH

Along the shore most anglers target black bream and cobbler with baits of fresh river bloodworms.

THE CAUSEWAY

Crossing the north side of the river to the south side over Herrison Island, the Causeway is one of Perth's top river-fishing spots. Black bream are the most sought after fish and some real thumpers can be hooked on blood worms or whole river prawns. Big mulloway are another regular catch, and keen anglers put in many hours after dark, fishing with heavy tackle, chasing them. Cobbler, tailor and crabs are also taken near the causeway.

BURSWOOD

Behind the casino there is some excellent black bream water where bait and lure anglers often catch some big fish weighing up to 2 kilograms. Cobbler are caught at night on bloodworms, while some good mulloway and occasional giant herring also turn up.

EAST PERTH

Like Burswood, this area is a very productive black bream fishing area. There are numerous spots within this fishing site that have mussel beds and old structures to attract the bream; best bait seems to be fresh bloodworms.

BELMONT

Black bream and occasional large mulloway are the prime targets at Belmont. Fishing is usually best from a small boat where anglers can fish the shore structures or snags for bream.

MAYLANDS

Maylands is an excellent black bream fishing area especially in summer when the fish are holding up-river. Fish the snags around fallen trees either early in the morning or late in the day to find some good bream. Each year there are several large mulloway taken from Maylands, usually by anglers fishing bony herring fillets set out on heavy gear.

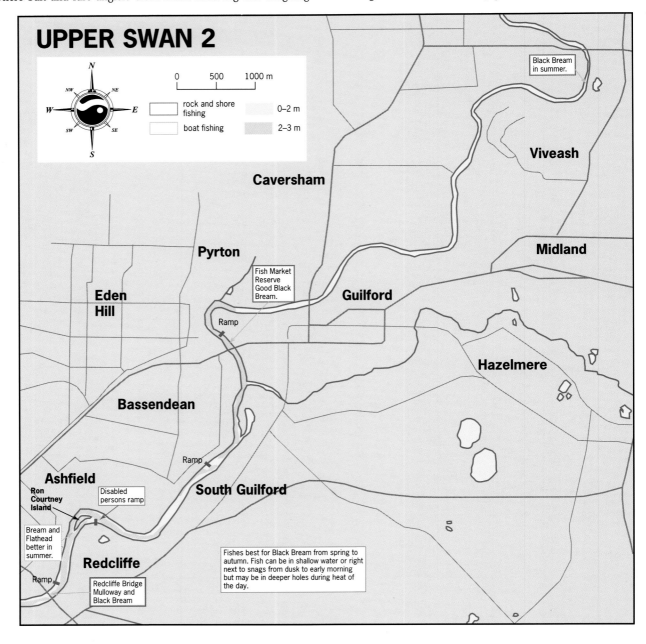

ASCOT

Mostly anglers targeting black bream and cobbler fish from locations around the shore or from small dinghies parked just out from the reeds. This area fishes best during summer and usually late in the afternoon. Just remember to take plenty of insect repellent, as the mosquitoes are very persistent.

UPPER SWAN

Above Ashfield, the river narrows and is heavily fished in summer for black bream around the gum tree snags and reeds that are along the shore. Really big black bream are taken from the upper reaches every year, mostly on baits of bloodworms, whole river prawns or live shrimps. Lure fishing is becoming much more popular for bream.

CANNING BRIDGE

The Canning River departs from the Swan and makes its way up under the Canning Bridge and beyond. The bridge itself is only narrow and has angler access built under the eastern side. This allows anglers to fish for many species, but the best catches seem to be when the tide slows and is about to change. Big mulloway can be hooked late at night on big fillets or live baits on heavy

lines. Some really big black bream live around the pylons but usually can only be tempted on live prawns, but once hooked it can be a job to pull them out. Smaller black bream are commonly caught on river prawns, and tailor and flathead also turn up regularly. Fishing nearby with a boat is also popular for tailor, mulloway and crabs, especially in spring and summer.

MT PLEASANT

Part of the Canning River, this stretch is a good location to fish for black bream, chopper tailor and flathead. Most of the fishing is from shore, under the trees or from one of several small jetties.

MT HENRY

A public jetty is the focal point of this area, and from it black bream, flathead, chopper tailor and mulloway can all be caught. A short distance up the main road the bridge also produces a few black bream for anglers casting from the shore, but most people with a boat fish the pylons for mulloway and black bream.

CANNING RIVER

Up from Mt Henry Bridge the Canning River shallows out into a wide area with a channel following the shore some distance.

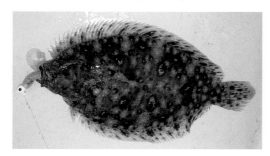

TOP: A Swan River flounder taken on a rubber-tail jig.

CENTRE: Black bream are a prize species from the Swan and Canning rivers.

BOTTOM: Over the warmer months bar-tailed flathead abound in the shallows of the Swan River and can be caught on minnow lures.

Giant herring have made the Swan River home and each summer these fish in the shallows thrill fly and lure anglers.

FISH FACTS

ROCK LOBSTER

There are several species of rock lobster found around the WA coastline but the most heavily fished is the Western Rock Lobster that is found from Shark Bay southwards. A massive commercial industry relies on these crayfish and a heavy recreational effort also takes place during the season.

A recreational fishing licence is needed before you attempt to take any crayfish from WA waters and there are strict size and bag limits that need to be followed. You should study all the rules prior to venturing out to catch a feed of lobsters, these vary during the season and can be answered when you get your licence from the Fisheries Department.

Most choose to drop baited pots around offshore reefs to catch these delicious crustaceans; this works well providing the reef has not had heavy commercial pressure put on it. Avoid the full moon as it is well known that rock lobster can be almost impossible to catch then and be prepared to get up early to check your pots that have been left from the day before. Some people prefer to dive for rock lobster armed with a noose that is positioned over the tail and tightened to snare the creature. This takes some practice but can be very effective at catching specimens hiding in reef ledges.

All rock lobster demand a high price in the markets as their unique flavour is considered by many to be the best in the world. Most boil them whole and then sit down to a delicious meal but they can be frozen and stored for later on.

ABOVE: Mulloway on fly from under the Narrows Bridge at night.

LEFT: The Narrows Bridge is a great mulloway and bream spot right in front of the city of Perth.

Most anglers chase black bream and small mulloway in the Canning, usually from shore spots that lead up to Shelly Bridge. Spots like Fifth Avenue and Mums Point allow shore anglers to set out baits for bream close to shore. Around Shelly Bridge and the old Riverton Bridge, black bream and mulloway are taken mostly by bait anglers fishing close to the pylons. Some big cobbler can also be taken at night, usually on fresh bloodworms. Above Riverton Bridge the river narrows and snakes its way up to the Kent Street weir; this area is fishable by small dinghy or canoe for black bream and cobbler.

FISHING BOAT HARBOUR

This smaller rock groyne to the south of South Mole is a good place to fish for herring, whiting, garfish, skippy, tarwhine and tailor. Just out from here, the weed and sand beds are top squid spots and they will also produce some very nice King George whiting.

SOUTH BEACH

This is the first sand beach to the south of Fremantle, and it provides anglers with the choice of fishing from the beach itself or from the small rock groynes nearby. From the beach it is possible to catch some big sand and yellowfin whiting, usually on light flick rods with small sinkers and hooks baited with cut prawn or squid but fish close to the shore. From the rock groyne and the beach, anglers target tailor and herring. At night there are usually big stingrays about, and occasionally there have been mulloway and small sharks taken.

COOGEE BEACH

The stretch of coast between South Beach and Coogee Beach is made up of shallow sand and limestone reefs that produce some herring, whiting and tailor. However, it is not until you reach Coogee Beach that the fishing opportunities improve, as this beach and its small jetty are well known for their catches of tailor, herring, whiting and garfish. At night from the jetty, squid and tailor make up the bulk of the catch but big stingrays and mulloway are always a chance with larger baits fished on the bottom.

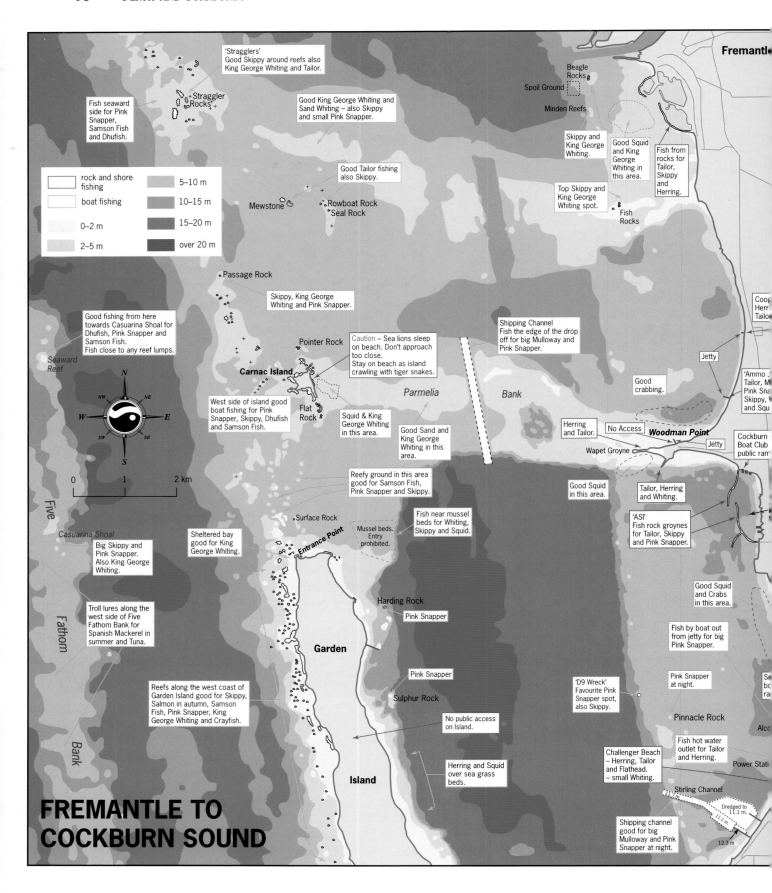

Legend:
- rock and shore fishing
- boat fishing
- 0–2 m
- 2–5 m
- 5–10 m
- 10–15 m
- 15–20 m
- over 20 m

FREMANTLE TO COCKBURN SOUND

Map labels:
- 'Stragglers' Good Skippy around reefs also King George Whiting and Tailor.
- Fish seaward side for Pink Snapper, Samson Fish and Dhufish.
- Straggler Rocks
- Good King George Whiting and Sand Whiting – also Skippy and small Pink Snapper.
- Good Tailor fishing also Skippy.
- Beagle Rocks
- Spoil Ground
- Minden Reefs
- Skippy and King George Whiting.
- Good Squid and King George Whiting in this area.
- Fish from rocks for Tailor, Skippy and Herring.
- Top Skippy and King George Whiting spot.
- Fish Rocks
- Fremantle
- Mewstone
- Rowboat Rock
- Seal Rock
- Passage Rock
- Good fishing from here towards Casuarina Shoal for Dhufish, Pink Snapper and Samson Fish. Fish close to any reef lumps.
- Seaward Reef
- Skippy, King George Whiting and Pink Snapper.
- Pointer Rock
- Caution – Sea lions sleep on beach. Don't approach too close. Stay on beach as island crawling with tiger snakes.
- Carnac Island
- Parmelia
- Bank
- Shipping Channel Fish the edge of the drop off for big Mulloway and Pink Snapper.
- Jetty
- Coog Herr Tailo
- 'Ammo' Tailor, M Pink Sna Skippy, and Squ
- Good crabbing.
- West side of island good boat fishing for Pink Snapper, Skippy, Dhufish and Samson Fish.
- Flat Rock
- Squid & King George Whiting in this area.
- Good Sand and King George Whiting in this area.
- Herring and Tailor.
- No Access
- Woodman Point
- Wapet Groyne
- Cockburn Boat Club public ram
- Jetty
- Reefy ground in this area good for Samson Fish, Pink Snapper and Skippy.
- Good Squid in this area.
- Tailor, Herring and Whiting.
- 'ASI' Fish rock groynes for Tailor, Skippy and Pink Snapper.
- Surface Rock
- Fish near mussel beds for Whiting, Skippy and Squid.
- Mussel beds. Entry prohibited.
- Entrance Point
- Sheltered bay good for King George Whiting.
- Casuarina Shoal
- Big Skippy and Pink Snapper. Also King George Whiting.
- Troll lures along the west side of Five Fathom Bank for Spanish Mackerel in summer and Tuna.
- Five Fathom Bank
- Harding Rock
- Pink Snapper
- Garden
- Good Squid and Crabs in this area.
- Fish by boat out from jetty for big Pink Snapper.
- Pink Snapper at night.
- Pink Snapper
- Sulphur Rock
- 'D9 Wreck' Favourite Pink Snapper spot, also Skippy.
- Pinnacle Rock
- Alco
- Reefs along the west coast of Garden Island good for Skippy, Salmon in autumn, Samson Fish, Pink Snapper, King George Whiting and Crayfish.
- No public access on Island.
- Herring and Squid over sea grass beds.
- Island
- Challenger Beach – Herring, Tailor and Flathead. – small Whiting.
- Fish hot water outlet for Tailor and Herring.
- Power Stati
- S bc ra
- Stirling Channel
- Dredged to 11.1 m.
- 12.3 m
- Shipping channel good for big Mulloway and Pink Snapper at night.

STRAGGLERS

This is a large area of breaking reef that is best fished only on calm days, as it can be very hazardous in rough seas. Big tailor, skippy, King George whiting and herring are the most common catches. The deeper water also produces dhufish, Samson fish and yellowtail kings at times.

MEWSTONES

A very popular big tailor location, these small rocks surrounded by breaking reef are home to some jumbo tailor at times. Casting poppers or baitcasting mulies across the whitewater is the best way to find out if there are any big tailor about. Herring, King George whiting, Skippy and squid are most common. Sometimes big Samson fish and yellowtail kings can turn up to wreak havoc with light tackle and there is always a chance of a salmon or two in autumn.

CARNAC ISLAND

This tiny island to the north of Garden Island is a pleasant place to visit by boat. Access on the island is limited to the beaches where large sea lions often sleep. It is not advisable to venture from the beach as the low scrub and dunes are home to large numbers of tiger snakes. Fishing around the island is pretty good for herring, garfish, whiting and squid. The deeper reefs to the west are good spots to try for dhufish and big Samson fish. In spring when the pink snapper run is on, fishing near the island is very worthwhile.

GARDEN ISLAND

Unfortunately this large island is off limits to the public as the navy controls the only access via the Causeway. By boat, Garden Island is a great place to fish with numerous shallow and deep reefs to try. The deeper reefs forming the Five Fathom Bank to the west of the island are excellent places to target dhufish, Samson fish, pink snapper and breaksea cod. The usual method is to drift fish over this ground but sometimes if the weather is suitable it is worth anchoring and berleying the fish, then floating down unweighted baits.

Closer to the island the reef holes and beaches can produce salmon during autumn and big skippy, herring and King George whiting at other times of the year. Any breaking reefs are worth prospecting for tailor with poppers or mulies baitcast into the white water.

On the Cockburn Sound side of the island the shallow sand and weed patches are popular King George whiting spots; these same areas also produce some great catches of squid and herring.

South Mole is a great place to fish for tailor, herring, tarwhine and skippy.

AMMUNITION JETTY

Originally built to load ammunition supplies for the navy at Garden Island, this jetty was opened to public use and has become one of the favourite jetties in Cockburn Sound. It is a large jetty with plenty of space, and is surrounded by a big parking area and picnic grounds and barbecue facilities. It attracts a huge number of anglers at times, and finding a spot in summer can be almost impossible.

From the jetty, catches of herring, garfish, whiting, skippy, yellowtail, tailor and squid are common. Bonito and big tailor make raids sometimes out from the end and at night big baits that have been set out have accounted for big mulloway, sharks, snapper and stingrays. Crabbing from the jetty is very popular and productive at times; baited drop nets are left on the bottom for ten minutes and then hauled up, trapping the crabs in the process.

WOODMANS POINT

This area is made up of a couple of rock groynes and shallow sand and weed beaches. From the deep water out on the middle rock groyne big mulloway and pink snapper have been taken, along with plenty of tailor and herring. The shallower areas are great places to target herring, whiting and squid. Crabbing through the shallows can be great fun, especially at night, and big cobbler can be found around the rocks and weed beds.

The big cement breakwall protecting the Cockburn Power Boat Club is also a great place to fish, with squid, crabs, herring, tailor, garfish and the occasional bonito turning up. At night in October and November there is the chance of picking up a big pink snapper from the rocks.

ASI GROYNE

This massive rock groyne, which protects the shipbuilding industries, is reputed to be the number one spot to catch big pink snapper during their spring run into Cockburn Sound. There is plenty of room to fish along the length of the groyne and snapper catches have come from all sides, so it is not important to get the best spot right out at the end. Big baits fished on the bottom, usually after a decent storm, is the best way to target the big pinkies that average 8–12 kilograms. Every now and then a big mulloway is also taken by this method.

Also from the rocks you can catch herring and skippy during the day, and late in the afternoon or at night some big tailor often show up.

A calm afternoon's fishing from a beach in Cockburn Sound.

Woodman's Point looking west towards Garden Island.

FISH FACTS

TREVALLY

Apart from the smaller silver trevally known as 'skippy' in the southwest of the State the big variety of northern species are usually known by their real names. Golden, Giant, Gold Spot, Big Eye, Bludger and Brassy trevally are probably the most commonly encountered species. The one thing all these species have in common is their fighting ability, which has earned them a favourite place amongst anglers fishing from Shark Bay northwards.

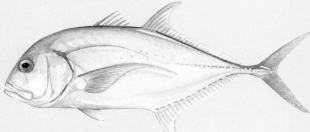

Giant Trevally

The giant trevally grows to the largest size, topping 50 kg but commonly encountered around the 10–25 kg mark. These big and powerful fish inhabit the shallow reef and coral areas of the north, often entering mangrove creeks in search of food. They feed heavily on other fish, usually mullet that they ambush with their bucket-sized mouths in the shallows, so lure fishing for these fish is the best way to encounter them. At Exmouth, anglers use beefed up spin gear with large surface poppers from the shore or small boats around the coral to entice massive giant trevally. The resulting surface strikes are very exciting but stopping such a powerful fish in shallow water amongst coral is almost impossible.

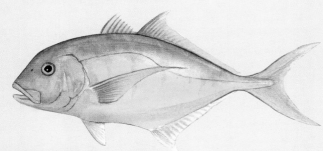

Golden Trevally

Golden trevally are another common species often taken on lures, saltwater fly and bait. These fish reach sizes over 20 kg but are usually under this and are considered the best eating fish of the trevally family. They have big rubbery lips that they use to sift through the sand and mud while searching for small invertebrates and fish. Goldens will also attack baitfish schools and as a result they can easily be caught on a number of lures or saltwater flies fished around bait balls.

Boat anglers have found that golden trevally can be brought almost to the back of the boat with berley, and it is a simple method of just dropping a baited hook out the back to tempt them. The fight of most trevally is a very powerful tussle that keeps anglers on their toes the whole time, especially if there is structure nearby for the trevally to drag the line around.

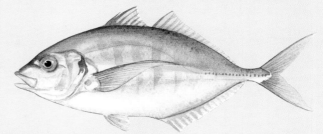

Skippy (Silver Trevally)

The name 'skippy' is unique to Western Australia, and it refers to our silver trevally, a species that is heavily targeted. Although found from north-west cape southwards, it is more common south of Kalbarri. Skippy can be found in big schools, especially in autumn around reefs where anglers attract them with berley.

Most of the fish found around the inshore reefs are under 0.5 kg, but along the south coast near Esperance bigger specimens are caught on heavier surf-fishing tackle. From a boat, good-sized skippy in the range 0.5–1.5 kg are taken around reefs on bluebait or whitebait fished on ganged hooks.

These fish put up a strong fight and can easily run your line through the reef if you don't put the brakes on them. Occasionally anglers chasing other species on the deep offshore reefs pick up some thumping big skippy up to 5 kilograms. These fish are rarely seen close to land and are an impressive sight. Skippy are often kept for the dinner table.

Other species

All the other species of trevally are just as aggressive and will also take lures, flies and baits. They are often found around reef lumps and wrecks and will hunt baitfish right into the shallows on the rising tide. Many sport fishers release the trevally they catch even though they are considered not too bad when eaten fresh.

COCKBURN SOUND

Boat anglers have the chance to target a wide range of species throughout Cockburn Sound. Probably the most awaited run of fish is the spawning run of the large pink snapper each spring into the Sound. These snapper range from about 5–15 kg and the resulting frenzy of anglers targeting these schooling fish has resulted in Fisheries WA imposing a closed season from September to the start of November to allow the fish a chance to aggregate and spawn. Big catches are still made in October and after November throughout the Sound, with several hot spots like the D9, a wreck sitting out from the Kwinana Industrial area.

Other productive spots are any lumps or gravel beds that can be picked up on the sounder. Anglers then anchor up and berley with chopped mulies to attract the fish. The Sound also produces good catches of crabs, squid, herring, garfish, skippy, tailor, bonito, mulloway and both King George and sand whiting through the year.

KWINANA INDUSTRIAL STRETCH

Heading south from ASI you enter the heavy industrial stretch of Kwinana, where coastal access is limited to a few beach locations. Challanger Beach, just south of the power station, is a favourite place to catch tailor, herring and small sand whiting. Kwinana Beach offers the same species and generally fishes

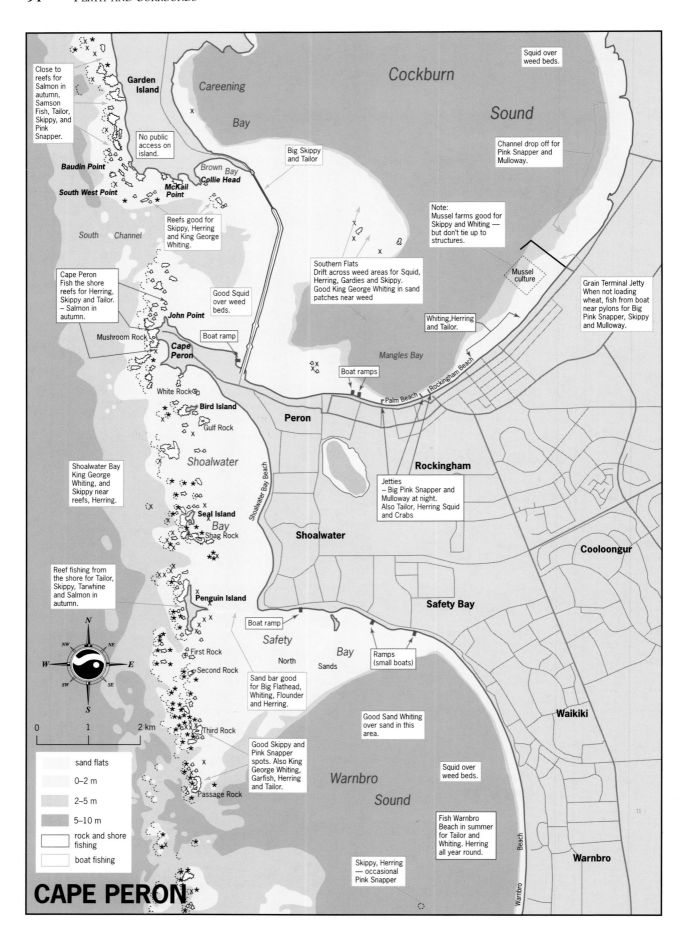

Close to reefs for Salmon in autumn, Samson Fish, Tailor, Skippy, and Pink Snapper.

Garden Island

Careening Bay

No public access on island.

Cockburn

Sound

Squid over weed beds.

Channel drop off for Pink Snapper and Mulloway.

Baudin Point

Brown Bay
Collie Head

McKail Point

South West Point

Reefs good for Skippy, Herring and King George Whiting.

South   Channel

Big Skippy and Tailor

Note: Mussel farms good for Skippy and Whiting — but don't tie up to structures.

Cape Peron Fish the shore reefs for Herring, Skippy and Tailor. – Salmon in autumn.

Good Squid over weed beds.

Southern Flats
Drift across weed areas for Squid, Herring, Gardies and Skippy. Good King George Whiting in sand patches near weed

Mussel culture

Grain Terminal Jetty When not loading wheat, fish from boat near pylons for Big Pink Snapper, Skippy and Mulloway.

John Point

Mushroom Rock

Boat ramp

Cape Peron

Whiting, Herring and Tailor.

Mangles Bay

White Rock

Boat ramps

Bird Island

Gulf Rock

Peron

Palm Beach   Rockingham Beach

Shoalwater Bay King George Whiting, and Skippy near reefs, Herring.

Shoalwater

Shoalwater Bay Beach

Rockingham

Jetties
– Big Pink Snapper and Mulloway at night.
Also Tailor, Herring Squid and Crabs

Seal Island

Bay

Shag Rock

Shoalwater

Cooloongur

Reef fishing from the shore for Tailor, Skippy, Tarwhine and Salmon in autumn.

Penguin Island

Safety Bay

N
NW   NE
W   E
SW   SE
S

Boat ramp

Safety

North

Sands

Bay

Ramps (small boats)

Waikiki

First Rock

Second Rock

Sand bar good for Big Flathead, Whiting, Flounder and Herring.

Good Sand Whiting over sand in this area.

0   1   2 km

Third Rock

Good Skippy and Pink Snapper spots. Also King George Whiting, Garfish, Herring and Tailor.

Warnbro

Sound

Squid over weed beds.

sand flats
0–2 m
2–5 m
5–10 m
rock and shore fishing
boat fishing

Passage Rock

Fish Warnbro Beach in summer for Tailor and Whiting. Herring all year round.

Skippy, Herring — occasional Pink Snapper

Warnbro Beach

Warnbro

CAPE PERON

better during the warmer months. The larger industrial jetties along this area are off limits to the public, but by boat some of them, like the Grain Terminal, can be fished. These jetties are dynamite pink snapper spots, and large numbers of big snapper often live around the pylons. Tailor, big skippy, bonito, herring and mulloway are also common species to be found around the jetties.

ROCKINGHAM

Lying at the southern end of Cockburn Sound, Rockingham is a popular fishing location. Its jetties are well known for producing big pink snapper and mulloway, usually at night on heavy lines. These jetties are only small but put the angler within reach of a deep drop off that follows the bay around. Smaller species like tailor, herring, blue mackerel, yellowtail, gardies, whiting, squid and crabs are all hauled up on the planks regularly.

The boat ramps at Rockingham are the first choice of many who launch their boats in search of pink snapper out in the Sound during the spring run. The weed beds out from these ramps are great spots to fish for squid, whilst the deeper water often produces plenty of King George whiting.

GARDEN ISLAND CAUSEWAY

This rock groyne that leads to a massive bridge is off limits to shore anglers, but by boat it is a great place to fish for King George whiting, very big silver trevally (skippy), big tailor and squid. Trolling small lures along the rocks will usually provide plenty of herring. Fishing close to the rocks with light tackle will produce tarwhine and leatherjackets but most boats fish the deep channels running along the pylons of the bridge. One of the best things to do here is to berley heavily and fish whole whitebait or pilchards on ganged hooks, with as little weight as possible. The big skippy and tailor will fall for this method, but lock-up tactics are needed at times to keep them away from the pylons.

POINT PERON

Just to the west of the Causeway, Point Peron is a prime reef-fishing spot, as it is made up of limestone cliffs and reef holes that attract a wide range of fish species. Large skippy, tailor, whiting and herring are year-round catches, and in autumn there are salmon caught from some of the reef holes and small beaches. Some walking is required to reach the better spots, and paths that lead through the low scrub to these.

PENGUIN ISLAND

Found to the south of Point Peron, this small island is home to hundreds of nesting terns and gulls, and a small rookery of fairy penguins. Fishing from the island is mostly done on the seaward side where impressive reef holes and sand beaches often produce big tailor, salmon and herring. Smaller baits fished on the bottom are usually taken by tarwhine but some big King George whiting and sand whiting can also be hooked.

Access to the island is by ferry or by wading across the sandbar leading out to the island. This should be done with extreme care, as several deep channels must be negotiated. Fishing from the sandbar is very popular with light spin tackle or fly gear for flathead, flounder, herring and whiting.

COVENTRY REEF

Reached by boat this area of shallow reef is a magnet to migrating salmon during autumn, when big schools take up residence and can be caught on baits and lures. Herring can be prolific around the reef and some nice tailor and Samson fish are also caught.

The reef shoreline around Point Peron is a good fishing spot for herring, skippy and tarwhine.

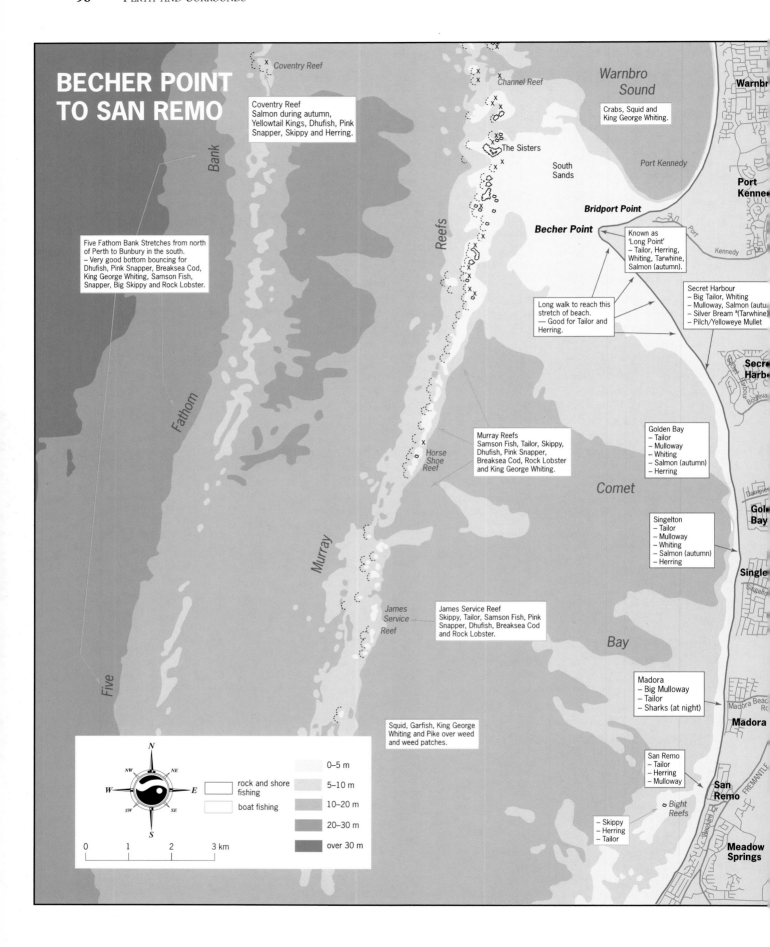

BECHER POINT TO SAN REMO

Coventry Reef

Channel Reef

Warnbro Sound

Warnbr

Coventry Reef
Salmon during autumn,
Yellowtail Kings, Dhufish, Pink
Snapper, Skippy and Herring.

Crabs, Squid and
King George Whiting.

The Sisters

South
Sands

Port Kennedy

Port
Kenne

Bank

**Five Fathom Bank Stretches from north
of Perth to Bunbury in the south.**
– Very good bottom bouncing for
Dhufish, Pink Snapper, Breaksea Cod,
King George Whiting, Samson Fish,
Snapper, Big Skippy and Rock Lobster.

Reefs

Bridport Point

Becher Point

Known as
'Long Point'
– Tailor, Herring,
Whiting, Tarwhine,
Salmon (autumn).

Secret Harbour
– Big Tailor, Whiting
– Mulloway, Salmon (autu
– Silver Bream *(Tarwhine)
– Pilch/Yelloweye Mullet

Long walk to reach this
stretch of beach.
— Good for Tailor and
Herring.

Secr
Harb

Fathom

*Horse
Shoe
Reef*

Murray Reefs
Samson Fish, Tailor, Skippy,
Dhufish, Pink Snapper,
Breaksea Cod, Rock Lobster
and King George Whiting.

Golden Bay
– Tailor
– Mulloway
– Whiting
– Salmon (autumn)
– Herring

Comet

Gol
Bay

Murray

Singelton
– Tailor
– Mulloway
– Whiting
– Salmon (autumn)
– Herring

Single

*James
Service
Reef*

James Service Reef
Skippy, Tailor, Samson Fish, Pink
Snapper, Dhufish, Breaksea Cod
and Rock Lobster.

Bay

Madora
– Big Mulloway
– Tailor
– Sharks (at night)

Madora

Squid, Garfish, King George
Whiting and Pike over weed
and weed patches.

San Remo
– Tailor
– Herring
– Mulloway

San
Remo

Five

*Bight
Reefs*

– Skippy
– Herring
– Tailor

Meadow
Springs

Legend

N NW NE W E SW SE S

0   1   2   3 km

rock and shore fishing	
boat fishing	

	0–5 m
	5–10 m
	10–20 m
	20–30 m
	over 30 m

SAFETY BAY / WARNBRO SOUND

Safety Bay provides excellent access for boat anglers intent on fishing Shoalwater Bay and Warnbro Sound. The boat fishing is good for a wide range of common species like herring, tailor, gardies and whiting. The annual spring run of pink snapper is also eagerly awaited as fish are regularly taken from several spots out in the bay usually located near several rocks running south from Penguin Island. The Murray Reefs lying offshore from Warnbro Sound are popular with boat fishers chasing dhufish, pink snapper, Samson fish, silver trevally, breaksea cod and big King George whiting. Warnbro Sound is under-rated for its blue manna crabs.

ROTTNEST ISLAND

To many Perth people Rottnest Island is the number one fishing spot locally. With its beautiful bays and beaches, the island is home to a mixture of tropical and temperate species. Lying just 20 km out from Fremantle, Rottnest is easily reached by mid to large boats, or by a regular ferry service. Once there you can hire a pushbike or catch the local bus to explore the island. There is plenty of accommodation available but you will need to book well in advance during peak season.

FISH FACTS

WAHOO

Related to the other mackerels, these torpedo-shaped fish are usually only found well offshore where they also hunt baitfish. Wahoo are capable of incredible bursts of speed, and their razor sharp teeth demand respect when handling.

Most wahoo are taken by anglers trolling for other species of gamefish, and have a nasty habit of slicing up expensive skirted lures being trolled for tuna and marlin. Once hooked, wahoo display a lightning fast burst of speed, which will have your reel screaming as several hundred metres of line disappears in seconds. Once the first few runs are finished these fish are usually too exhausted to give the angler too much trouble near the boat. Although they are sometimes caught in good numbers from the Rottnest Trench to the west of Perth, they are more common in northern waters.

Rottnest Island is a popular holiday and fishing spot just off the coast from Perth.

Fishing from the shore around Rottnest is a great way to experience beach and rock fishing. The most common species caught here would be herring, as these fish seem to be all around the island and respond well to berley. Light tackle is a great way to fish for herring, and other species also commonly encountered are tarwhine, silver trevally (skippy), King George and sand whiting and garfish. During autumn it is worth fishing heavier tackle and the deeper reef holes for salmon which often hold up around the island in big numbers.

THOMSON BAY

Ferries arrive and depart at Thomson Bay, carrying visitors to and from the island; it is also where the main settlement is situated with several small shops, accommodation and a pub. Fishing for herring, garfish and tarwhine from the ferry jetty is popular during the day. At night chopper tailor, silver trevally and squid often show up to please any anglers trying their luck.

BATHURST POINT

Bathurst Point, at the northern end of Thomson Bay is a good place to catch herring, gardies and the occasional King George whiting. It is a good spot to fish last thing in the afternoon prior to your ferry leaving for the mainland, as having a flat tyre on your pushbike at the other end of the island an hour before you are meant to leave can be very stressful.

THE NATURAL JETTY

The Natural Jetty is a line of reef running out from shore at the southern end of Thomson Bay, and produces mixed bags of silver trevally, tailor, herring, garfish and tarwhine. Casting a popper around the white water late in the day often produces some nice tailor.

PARKER POINT

Boat anglers chase big yellowfin tuna, shark mackerel, Samson fish and yellowtail kings at Parker Point. Trolling big minnow lures around this Point has accounted for some great captures on the mentioned species. Fishing from the rocks is reasonable for smaller species like herring, silver trevally and tailor. There is a small sanctuary zone at Parker Point.

SALMON BAY

Salmon Bay provides shore anglers with some of the best beach and reef fishing on the island, with tailor, mulloway, salmon, flathead, yellowfin, sand and King George whiting, silver trevally and herring all showing up at various times of the year. Autumn and winter seem to provide the best fishing especially for mulloway, silver trevally and salmon. Surf rods should be used and be prepared to wade out onto the shore reefs to fish the deeper holes where these fish feed. Take care during rough conditions as it is easy to get washed into a reef hole, especially if the tide is rising and the waves are big. Use a simple rig of a small ball or bean sinker running down to a short leader of monofilament line with a set of four or five ganged hooks to suit the bait. Best baits are whole pilchards, whitebait or bluebait.

NANCY COVE

A pleasant little spot to try for silver trevally, herring, sand and King George whiting, Nancy Cove also occasionally provides salmon around the reefs in autumn. A jetty gives access for the elderly or disabled.

STRICKLAND BAY

The shore angler has many spots to target herring, silver trevally, sand and King George whiting in Strickland Bay. Small ganged hooks baited with whitebait or bluebait should be used with a small sinker that allows the bait to be cast into sand patches between the reefs. A light flick rod is all that is needed, and try to berley up with pollard and oil for better results.

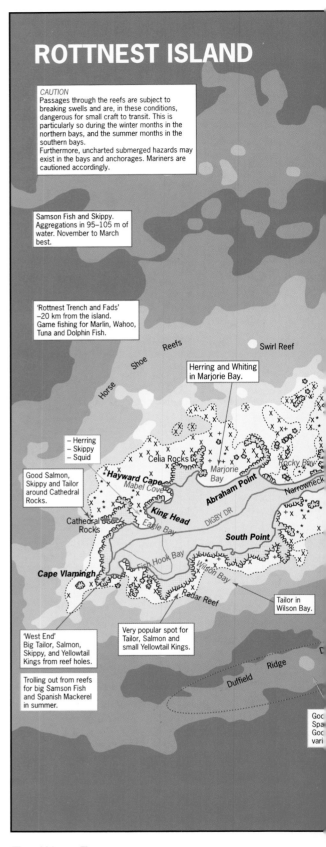

ROTTNEST ISLAND

CAUTION
Passages through the reefs are subject to breaking swells and are, in these conditions, dangerous for small craft to transit. This is particularly so during the winter months in the northern bays, and the summer months in the southern bays.
Furthermore, uncharted submerged hazards may exist in the bays and anchorages. Mariners are cautioned accordingly.

Samson Fish and Skippy. Aggregations in 95–105 m of water. November to March best.

'Rottnest Trench and Fads' –20 km from the island. Game fishing for Marlin, Wahoo, Tuna and Dolphin Fish.

Herring and Whiting in Marjorie Bay.

– Herring
– Skippy
– Squid

Good Salmon, Skippy and Tailor around Cathedral Rocks.

Tailor in Wilson Bay.

'West End' Big Tailor, Salmon, Skippy, and Yellowtail Kings from reef holes.

Very popular spot for Tailor, Salmon and small Yellowtail Kings.

Trolling out from reefs for big Samson Fish and Spanish Mackerel in summer.

THE WEST END

The West End of Rottnest Island fishes well for a number of species. Along with salmon there is the chance of hooking some big tailor, yellowtail kingfish, dhufish and Samson fish, especially from the West End reefs.

Care is needed when fishing these reefs as in rough weather they can be very dangerous, but the advantage with Rottnest is that there is always somewhere else to

North Point Reef

Fish by boat on reefs surrounding island for big Dhufish, Pink Snapper, Samson Fish, Breaksea Cod, Queen Snapper and Skippy.
– Good crayfish on reefs during season.

The shores, reefs and islands of Rottnest form a natural hazard that has claimed vessels since 1842. Underwater and land plaques have been positioned giving details of the wrecks around Rottnest, refer to West Australian Museum and Rottnest Island Authority publication.

Popular mooring spot.

Herring and Skippy

Herring and Gardies

Kingston Reefs

Kingston Spit

Herring

Parakeet I.

North Point

Parakeet Bay

Point Clune

Longreach Bay

Geordie Bay

Bathurst Point

Duck Rock

Mushroom Rock

Transit Rocks

Ferry Jetty

Thomson Bay

Kingston Reefs

Armstrong Point

WAY

BOVELL

Charlotte Point

Ricey Beach

Lake Baghdad

Garderi Lake

Lake Negri

Lake Sirius

Lake Vincent

Herschel Lake

Pearse Lake

Phillip Rock

King George Whiting close to reef.

Pink Lake

DIGBY DR

Rottnest Island

Government House Lake

Phillip Point

Bickley Bay

Tailor and Skippy

Note:
Herring are very common from most of the bays and reefs around the island. Salmon are common around many reefs in autumn.

Lake Timperley

Serpentine Lake

Airstrip

No cars on the island – transport is by pushbike or island bus.
No boat ramps or illegal mooring allowed.

Herring

Bickley Point

Jubilee Rocks

Wallace Island

Twin Rocks

PARKER

DIGBY DR

Nancy Cove

Fairbridge Bluff

POINT

Henrietta Rocks

Joan Rock

ROAD

Vlamingh Landing

Porpoise Bay

Dyer Island

Kitson Point

Vera Rocks

Salmon Bay

Pocillopora Reef

Fish the beaches and reef holes of Salmon Bay for Salmon, Tailor, Whiting, Herring, Skippy and Mulloway.

Salmon Point

Tailor and Skippy in Mary Cove.

Parker Point

Troll out from reefs for big Yellowfin Tuna and occasional Spanish Mackerel.

– Snapper
– Breaksea Cod
– Samson Fish

jetties
roads
rock and shore fishing
boat fishing

0–5 m
5–10 m
10–20 m
20–30 m
over 30 m

N
NW NE
W   E
SW SE
S

0   0.5   1 km

fish that is sheltered and out of the wind. Spots worth trying at the West End are Wilson Bay, Radar Reef, Fish Hook Bay and Cathedral Rocks.

Autumn is a popular time to fish this area by anglers chasing salmon. Boat anglers target Spanish mackerel out from the West End reefs by trolling minnow lures not far from shore. Other species like tuna and yellowtail kingfish are also taken with this method.

MARJORIE, ROCKY & STARK BAYS

These bays all produce plenty of herring once berley is added to the water. Other species like silver trevally, sand and King George whiting and flathead are often welcome additions to the bag.

RICEY BEACH

Ricey Beach is well known for holding salmon in the reef holes during their autumn run north. Big tailor can also be taken on baits and lures like poppers cast into the reef holes at first or last light. Herring can easily be caught all along the beach and shore reefs and the occasional run of silver trevally makes Ricey Beach a popular fishing spot.

GEORDIE BAY

A popular mooring spot for holiday boat anglers, Geordie Bay's shore settlement is often booked out months in advance. Fishing from a boat or shore, anglers will have no trouble catching a feed of herring that are abundant in the bay. At night a squid jig cast over the side of the boat can provide a feed of fresh calamari for breakfast or be used for bait to tempt the island's King George whiting or possibly a big dhufish from the offshore reefs. A live herring set out on a heavy rod can be all too tempting for the occasional big Samson fish. Once hooked, these educated Samson fish will then run your line through the maze of moorings in the bay.

OFFSHORE

The island rarely disappoints a visiting angler, but fishing its waters by boat is when some of the real prizes turn up. Big dhufish are a favourite capture in Rottnest waters, and if you get a licence during the season the place is crawling with crayfish. The deeper reefs provide excellent bottom fishing for dhufish, queen snapper, pink snapper, breaksea cod, Samson fish, yellowtail kingfish and small sharks.

Gamefishing on a larger scale takes place at a location called 'The Trench' another 20 km out to sea from Rottnest. There have been some FADs (Fish Attracting Devices) dropped out in this deep water each year, which have attracted dolphin fish, wahoo and marlin. Trolling big lures for the marlin is the most popular method, while whole pilchards or live herring are used to catch the dolphin fish attracted to the FADs. They will respond to lures and saltwater flies but become very shy when too many boats are about.

BOAT RAMPS & TACKLE STORES

Like any capital city, Perth has a huge boating population that takes advantage of the coastal waters and the Swan and Canning rivers. South of Perth the cities of Mandurah and Bunbury also attract huge numbers of boating anglers that have a choice of numerous launching facilities provided. In summer many of the popular ramps become very crowded along the coast and in the rivers and estuaries. Places like Rottnest Island or the Peel Estuary can be so crowded during these periods that they resemble a busy highway. Boating is popular all year round but the summer months are favoured by many due to the warm conditions, however gusting easterly winds blow hard in the mornings only to be replaced by strong southwest sea breezes in the afternoons. Many keen offshore anglers prefer the calm conditions that can be experienced in autumn and early winter but once the strong winter storms set in many retire their boats until later in the year.

RAMPS

Two Rocks – Boat harbour
Mindarie Keys – Marina
Ocean Reef – Marina
Hillarys – Boat Harbour
Woodmans Point – Near Cockburn Sea Rescue
Naval Base – Hogg Road
Kwinana Beach – reserve
Rockingham – Palm Beach and Point Peron
Safety Bay – Bent Street, Donald Drive and Carlisle Street

SWAN RIVER RAMPS

Guildford – Swan Street and Fish Market Reserve (unsealed ramp)
Bayswater Claughton Reserve
Maylands – Clarkson Road
Belmont – Abernethy Road (unsealed ramp)
Bassendean – Pickering Park (unsealed ramp)
Rivervale – Goodwood Parade
South Perth – Coode Street
Subiaco – Hackett Drive
Mosman – Johnston Street
Point Walter – East Fremantle
Leeuwin – across from Army Barracks

CANNING RIVER

Deepwater Point – Mt Pleasant
Manning – Cloister Ave (unsealed ramp)

TACKLE STORES — PERTH NORTH

Got Ya Tackle & Camping
Shop 3, 89 Erindale Road,
Balcatta WA 6021
Tel: (08) 9240 6000

The Lure
25 Winton Road,
Joondalup WA 6027
Tel: (08) 9301 5873

Joondalup Fishing & Outdoors
Shop 13, 200 Winton Road,
Joondalup WA 6027
Tel: (08) 9300 2588

The Hunters Den
170 Winton Road,
Joondalup WA 6027
Tel: (08) 9300 3434

Bluewater Tackle
140 Russel Street,
Morley WA 6062
Tel: (08) 9375 9800

Bluewater Tackle
21 Scarborough Beach Road,
Scarborough WA
Tel: (08) 9245 1313

Bluewater Melville
248 Leach Highway
Myaree WA
Tel: (08) 9330 7766

Graeme Harris Guns
170 Great Eastern Highway,
Midland WA 6056
Tel: (08) 9274 5699

Joe's Fishing Tackle
500 Charles Street,
North Perth WA
Tel: (08) 9201 0660

Campbell's Protackle
171 Oxford Street,
Leederville WA 6007
Tel: (08) 9444 3710

Fleet's for Tackle
141 Walter Road,
Morley WA 6062
Tel: (08) 9276 2389

The Tackle Shack, Morely
8 Cassia Way
Morely WA 6062
Tel: (08) 9377 3369

Getaway Camping, Fishing & Boating
3/516 Alexander Drive,
Malaga WA 6090
Tel: (08) 9209 1773

The Tackle Shack
Shop 76, Malaga Markets,
Alexander Drive,
Malaga WA 6090
Tel: (08) 9248 3800

Allsports
44 Hutton Street,
Osborne Park WA
Tel: (08) 9444 9633

Urban Angler
Unit 1, 44 Hutton Street,
Osborne Park WA
Tel: (08) 9444 9633

Salmon Bay at Rottnest Island where anglers can fish the reef for many species.

BOAT RAMPS & TACKLE STORES

City Boat & Tackle
The Basement,
790 Hay Street,
Perth WA 6000
Tel: (08) 9321 7300

Allsport Tackle & Marine
Unit 4/364 South Street
O'Connor WA
Tel: (08) 9337 5682

TACKLE STORES — PERTH SOUTH

Carrington Street Tackle & Marine
429 Carrington Street,
Hamilton Hill WA 6163
Tel: (08) 9336 2138

Allsports Tackle & Marine
4/364 South Street,
O'Connor WA 6163
Tel: (08) 9337 5682

Carry On Camping
2880 Albany Highway,
Kelmscott WA 6111
Tel: (08) 9495 1940

Anglers Fishing World
221 Albany Highway,
Victoria Park WA 6100
Tel: (08) 9355 0575

The Complete Fisherman
2 Bulimba Road
Nedlands WA
Tel: (08) 9389 1337

Breammaster
929 Beaufort Street
Inglewood WA
Tel: (08) 9271 0555

Victoria Park Tackle
459 Albany Highway,
Victoria Park WA
Tel: (08) 9362 3162

Jets Cycles & Tackle
2280 Albany Highway,
Gosnells WA 6110
Tel: (08) 9398 2359

Rays Sportspower Albany
288 York Street
Albany WA
Tel: (08) 9842 2842

Sports Marine
113 Victoria Street
Bunbury WA
Tel: (08) 9721 4961

Oliver's Cycle & Tackle Mart
2/1440 Albany Highway,
Cannington WA
Tel: (08) 9458 7716

Attfield Tackle & Sports
2/38 Attfield Street,
Maddington WA 6109
Tel: (08) 9493 6553

Anglers Anonymous
4/255 Bannister Road,
Canning Vale WA 6155
Tel: (08) 9455 2521

Getaway Camping, Fishing & Boating
2/190 Bannister Road,
Canning Vale WA
Tel: (08) 9455 5875

Fisherman's Paradise
793a Canning Highway,
Applecross WA
Tel: (08) 9364 8330

Custom Networks
84 Hampton Road,
Fremantle WA 6162
Tel: (08) 9335 2492

Fleets for Tackle
2/64 Adelaide Street,
Fremantle WA 6160
Tel: (08) 9430 8188

The Chart Map Shop
14 Collie Street
Fremantle WA 6160
Tel: (08) 9335 8665

Rockingham Fishing & Camping World
81 Dixon Road,
Rockingham WA 6168
Tel: (08) 9528 5255

West Coast Tackle
Shop 2, Rockingham Arcade,
Kent Street,
Rockingham WA
Tel: (08) 9527 7919

Freerange Supplies
112 Brookman Street
Kalgoorlie WA 6430
Tel: (08) 9093 1099

Esperance Diving & Fishing
72 The Esplanade
Esperance WA 6450
Tel: (08) 9071 5111

CHAPTER 8

MANDURAH TO BUSSELTON

MANDURAH

LONG POINT

To the south of Safety Bay is a stretch of shallow beach leading up to Long Point where, in the past, 4WD access allowed anglers to explore and fish a wide area. In recent times the access to the beach has been by foot only and anglers tend to only fish a small portion of this area.

Long Point has always been a very good spot to fish for tailor and herring, especially in the evenings as the fish move into the surf to feed. Other species like whiting, flathead, flounder, silver bream and the occasional mulloway and salmon have all been caught here.

SECRET HARBOUR

The big housing development established here has opened up a very productive section of surf beach that seems to have taken the place of Long Point as a favourite amongst many beach anglers. The beach has deeper water than Long Point, with some good gutters and channels to attract fish. Big tailor are a regular catch at certain times of the year, and in summer chopper tailor are nearly always on the bite in the afternoons when the sea breeze blows. Herring, whiting and silver bream are found in good numbers, and big mulloway and small sharks are always a chance on larger baits fished at night. In autumn, salmon can be caught as they migrate north and big schools of yellow eye mullet (pilch) show up each winter.

GOLDEN BAY

Like Secret Harbour, Golden Bay is a fantastic beach to fish, with a deep gutter running along the beach and a sandbar further out to break the waves. Tailor are the main species fished for, but big mulloway, small sharks, herring, pilch and whiting are all caught from this beach.

SINGELTON BEACH

This smaller stretch of beach is another good tailor and mulloway spot, with deep gutters cutting in close to shore.

MADORA BEACH

Madora Beach has earned the reputation of being the number one spot to hook a big mulloway in the surf close to Perth. Some very big fish upwards of 20 kg

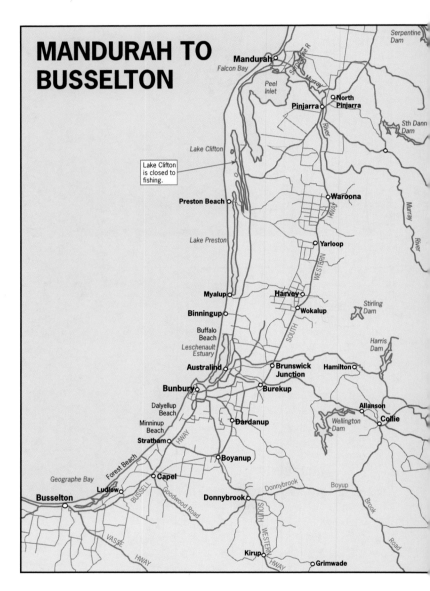

can be hooked on large baits fished usually after dark on a rising tide. Small sharks and rays are also commonly caught by anglers using heavy tackle at night, and the summertime chopper tailor runs make Madora a very popular angling beach.

SAN REMO

Although not as popular as Madora, San Remo is also a very good beach to fish for mulloway and many big fish are hooked here each year. Tailor, herring, whiting and silver bream also turn up regularly along with pilch and the occasional salmon in the cooler months.

HALLS HEAD

Fishing from the shore into the broken surf and reef is reasonably productive for tailor, herring and big mulloway at night. There are reasonable fishing

MANDURAH TO DAWESVILLE CHANNEL

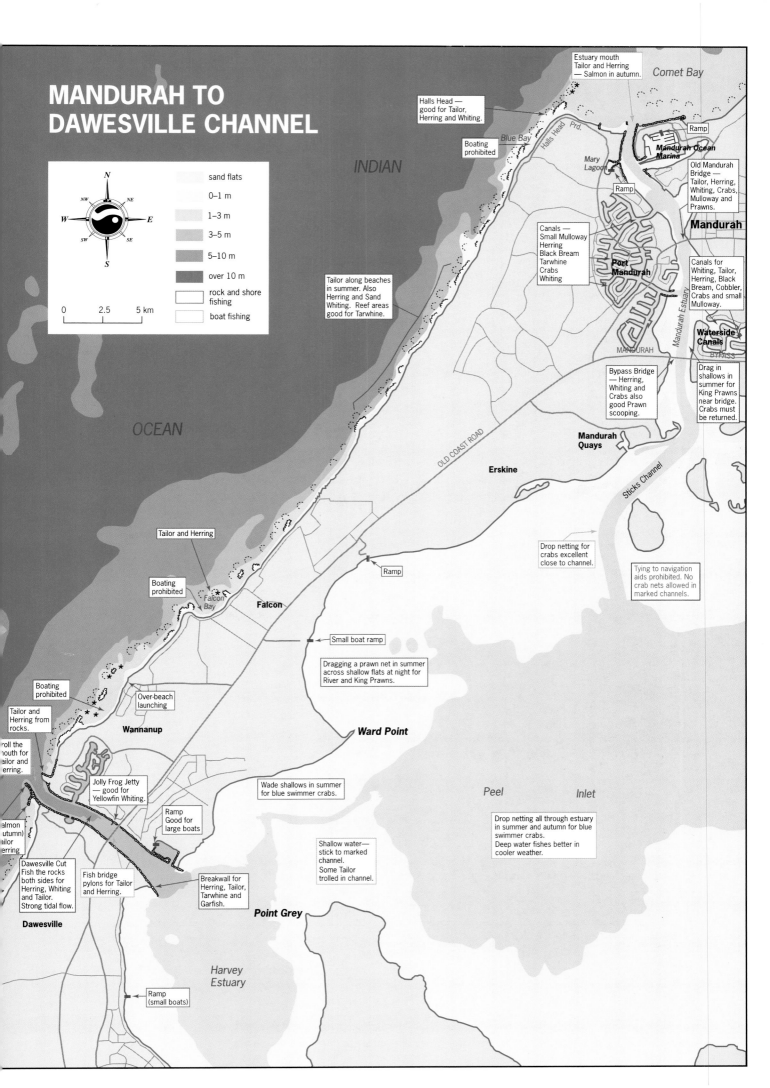

Estuary mouth
Tailor and Herring
— Salmon in autumn.

Comet Bay

Halls Head —
good for Tailor,
Herring and Whiting.

Boating
prohibited

Blue Bay

Ramp

Mandurah Ocean Marina

Mary Lagoon

Ramp

Old Mandurah
Bridge —
Tailor, Herring,
Whiting, Crabs,
Mulloway and
Prawns.

INDIAN

Mandurah

Canals —
Small Mulloway
Herring
Black Bream
Tarwhine
Crabs
Whiting

Port Mandurah

Canals for
Whiting, Tailor,
Herring, Black
Bream, Cobbler,
Crabs and small
Mulloway.

Waterside Canals

Tailor along beaches
in summer. Also
Herring and Sand
Whiting. Reef areas
good for Tarwhine.

MANDURAH

BYPASS

Drag in
shallows in
summer for
King Prawns
near bridge.
Crabs must
be returned.

Bypass Bridge
— Herring,
Whiting and
Crabs also
good Prawn
scooping.

Mandurah Quays

OCEAN

Erskine

Sticks Channel

OLD COAST ROAD

Drop netting for
crabs excellent
close to channel.

Tying to navigation
aids prohibited. No
crab nets allowed in
marked channels.

Tailor and Herring

Ramp

Boating
prohibited

Falcon Bay

Falcon

Small boat ramp

Dragging a prawn net in summer
across shallow flats at night for
River and King Prawns.

Boating
prohibited

Over-beach
launching

Wannanup

Ward Point

Tailor and
Herring from
rocks.

roll the
mouth for
ailor and
erring.

Jolly Frog Jetty
— good for
Yellowfin Whiting.

Wade shallows in summer
for blue swimmer crabs.

Peel   Inlet

Ramp
Good for
large boats

Drop netting all through estuary
in summer and autumn for blue
swimmer crabs.
Deep water fishes better in
cooler weather.

almon
utumn)
ailor
erring

Dawesville Cut
Fish the rocks
both sides for
Herring, Whiting
and Tailor.
Strong tidal flow.

Fish bridge
pylons for Tailor
and Herring.

Breakwall for
Herring, Tailor,
Tarwhine and
Garfish.

Shallow water—
stick to marked
channel.
Some Tailor
trolled in channel.

Dawesville

Point Grey

Harvey Estuary

Ramp
(small boats)

Legend

N
NW   NE
W   E
SW   SE
S

0   2.5   5 km

	sand flats
	0–1 m
	1–3 m
	3–5 m
	5–10 m
	over 10 m
	rock and shore fishing
	boat fishing

Anglers fishing for salmon from the reef at Tims Thicket, which is just to the south of Mandurah.

Breaksea cod are often taken by anglers fishing the offshore reefs and are highly regarded for their eating qualities.

spots all the way down to Falcon where tailor, herring, whiting and silver bream can be caught.

PEEL ESTUARY MOUTH

This is where the Peel Estuary at Mandurah meets the Indian Ocean to the north. The rock groynes at the mouth are top tailor and herring spots, especially when the tide turns.

PEEL ESTUARY

This is the crabbing capital in Western Australia, with thousands of anglers targeting Mandurah's big blue manna crabs each summer. The estuary is very large and shallow, and provides an excellent nursery for the crabs to breed and grow. Most anglers use baited drop nets from the shore, bridges or boats to catch a feed, however wading through the shallows with a wire scoop can be very productive, especially at night with a torch.

Fishing in the estuary takes second place to crabbing, but there are plenty of herring, tailor, whiting, cobbler, flounder and small mulloway swimming in this system to make wetting a line worthwhile. Runs of tasty king prawns also

Blue swimmer crabs are locally known as blue manna crabs.

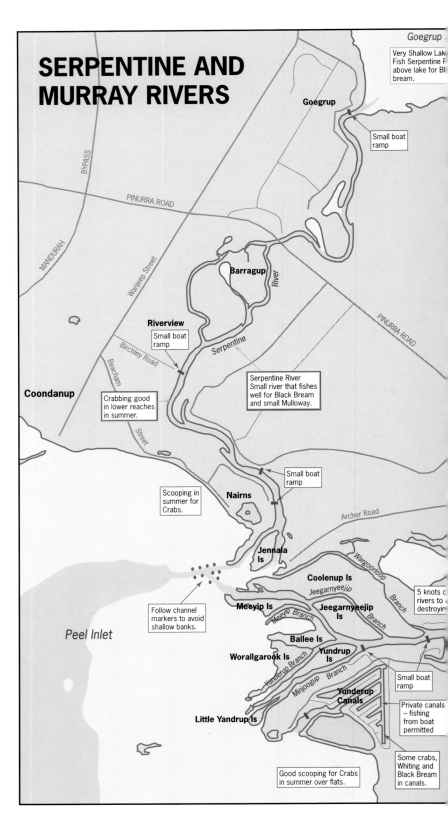

SERPENTINE AND MURRAY RIVERS

(map labels)

Goegrup

Very Shallow Lak Fish Serpentine F above lake for Bl bream.

Goegrup

Small boat ramp

BYPASS

MANDURAH

PINURRA ROAD

Wanjeep Street

Barragup

River

Riverview

Small boat ramp

Birchley Road

Serpentine

PINURRA ROAD

Beacham

Coondanup

Serpentine River
Small river that fishes well for Black Bream and small Mulloway.

Crabbing good in lower reaches in summer.

Street

Small boat ramp

Scooping in summer for Crabs.

Nairns

Archer Road

Jennala Is

Wagoorloop

Coolenup Is

Jeegarnyeejip

Branch

5 knots o rivers to destroyin

Meeyip Is

Meeyip Branch

Jeegarnyeejip Is

Follow channel markers to avoid shallow banks.

Peel Inlet

Ballee Is

Worallgarook Is

Yunderup Branch

Yundrup Is

Small boat ramp

Minjoogup Branch

Yunderup Canals

Private canals – fishing from boat permitted

Little Yandrup Is

Good scooping for Crabs in summer over flats.

Some crabs, Whiting and Black Bream in canals.

attract thousands of hopefuls with long scoop nets and lanterns at night.

OLD TRAFFIC BRIDGE

The Old Traffic Bridge is Mandurah's most famous fishing landmark, as thousands of anglers, both young and old, take advantage of the fishing platforms built under this structure. There must have been thousands of crabs hauled up in drop nets each year, and on the nights when the king prawns are running, it is shoulder-to-shoulder with scoop nets and lanterns everywhere. Herring, tailor, whiting and silver bream are usually caught on lighter tackle while late at night many a big mulloway has been hooked but often lost around the pylons of the bridge.

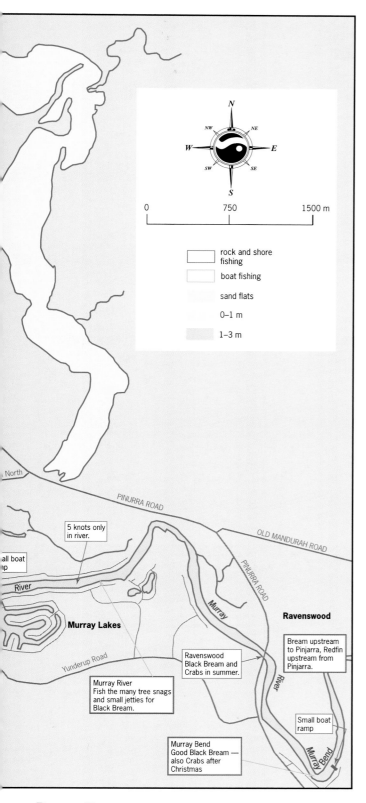

The Peel Estuary is a popular crabbing and fishing spot.

many trees that provide excellent snags for black bream, but a quiet approach is needed as these rivers are very shallow and the bream are very timid. There are also plenty of mullet and the crabs in summer can be caught a fair way up from the estuary. The speed limit is just 5 knots to prevent bank wash erosion. Black bream are found all the way up to Pinjarra—use baits of river prawns or blood worms. Small minnow lures or soft plastic jigs also take plenty of fish.

DAWESVILLE CUT

This massive channel cut through to the ocean from the Peel Estuary has not only flushed out the whole system it has created a very important recreational fishing spot. There are hundreds of metres of rock walls to the north and south that are easily accessed and fished by hundreds of anglers each year. Herring make up the bulk of the catch, and these popular little fish seem to congregate in big numbers especially during winter. Tailor can be caught all along the channel but seem to be most prolific from the mouth of The Cut and also close to the pylons of the major traffic bridge. Big yellowfin whiting turn up from the small jetty at the 'Jolly Frog' near the northern side of the bridge and juvenile salmon provide some sport in winter.

Small and large boats have access to the productive Bouvard Reefs found out from The Cut and down towards Bunbury. Big dhufish, Samson fish, pink snapper, breaksea cod, queen snapper and skippy are regular catches from the offshore reefs. There is also good diving for rock lobsters with pots being less successful from Mandurah south.

BYPASS BRIDGE

This bridge was built to divert the bulk of the traffic heading south around the main town, and like the Old Traffic Bridge it has angling platforms built underneath to allow safe fishing access to the Peel Estuary. Crabs and king prawns make up the bulk of the catches from this bridge, however herring, tailor and whiting are often landed.

SERPENTINE AND MURRAY RIVERS

These flow into the eastern side of the estuary and are popular crabbing spots. Further up these rivers the banks are lined with

The Old Traffic Bridge at Mandurah is a good place to spend a few hours crabbing or fishing.

FISH FACTS

BREAM

Black bream are an estuary species found from the Murchison River at Kalbarri all the way down to the Great Australian Bight. They are rarely caught outside of an estuary, and are heavily fished by many anglers.

A schooling fish, these bream have a reputation for being very cunning and hard to catch, especially the large ones, which can reach 3 kilograms. Most fish encountered in rivers and estuaries range from a few hundred grams to about 1.8 kg, with a 2 kg fish being a prize specimen.

Bream move upstream in summer where thay can be caught well above the tidal influence. Autumn rains push the fish down the estuaries to breed.

Most anglers target these fish with bait, usually a whole river prawn, bloodworm or cut fish fillet, which is fished around structures like jetties, bridge pylons, fallen trees and rock bars. A small hook around the number 2 size is rigged on 4–6 kg line and cast out with a tiny ball sinker as close as possible to the snags. Anglers allow the fish a few metres of slack line before the hook is set; otherwise it will be easily pulled from the lips of the bream.

In recent years anglers have targeted these fish with lures and flies with exceptional results. The bream's predatory nature leads it to readily attack a small fish or prawn, so a small minnow lure, rubber jig or saltwater fly can be deadly at times.

The good eating qualities of bream mean that they are often kept for the table.

Large fish should be released as breeding stock as they are slow growing and can be 20 years old by the time they reach 2 kilos in weight.

FINGERMARK BREAM

Also known as golden snapper, fingermark bream are closely related to mangrove jacks and red emperor, and are a big favourite amongst many anglers fishing for bottom fish in the northwest. Fingermark bream are usually found on offshore reefs and wrecks where anglers fish for them with baited lines. Closer to shore they will inhabit deep channels and rock bars, usually around the mouths of creeks. They will take lures and saltwater flies in shallower waters and can put up a mean fight around rocks and snags.

Many anglers only target these fish for the table and their eating qualities are excellent.

FISH FACTS

FLOUNDER

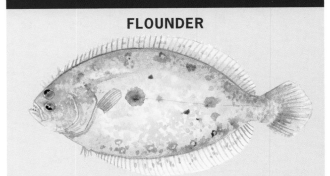

These fish are usually caught over the summer months in the estuaries and shallow sheltered waters of bays. A flounder is considered big when it reaches 'dinner plate' size, and their delicate flavour makes them a popular catch amongst most anglers.

Flounder are very aggressive fish that will lie in wait on the bottom where they blend in, making them invisible to predators and prey alike. A small lead-head jig or weighted saltwater fly bounced along the bottom is the best method to tempt these fish, and once hooked on light tackle they put up a surprisingly tough fight. Flounder will also take a variety of baits—prawn, squid and whitebait—that are usually fished on the bottom for other species like whiting.

Some of the biggest flounder caught each year come from Geographe Bay out from Busselton, where the shallow sand and seagrass beds attract plenty of these strange looking fish. The other hot spot is the Swan River in summer where big numbers of flounder move onto the shallow sand areas to feed.

FISH FACTS

GARFISH

'Gardies' as they are more commonly called, are a very popular species amongst Western Australian anglers, both for food and bait. Big schools of these fish inhabit coastal waters where they are easily caught from boat or shore. Gardies respond to berley well, and a mixture of pollard, water and oil is crushed into a berley cage that is used as a casting weight from the shore. A long fine leader down to a small hook baited with live maggots or a small piece of prawn is deadly on these fish and large catches can be made in periods of calm weather.

Most anglers target gardies from rock groynes or from a small dinghy anchored over sea grass beds. These fish have very small mouths so a long shanked hook in a small size ensures a quick hook and also helps easy removal of the hook.

Many anglers enjoy a feed of fresh garfish, and if prepared correctly and lightly fried in flour and oil they are delicious. Others choose to keep their gardies whole for bait when fishing for big tailor or when heading north chasing mackerel.

During the summer months crabs can be found in good numbers from the estuaries and inshore waters from Mandurah southwards to Busselton.

TIMS THICKET

To the south of The Cut, beaches stretch to the south towards Bunbury, and the first popular spot is a section of shore reef called Tims Thicket. This spot is a dynamite salmon location each autumn when big schools of migrating salmon hold up on the reef, providing some excellent action for beach anglers. Tailor and mulloway are also taken here at times, whilst herring and whiting seem to be a year round proposition.

WHITE HILLS

This beach is easily accessed by 4WD and has plenty of prime spots to target mostly tailor and herring. In autumn a big salmon is a possibility and large baits at night seem to catch mostly small sharks with only the occasional mulloway.

The bypass bridge crossing the Peel Estuary at Mandurah.

PRESTON

This large, popular stretch of beach is best explored by 4WD. Tailor attract plenty of anglers in summer. While herring, whiting and silver bream can be caught during the day, at night big rays, small sharks and mulloway are possibilities on large baits set out in the deep gutters.

MYALUP AND BINNINGUP

Like Preston, these beaches are popular with Bunbury anglers who target mostly tailor and herring from the surf. Salmon show up during their autumn migration and mulloway and sharks are hooked at night.

BUNBURY

THE CUT

This is the mouth of the Leschenault Inlet and is a popular shore spot to target tailor, herring, mulloway and the occasional salmon in season.

LESCHENAULT INLET

Like the Peel and Harvey estuaries to the north, the Leschenault is famous for blue swimmer crabs. Big catches of these tasty crustaceans can be made during the warmer months by drop netting from a boat or shore, or scooping in the shallows. Fishing in the estuary is good for small King George whiting, silver bream, herring and garfish.

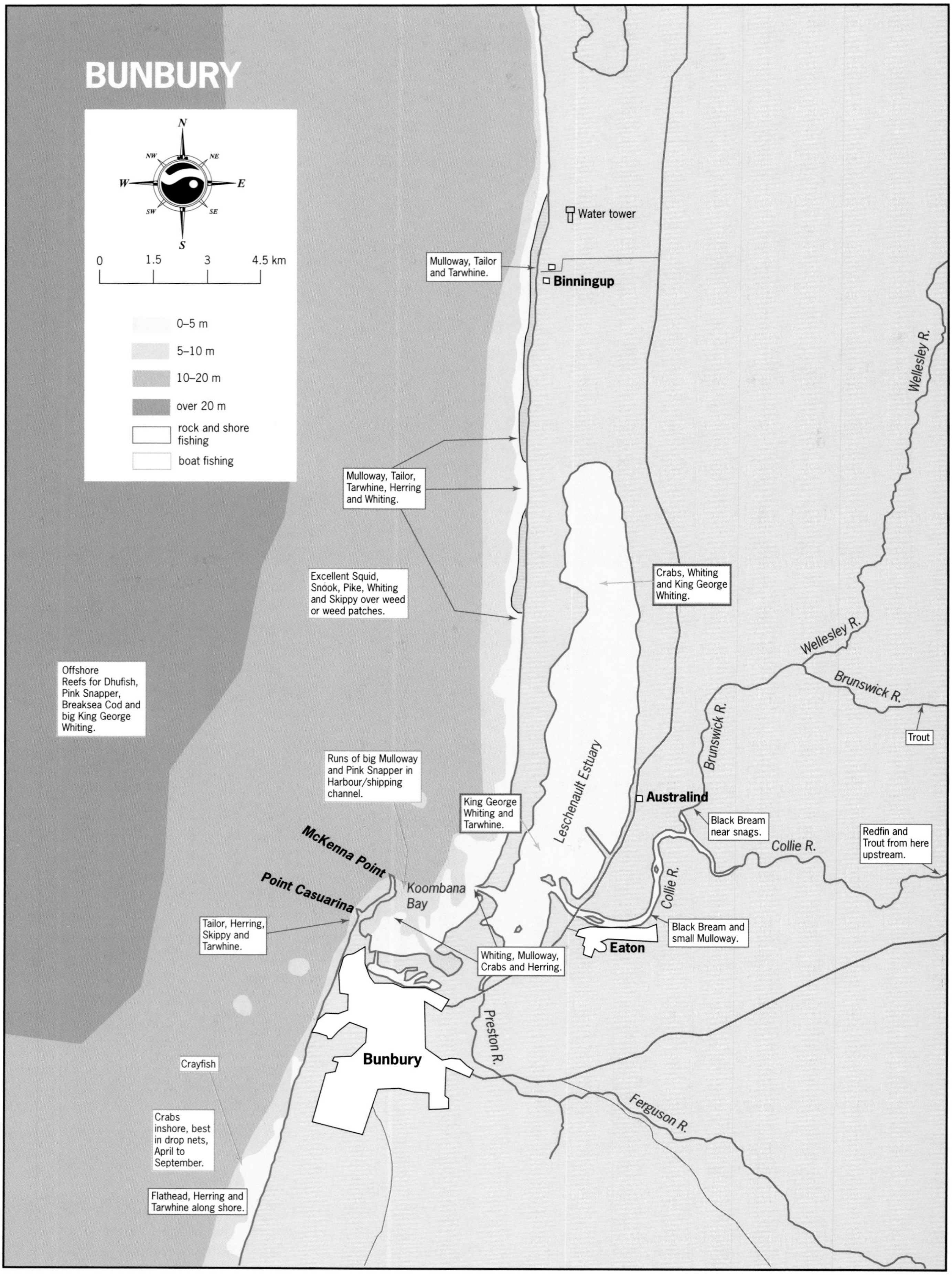

BUNBURY

N
NW   NE
W   E
SW   SE
S

0   1.5   3   4.5 km

0–5 m
5–10 m
10–20 m
over 20 m
rock and shore fishing
boat fishing

Water tower

Mulloway, Tailor and Tarwhine.

Binningup

Wellesley R.

Mulloway, Tailor, Tarwhine, Herring and Whiting.

Crabs, Whiting and King George Whiting.

Wellesley R.

Excellent Squid, Snook, Pike, Whiting and Skippy over weed or weed patches.

Brunswick R.

Offshore Reefs for Dhufish, Pink Snapper, Breaksea Cod and big King George Whiting.

Leschenault Estuary

Trout

Runs of big Mulloway and Pink Snapper in Harbour/shipping channel.

Australind

Black Bream near snags.

Collie R.

Redfin and Trout from here upstream.

McKenna Point

King George Whiting and Tarwhine.

Collie R.

Point Casuarina

Koombana Bay

Black Bream and small Mulloway.

Tailor, Herring, Skippy and Tarwhine.

Eaton

Whiting, Mulloway, Crabs and Herring.

Preston R.

Crayfish

Bunbury

Crabs inshore, best in drop nets, April to September.

Ferguson R.

Flathead, Herring and Tarwhine along shore.

From Cape Naturaliste south the coastline becomes very hazardous for rock anglers and extreme care should be taken at all times. Lives unfortunately are lost almost every year.

A nice blue-spot flathead taken on light tackle from the shore at Busselton.

BUNBURY HARBOUR

Fishing is mostly done from the breakwalls where big tailor and mulloway are caught. Inside the harbour, there are herring, garfish, silver bream and whiting. The deep shipping channel is well known for producing big mulloway at night, and boats anchor along the edge and fish with live baits or whole mulies on heavy tackle.

COLLIE RIVER

The Preston and Collie rivers to the north of the town are prime black bream spots. The Collie also produces small mulloway at times but the big black bream attract most anglers. Fishing is mostly done by small boat and the best spots seem to be the fallen tree snags that line the banks further up. A whole river prawn lightly fished amongst these snags is the best way to hook these fish, and bream up to 2 kg are not uncommon.

BACK BEACH

South of the harbour breakwalls is the back beach, which is a popular and close spot for local anglers chasing most of the common species. Herring and tailor make up the bulk of the catches but the occasional big mulloway and small shark turn up at night and during autumn there are always a few migrating salmon passing through.

BUSSELTON

CAPEL RIVER

This tiny river is mostly fished from the shore or by small boats for black bream, however the fish are usually very small and undersize. At the mouth the fishing can improve for tailor, herring and whiting. After heavy rains the river mouth is a good place to try for mulloway that are attracted to the dirty water flowing out into the ocean, which brings smaller fish with it.

PEPPERMINT GROVE

To the south of the Capel River lies Peppermint Grove Beach, a popular holiday spot for anglers in summer. This beach provides excellent fishing for chopper tailor, herring, whiting, flathead, flounder, skippy, crabs and squid.

FORREST BEACH

Forrest Beach is another favourite fishing spot that produces the same species as Peppermint Grove but also fishes well for mulloway and small sharks when the small creeks break through and push the dirty water out to sea after heavy rains.

WONNERUP BEACH AND ESTUARY

During the day, the beach is popular for smaller species such as flathead, herring, skippy and whiting, whilst after dark, the chance of a big mulloway from the mouth of the estuary makes it worth fishing. From small boats, crabbing and squidding can be excellent. Wonnerup and Vasse estuaries are mostly shallow fish nurseries for black bream, silver bream, silver trevally and King George whiting.

FISH FACTS

AUSTRALIAN SALMON

Thousands of recreational and a handful of professional fishers eagerly pursue the autumn run of the Australian salmon along the southwest coast, each year. Easter is prime salmon time in the southwest while the 'run' starts as early as January around Esperance. Big schools of these fish migrate close to the shore providing numerous shore and boat anglers with the chance to target them. These fish average 3–6 kg but bigger specimens turn up at times and once hooked they put up a powerful fight, interrupted with plenty of head shakes and leaps.

Salmon schools can usually be spotted as big black masses moving along the beaches and around rocky headlands of the south coast. They usually make it up as far as Perth and places like Rottnest Island become popular salmon fishing spots.

Salmon are predators that respond to baits of whole pilchards, fish fillets and squid. A live whiting or herring fished under a blob float will nearly always draw a strike from passing salmon, as will a fresh fillet of herring which seems to be their preferred prey species.

Casting or trolling lures for salmon is great fun, and once a school is seen it can be nearly too easy to get a strike once you get within casting range. Minnow lures, metal slices, jigs, poppers and saltwater flies will all catch salmon, and their competitive nature usually means that you will have several fish all pushing each other to get to the lure or fly first.

As these fish are capable of putting up a strong fight most anglers choose to fish for them from the shore with heavy surf fishing tackle and bait. Lure and fly anglers will use lighter gear.

Unfortunately the salmon run varies from year to year because of water temperatures, and the fish must survive the commercial netting along the southwest coast. Recreational anglers also take big numbers of salmon each year, usually for their own consumption, but thankfully many anglers are now releasing most of the salmon they catch.

Salmon are not rated very highly as an eating species, as a result most of the commercial catch goes to cat food and cray bait. When bled soon after capture and eaten fresh they are considered by many to be good tucker.

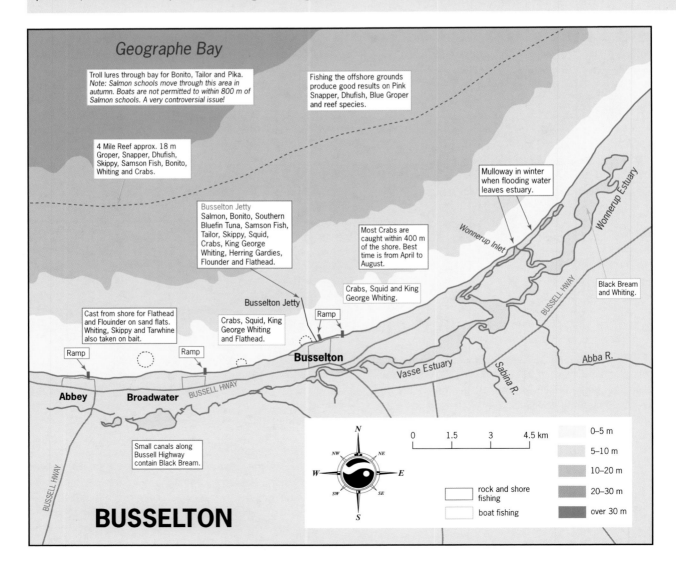

Geographe Bay

Troll lures through bay for Bonito, Tailor and Pika.
Note: Salmon schools move through this area in autumn. Boats are not permitted to within 800 m of Salmon schools. A very controversial issue!

Fishing the offshore grounds produce good results on Pink Snapper, Dhufish, Blue Groper and reef species.

4 Mile Reef approx. 18 m Groper, Snapper, Dhufish, Skippy, Samson Fish, Bonito, Whiting and Crabs.

Busselton Jetty
Salmon, Bonito, Southern Bluefin Tuna, Samson Fish, Tailor, Skippy, Squid, Crabs, King George Whiting, Herring Gardies, Flounder and Flathead.

Mulloway in winter when flooding water leaves estuary.

Wonnerup Inlet

Wonnerup Estuary

Most Crabs are caught within 400 m of the shore. Best time is from April to August.

Crabs, Squid and King George Whiting.

Black Bream and Whiting.

Busselton Jetty

Cast from shore for Flathead and Flounder on sand flats. Whiting, Skippy and Tarwhine also taken on bait.

Crabs, Squid, King George Whiting and Flathead.

Ramp

Busselton

BUSSELL HWAY

Vasse Estuary

Sabina R.

Abba R.

Ramp

Ramp

Abbey   Broadwater   BUSSELL HWAY

Small canals along Bussell Highway contain Black Bream.

BUSSELL HWAY

BUSSELTON

N
NW NE
W   E
SW SE
S

| 0 | 1.5 | 3 | 4.5 km |

rock and shore fishing

boat fishing

0–5 m
5–10 m
10–20 m
20–30 m
over 30 m

FISH FACTS

YELLOWTAIL KINGFISH

Although not as common as Samson fish, the yellowtail kingfish is a species that is encountered in much the same locations. The west-end of Rottnest Island is home to a healthy population of these fish that range from small specimens of only a few kilograms to massive 20 kg monsters that usually find their freedom amongst the reefs.

At Steep Point big yellowtail kingfish patrol the base of the cliffs where they can be seen but are rarely hooked on lines. If one does make a mistake it is usually a short battle in favour of the fish as it dives and drags the line through the rocks.

Tackle needs to be on the heavy side to effectively stop a big yellowtail kingfish, so at least 10–15 kg line is needed to stand at least a slim chance from the shore. The south coast is a good place to find these fish, and they often turn up on live baits fished under balloons for Samson fish from rocky headlands. Reported to be good eating in WA, most yellowtail kingfish find their way to the dinner table.

BUSSELTON

Busselton is a pleasant and neat town that caters for tourists with numerous hotels, motels and caravan parks. The beach in front of the town and westwards towards Seista Park is characterised by shallow weed and sand flats and is mostly protected. Very good fishing can be found all along this stretch, with flathead, flounder, King George, sand and yellowfin whiting available. Herring and chopper tailor turn up at times in big numbers, whilst the crabbing and squidding over the weed beds is well worth the effort from a small boat.

BUSSELTON JETTY

Probably the focal point for recreational fishing, this long jetty provides plenty of access for anglers chasing a huge range of species. From the shallows closer to shore herring, gardies, whiting, skippy, tarwhine, crabs and squid are all common catches. The deep water out from the end is a fantastic spot to spin for bonito and southern bluefin tuna. Big Samson fish, mulloway, yellowfin tuna and sharks are all hooked on live baits fished on heavy lines out from the end, and a live squid is one of the first choices of bait when targeting these bigger species. Half way along the jetty is a mulloway hot spot, and each year runs of mulloway see many fish hooked from the jetty on heavy hand lines or rods after dark. Big John dory are also a regular catch on small live baits fished near the pylons.

BOAT RAMPS & TACKLE STORES

MANDURAH / PEEL ESTUARY RAMPS

Mary Street
Dolphin Pool
Dawesville – northern marina at channel and ramp at south of channel
Waterside Canals
Yunderup Canals
Falcon
Murray Lakes Canals – Murray River
North Yunderup – Cullenup Road
South Yunderup – River Road
Murray Bend – Ravenswood
Pinjarra – Henry Street
Serpentine River – Riverside Gardens, Nairns, Riverview and Furnissdale

MANDURAH / PEEL ESTUARY TACKLE SHOPS

Bailey's Baitbox
Shop 2, 369 Warnbro Sound Avenue,
Port Kennedy WA 6172
Tel: (08) 9524 6863

Mandurah Tackle Mart
Shop 4 Meadow Springs Shopping Centre
Mandurah WA 6210
Tel: (08) 9581 6484

Miami Marine & Hardware
Shops 5 & 6, Miami Village,
Old Coast Road,
Falcon WA 6210
Tel: (08) 9534 2787

Totally Wild Fishing & Camping
13-77 Reserve Drive,
Mandurah WA 6210
Tel: (08) 9581 8877

Fishing & Camping World
78 Pinjarra Road,
Mandurah WA 6210
Tel: (08) 9586 2749

Tuckey's Tackle
2 Mandurah Terrace,
Mandurah WA 6210
Tel: (08) 9535 1228

BUNBURY RAMPS

Stirling Street
Power Boat Club
Casuarina Boat Harbour
Turkey Point – Cut
Collie River – Elbow Reserve, Taylor Road and Pratt Road, Eaton
Australind – Ridley Place

BUNBURY TACKLE SHOPS

Bunbury Sportsmarine
113 Victoria Street,
Bunbury WA 6230
Tel: (08) 9271 4961

Gun-Mart
Blair Street,
Bunbury WA 6230
Tel: (08) 9721 6366

Collie Sports & Leisure
Shop 11 Boulavarde Shopping Ctre
Collie WA 6225
Tel: (08) 9734 5022

Bunbury Camping & Fishing
Unit 5&6 99 King Street
Bunbury WA
Tel: (08) 9791 9306

BUSSELTON RAMPS
Dolphin Road
Georgette Street
Newtown Beach
Scout Road
Port Geographe
Wonnerup

BUSSELTON TACKLE SHOPS

Outdoor Sports & Leisure Busselton
29 Queen Street
Busselton WA
Tel: (08) 9752 4044

Busselton Sports Power
99 Queen Street
Busselton WA 6280
Tel: (08) 9752 2457

Busselton Army Surplus
Unit 1/17 Bussell Highway
Busselton WA 6280
Tel: (08) 9754 2909

CHAPTER 9

DUNSBOROUGH TO WINDY HARBOUR

DUNSBOROUGH

Dunsborough is another very popular holiday fishing destination where anglers can take advantage of the excellent shore- and boat-fishing opportunities available. In autumn, salmon-run anglers position themselves on one of the many beaches or small rocky sections to fish for these great sport fish. Spinning with lures or fishing baits such as whole pilchards on ganged hooks under a blob float or on the bottom with a sinker, is the way to catch a salmon. Good reliable tackle is needed as these fish will fight strongly, and a landing net is always handy to have when the fish tires and is ready to be landed.

Some of the most popular locations to try close to town are Casle Bay and Meelup. Catching herring is almost too easy, as large numbers of these fish can be attracted by a little berley, and during the salmon run it is worth putting out a live herring on a larger rod as this is the number one salmon bait. Tailor often turn up from the shore late in the afternoons whilst skippy, gardies and whiting are also there for the taking.

There is plenty of accommodation available—from holiday homes to caravan parks —but booking early is a must in summer.

EAGLE BAY, ROCKY POINT, BUNKER BAY

This stretch of coast heading towards Cape Naturaliste, is a fantastic spot to fish for salmon during the autumn run. Big schools of salmon make their way around the cape and follow close to the coast where they are easily targeted from the many rocky outcrops in this area. This area is a safe place to fish when the western side of the cape is blown out by the sea breeze. Only a very large swell can cause problems in this area, especially around Bunker Bay where care must be taken. Herring, King George whiting, flathead, skippy and tailor are also very common from the rocks, small beaches or from a small boat that can be launched at Dunsborough. Trolling in the bay is a great way to catch a few bonito that can be about in big numbers, along with the occasional southern bluefin tuna. Closer to shore big pike often take trolled lures over the weed beds, and during the season salmon are commonly hooked.

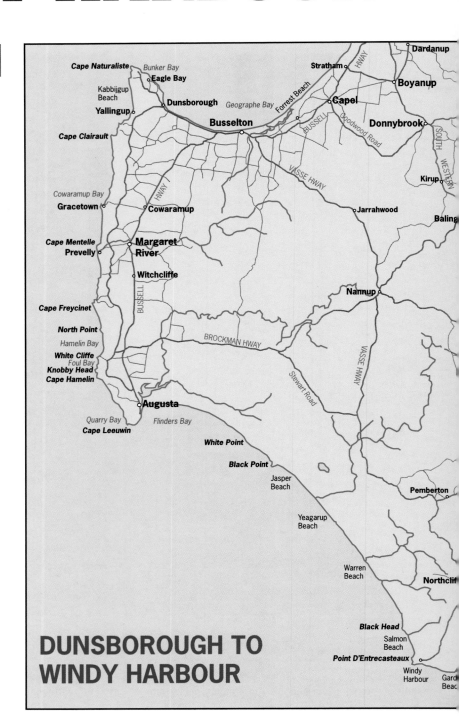

DUNSBOROUGH TO WINDY HARBOUR

FOUR MILE REEF

This reef, found only a few kilometres offshore, is a favourite place for boat anglers chasing big Samson fish, pink snapper, the occasional dhufish and skippy. Anchoring up and setting a good berley trail is the secret to success here, but good weather is needed, as this reef becomes very dangerous in a big swell.

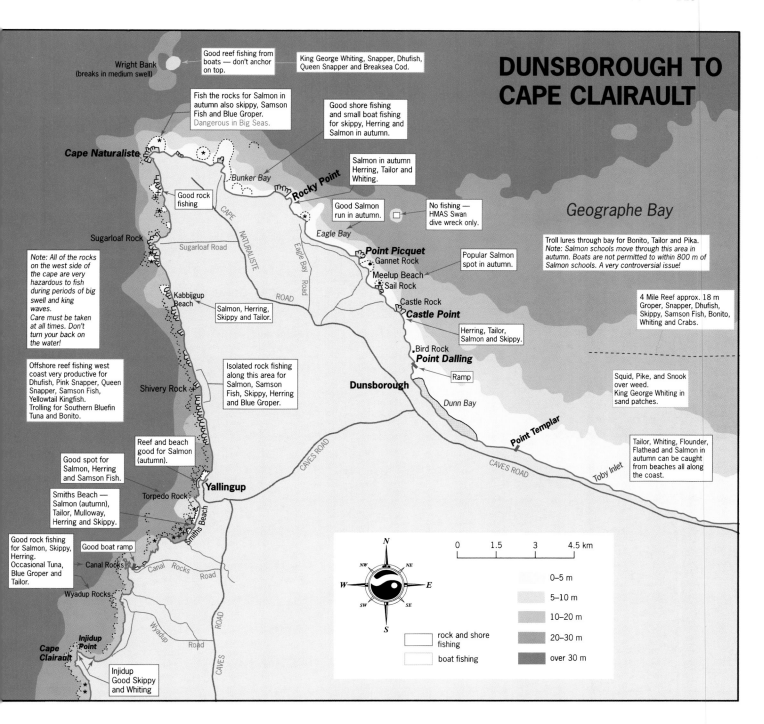

DUNSBOROUGH TO CAPE CLAIRAULT

Wright Bank (breaks in medium swell)

Good reef fishing from boats — don't anchor on top.

King George Whiting, Snapper, Dhufish, Queen Snapper and Breaksea Cod.

Fish the rocks for Salmon in autumn also skippy, Samson Fish and Blue Groper. Dangerous in Big Seas.

Good shore fishing and small boat fishing for skippy, Herring and Salmon in autumn.

Cape Naturaliste

Bunker Bay

Rocky Point

Salmon in autumn Herring, Tailor and Whiting.

Good rock fishing

No fishing — HMAS Swan dive wreck only.

Good Salmon run in autumn.

Eagle Bay

Geographe Bay

Sugarloaf Rock

Sugarloaf Road

CAPE NATURALISTE

Eagle Bay Road

Point Picquet
Gannet Rock

Popular Salmon spot in autumn.

Troll lures through bay for Bonito, Tailor and Pika. Note: Salmon schools move through this area in autumn. Boats are not permitted to within 800 m of Salmon schools. A very controversial issue!

Note: All of the rocks on the west side of the cape are very hazardous to fish during periods of big swell and king waves. Care must be taken at all times. Don't turn your back on the water!

Meelup Beach
Sail Rock

Castle Rock
Castle Point

4 Mile Reef approx. 18 m Groper, Snapper, Dhufish, Skippy, Samson Fish, Bonito, Whiting and Crabs.

Kabbijup Beach

ROAD

Salmon, Herring, Skippy and Tailor.

Herring, Tailor, Salmon and Skippy.

Bird Rock
Point Dalling

Offshore reef fishing west coast very productive for Dhufish, Pink Snapper, Queen Snapper, Samson Fish, Yellowtail Kingfish. Trolling for Southern Bluefin Tuna and Bonito.

Isolated rock fishing along this area for Salmon, Samson Fish, Skippy, Herring and Blue Groper.

Dunsborough

Ramp

Squid, Pike, and Snook over weed. King George Whiting in sand patches.

Shivery Rock

Dunn Bay

Point Templar

CAVES ROAD

Toby Inlet

Tailor, Whiting, Flounder, Flathead and Salmon in autumn can be caught from beaches all along the coast.

Reef and beach good for Salmon (autumn).

Good spot for Salmon, Herring and Samson Fish.

Yallingup

Smiths Beach — Salmon (autumn), Tailor, Mulloway, Herring and Skippy.

Torpedo Rock

Smiths Beach

Good rock fishing for Salmon, Skippy, Herring. Occasional Tuna, Blue Groper and Tailor.

Good boat ramp

Canal Rocks

Canal Rocks Road

Wyadup Rocks

Wyadup Road

CAVES ROAD

Injidup Point
Cape Clairault

Injidup Good Skippy and Whiting.

N
NW NE
W E
SW SE
S

0	1.5	3	4.5 km

0–5 m
5–10 m
10–20 m
20–30 m
over 30 m

rock and shore fishing

boat fishing

CAPE TO CAPE

CAPE NATURALISTE

This is the northern cape where the coast takes on its characteristic form of big sloping granite boulders that are often fronted with deep blue water. From here south, the coast is very treacherous and many lives have been lost, mostly with anglers slipping or being washed off the slippery rocks into a very powerful ocean. Anglers should only fish here on days when the swell is low and when others accompany them—they should never fish alone. It is advisable to keep well away from the wet, slippery rocks closer to the ocean. Good footwear that will grip on the rocks is essential.

Cape Naturaliste attracts many tourists who want to visit the lighthouse and look out over the fantastic scenery, but the whole area has a greater appeal for anglers as the rock fishing is first class. Big schools of salmon pass by, making their way around the cape each autumn, and lures or baits cast from the rocks into the deep blue water often bring results. Big Samson fish and yellowtail kingfish patrol close to the rocks especially early in the mornings, and captures of herring and skippy are very common with lighter tackle. A rough, 4WD track heads south close to the coast, allowing anglers to explore and find secluded spots.

SUGARLOAF ROCK

This is a famous rock-fishing location that is only to be fished in calm conditions with little or no swell. It can be reached by taking the turn-off from the Cape Naturaliste road, allowing easy access to this location with 2WD cars. This is a popular place to live bait a herring out on heavy tackle for big Samson fish,

Canal Rocks provides some shelter from the ocean by having large rock islands just offshore for protection. This is a good salmon spot in autumn.

yellowtail kingfish, sharks, salmon, bonito and southern bluefin tuna. Spinning from the rocks is also productive on salmon, bonito and southern bluefin tuna, while lighter tackle will produce plenty of herring. Big skippy and tailor turn up at times while a large bait fished on the bottom will occasionally attract pink snapper, dhufish, mulloway and blue groper. The rough 4WD track continues its way south from Sugerloaf Rock towards Yallingup, and all along this stretch, great fishing locations can be found.

YALLINGUP

Yallingup is a very popular surfing location that also has plenty of fans amongst anglers. It has a caravan park and a small shop, and easy 2WD access to many of the close fishing locations makes it an easy place to fish. Yallingup Beach is reached by a short walk from the car park and is a top place to fish for salmon and herring in autumn. The beach also produces skippy, tailor, whiting and the occasional mulloway and small shark. The reef is also a good place to try for skippy, salmon, tailor and herring.

TORPEDO ROCKS

From the car park at the sealed road a goat track leads anglers down to Torpedo Rocks where fishing from the sloping boulders into the deep blue ocean is often rewarding for several species. Salmon and herring are about in good numbers in autumn, while a big bait set out on the bottom has produced pink snapper, Samson fish, dhufish, queen snapper and small sharks at times. This is another dangerous location to fish in a big sea, and extreme care must be taken to avoid walking on the slippery rocks near the water. Take a rope gaff or a long pole gaff to land large fish rather than get too close to the water.

Torpedo Rocks is another famous rock fishing spot near Yallingup, but the sloping smooth rocks can be very dangerous in big seas.

Bonito are a regular catch on trolled lures along with southern bluefin tuna and salmon.

SMITHS BEACH

A very pleasant place to spend a few hours, days or even weeks fishing, Smiths Beach is well known for producing large numbers of salmon as they migrate along the coast each autumn. Mulloway are a regular catch in the surf mostly in the winter months, big tailor are often found in the summer months, and skippy, herring, flathead and whiting can also be taken.

Holiday accommodation is available at Smiths Beach but early bookings are essential.

CANAL ROCKS

A great spot for rock anglers who fish into the natural canal formed by the line of rocks just off the coast, providing sheltered conditions from the big swells that can plague this area. Salmon are the favourite species targeted here, as large numbers of fish move into the sheltered canal where they will respond to baits or lures. Herring, skippy and whiting are also taken from the shore, but a small boat ramp allows anglers to fish further out and on the western side of the rocks. Big Samson fish, dhufish, pink snapper, queen snapper, salmon, bonito, blue groper and southern bluefin tuna are often taken not far from shore.

WYADUP ROCKS

Reached by a sealed road, Wyadup Rocks fish well for salmon,

FISH FACTS

COBBLER

The cobbler or estuarine catfish in the Canning and Swan rivers has a keen following amongst anglers. These fish are found in good numbers in estuaries and river systems from Kalbarri southwards and can reach about 3 kg but are more usually caught at 1 kilogram.

Being a species of catfish, they possess three poisonous spines, the first on the dorsal fin and the others on the pectoral fins, and all three deserve the utmost respect. A sting from a cobbler is reported to be very painful, often resulting in a trip to the hospital. Recommended first aid to apply heat to 'cook' the proteins in the poison but not so hot as to cause scalds.

Cobbler are not the most attractive fish with a mouth surrounded by rubbery barbels and a colouration that is usually dark and blotchy, but their delicate flesh is regarded by many to be one of the best eating fish from the river. Most anglers fish for cobbler after dark when they venture out to feed on small invertebrates in the shallows; freshly dug bloodworms are the number one bait. The same rig that is used for black bream is often used for cobbler, and the two species are often caught in the same locations.

FISH FACTS

CRABS

Blue Swimmer Crabs

Otherwise called 'blue manna crabs' by many West Australians, these crabs are heavily fished for along the southwestern part of the State. In the Swan River or at Mandurah large numbers of crabs are caught each summer by anglers using drop nets or wire scoops either from the shore or boat.

A drop net baited with fresh mullet or other baits is lowered to the bottom and left for 10 minutes whilst the crabs crawl in to feed. It is then hauled up to the top quickly, trapping the crabs on the way. Scooping is done with a wire scoop net that is used to capture the crab spotted in the shallow water of the estuary. This is a very popular pastime in WA, and the resulting feed of fresh crabs is well worth the effort.

Mud Crabs

If ever there was an excuse to venture into a hot mangrove creek that is teeming with sandflies then a feed of mud crabs would have to be it. In recent years they have turned up as far south as the Collie River but generally good catches are not made until you reach Carnarvon in the north.

Mud crabs have a fierce reputation that deserves respect, as the power in their claws is enough to remove fingers and crush fishing rod blanks carelessly left to close to them. Dangers aside, the mud crab is fun to catch and is highly rated for its eating qualities. Drop nets (the only legal form of trap in WA) are used to catch them or coaxing them out of the mud at low tide with a blunt wire hook. Both methods will work well in different areas, and the warmer months seem to be the time when the crabs are easier to find.

There are two closely related species that are found in WA, the brown and the green mud crabs.

bonito and southern bluefin tuna on lures or baits cast from the rocks. A live herring set out under a balloon can attract big Samson fish, bonito or salmon, whilst skippy, herring and tailor can be fished for on lighter bait tackle. Once again this area is very dangerous during a big swell.

INJIDUP POINT

Injidup Point has the same potential as Wyadup Rocks and provides herring, skippy, whiting, tailor and the occasional salmon and mulloway. It should only be fished in calm conditions; Wyadup Beach is a safer option.

MOSES ROCK

South from Injidup a rough 4WD track continues south along the coast past Quininup Beach towards Willyabrup Beach where anglers can target salmon, herring, skippy, tailor, whiting and mulloway from numerous locations. Moses Rock is between the two and it is a bit of a walk to reach the fishing platforms where salmon, herring and skippy are often caught. Big Samson fish are often about in good numbers here and a live bait fished out under a balloon should get their attention, but heavy tackle is needed to stand any sort of a chance of beating one.

Squid can be caught from jetties or boats and can make great bait for many species or be kept for the dinner table.

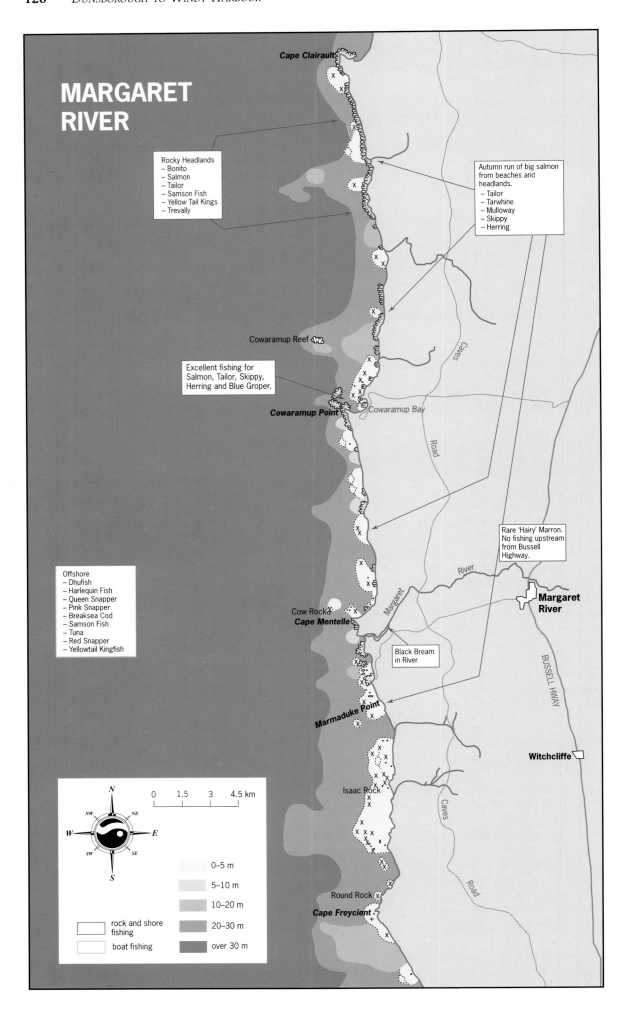

MARGARET RIVER

Rocky Headlands
– Bonito
– Salmon
– Tailor
– Samson Fish
– Yellow Tail Kings
– Trevally

Autumn run of big salmon from beaches and headlands.
– Tailor
– Tarwhine
– Mulloway
– Skippy
– Herring

Cape Clairault

Cowaramup Reef

Excellent fishing for Salmon, Tailor, Skippy, Herring and Blue Groper.

Cowaramup Point

Cowaramup Bay

Caves Road

Rare 'Hairy' Marron. No fishing upstream from Bussell Highway.

Offshore
– Dhufish
– Harlequin Fish
– Queen Snapper
– Pink Snapper
– Breaksea Cod
– Samson Fish
– Tuna
– Red Snapper
– Yellowtail Kingfish

River

Margaret

Margaret River

Cow Rock
Cape Mentelle

Black Bream in River

BUSSELL HWY

Marmaduke Point

Witchcliffe

Isaac Rock

Caves Road

N
NW   NE
W   E
SW   SE
S

0   1.5   3   4.5 km

Round Rock

Cape Freycient

0–5 m
5–10 m
10–20 m
20–30 m
over 30 m

rock and shore fishing

boat fishing

During big seas it is safer to fish from the beaches than the slippery rocks along this stretch of coast.

FISH FACTS

BLUE GROPER

This name has been given to several similar species of fish from the tuskfish family, with the Black Spotted Tusk Fish being most commonly encountered in northern waters. In the south the baldchin groper is a similar species that is also targeted in much the same way. All of these fish are popular with anglers because of their fine eating qualities.

Blue groper can be targeted over reefs by boat anglers using heavy lines with any of a variety of baits that include cut or whole fish like pilchards, octopus and squid. Once hooked these fish will put up a very strong fight that is usually an attempt to find a reef hole to dive into a spot where they can be impossible to move.

From the shore they can be targeted when the rising tide brings blue groper in close to shore to feed. Again a strong line is recommended and the best bait for shore fishing is a whole rock or ghost crab.

COWARAMUP BAY

A very picturesque spot, Cowaramup Bay is a great place to fish from the shore for herring, skippy and whiting. From the rocks at the point salmon, skippy, herring and Samson fish can be found, but this bay should only be fished in calm conditions with no swell. Small boats launch from the beach in the bay to take advantage of the great offshore fishing for dhufish, pink snapper, queen snapper, blue groper and harlequin fish. A caravan park and holiday accommodation is available if you book in advance.

South of here a 4WD track allows the many surfers and anglers to explore remote spots all the way to Margaret River.

MARGARET RIVER

This small settlement is famous world wide for its surfing and wines, however anglers also have a soft spot for it. Most of the common species are found here and numerous beach and rock locations provide excellent fishing in periods of low swell. Boat anglers often catch big dhufish, queen snapper, pink snapper, groper, Samson fish, harlequin fish and sharks. There is plenty of accommodation available and easy access to most of the best fishing spots. The river mouth fishes well for tailor, mulloway, herring and salmon in autumn, whilst its upper reaches have some big black bream hiding in the snags.

Redgate, Bobs Hollow, Conto Spring

Stretching to the south from Margaret River these pretty little fishing spots provide beach and rock fishing for herring, tailor, skippy, salmon and mulloway.

Boranup Beach

Most of the common species are found at Boranup Beach and it fishes best from summer through to autumn when the salmon start to run. This area is best explored by 4WD as there are several tracks following the coast to the north and south.

Hamelin Bay

This is a small-boat angler's dream location with a good little boat ramp and caravan park that is always well booked in summer when the fishing and weather are at their best. Close to shore there are plenty of herring, whiting, skippy and squid to keep anglers happy, while further out the reefs and wrecks are top spots to fish for dhufish, pink snapper, groper, Samson fish, yellowtail kings and queen snapper. Beach fishing is productive for herring, tailor, skippy and whiting. Salmon turn up late summer to autumn and mulloway are a possibility at any time.

Cosy Corner to Deepene

Just south of Hamelin Bay these top little fishing spots can be reached by taking the track to Cosy Corner from the Caves Road. Beach fishing is excellent for herring and salmon late summer to autumn, and a 4WD is a big advantage when venturing further along the coast to find fishing spots.

Skippy Rock to Cape Leeuwin

This part of the coast should only be fished in calm conditions with little or no swell. There is some good rock fishing for herring, salmon, tailor, skippy and big Samson fish. Blue groper, pink snapper and occasionally dhufish can be caught from the shore but chances improve when fishing from a boat into deeper water.

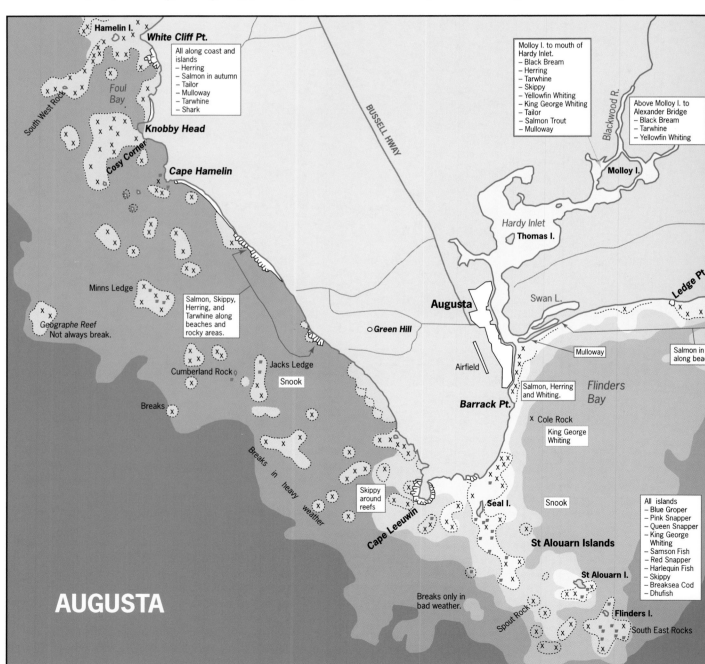

RIGHT: Offshore fishing is good for a wide range of species, including big King George whiting.

BELOW RIGHT: Yellowtail kingfish are not as common as Samson fish in WA but the south coast still produces some decent specimens at times.

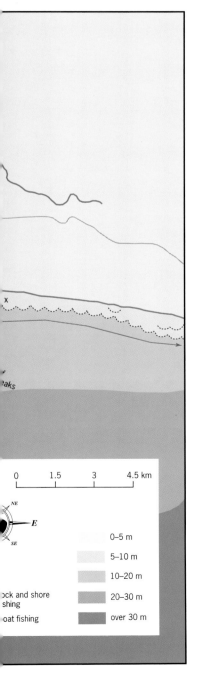

0   1.5   3   4.5 km

NE

E

SE

ck and shore
shing

oat fishing

0–5 m

5–10 m

10–20 m

20–30 m

over 30 m

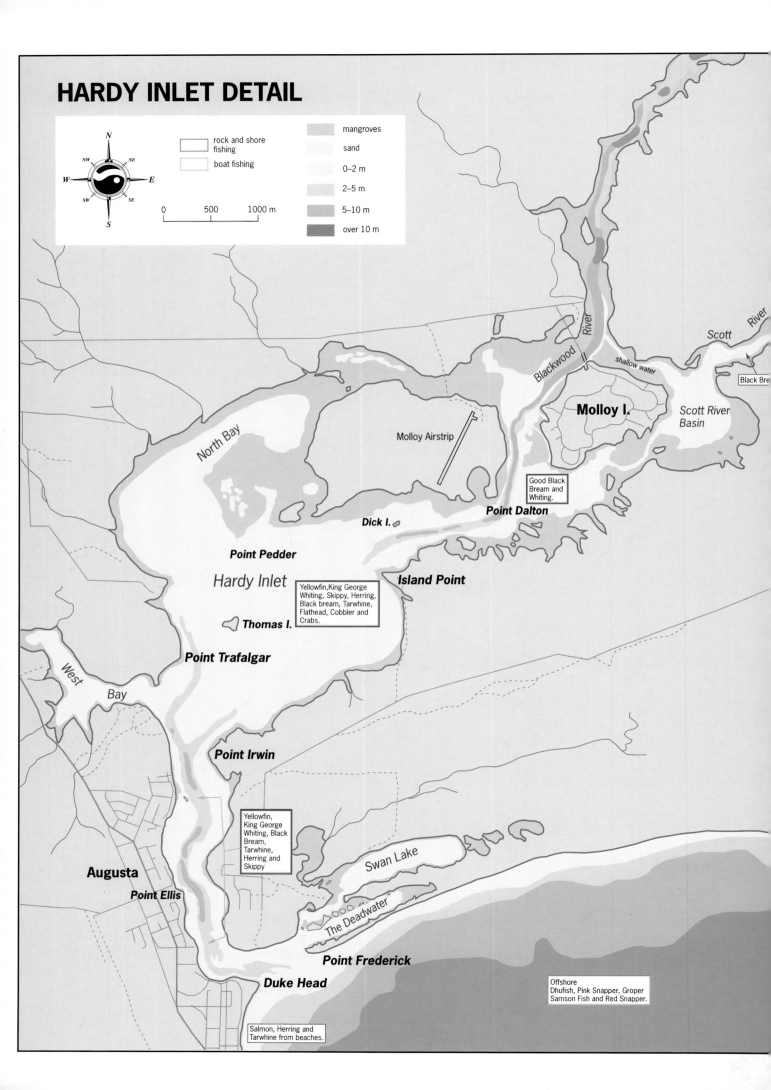

HARDY INLET DETAIL

Legend:
- rock and shore fishing
- boat fishing
- mangroves
- sand
- 0–2 m
- 2–5 m
- 5–10 m
- over 10 m

N NE E SE S SW W NW

0   500   1000 m

Scott River

Blackwood River

Molloy I.

Scott River Basin

shallow water

Black Bre[...]

Molloy Airstrip

Good Black Bream and Whiting.

North Bay

Dick I.

Point Dalton

Point Pedder

Hardy Inlet

Island Point

Yellowfin, King George Whiting, Skippy, Herring, Black bream, Tarwhine, Flathead, Cobbler and Crabs.

Thomas I.

Point Trafalgar

West Bay

Point Irwin

Yellowfin, King George Whiting, Black Bream, Tarwhine, Herring and Skippy.

Swan Lake

Augusta

Point Ellis

The Deadwater

Point Frederick

Duke Head

Offshore
Dhufish, Pink Snapper, Groper Samson Fish and Red Snapper.

Salmon, Herring and Tarwhine from beaches.

FISH FACTS

HERRING/TOMMY ROUGH

Herring are known as tommy rough in other Australian States. This is a popular and common species that inhabits the southern coastal waters and large numbers of them can often be found on the south coast and at Rottnest Island. They can be found on reefs, beaches, offshore islands, estuaries and harbours.

Herring rarely exceed a few hundred grams although the largest specimens are known as 'bull herring'. They are heavily targeted from Perth to the south coast, and thankfully they seem to be found in big schools. Herring are opportunistic feeders and will take a huge variety of baits, lures and flies and can usually be attracted to an area with a berley trail of pollard and oil. They are usually caught on or near the surface but occasionally will take baits on the bottom.

Most anglers fish for herring with a medium rod around the 2.5 m mark and use 6 kg line, but with a lighter outfit you will have an absolute ball on these fish. They put up a spirited fight for their size, with plenty of head shaking jumps that quite often result in them throwing the hooks.

A bunch of live wriggling maggots really drives these fish crazy, but a piece of prawn or whitebait on a hook is rarely refused. Even whole pilchards will not deter a hungry herring and many a beach angler who is chasing tailor has ended up with a few herring in the bag at the end of the session.

Small lures of almost any description will tempt herring, but one of the all-time favourites is a small piece of fluoro green straw on a single hook. This is slowly retrieved behind a float or berley cage for devastating results.

A feed of herring is enjoyed by thousands of West Australians each year, as they have a very tasty and oily flesh. As a result it can also be pickled as rollmops or filleted down and fried in breadcrumbs.

AUGUSTA

HARDY INLET

This pretty estuary, which is fed by the Blackwood and Scott rivers at Molloy Island, is an excellent place to fish for a wide range of species. Fishing the inlet itself is best done by small dinghy and using light tackle for species like black bream, King George whiting, yellow finned whiting, silver bream, skippy (silver trevally), herring, flathead and flounder. The best results come from anchoring up and berleying the fish to you, then allowing light line and small hooks to do the rest. The town of Augusta is a very popular holiday spot for many people, so booking your accommodation is best done early on to avoid disappointment.

BLACKWOOD RIVER

This river is well known for producing big black bream from the snags along the shore around Molloy Island right up to Alexander Bridge. Whole river prawns fished into the snags is the best way to target these fish but heavier line might be needed to stop hooked fish from breaking you off. King George and yellowfin whiting are also taken from the Blackwood River, usually on smaller hooks baited with cut prawn pieces or whole whitebait. Many anglers are now targeting black bream in this river with small minnow lures, soft plastic jigs or fly tackle. By quietly moving along the snags in a small boat, preferably with an electric outboard, the angler can cover all of the likely spots with stealth. The river above Molloy Island can produce some really large bream to over 2 kg, but they can be hard work and one of the local guides is worth the investment. A restocking program for black bream should ensure quality fishing in the future.

AUGUSTA OFFSHORE FISHING

By launching from the Flinders Bay boat ramp you can negotiate the bar at the mouth of the inlet to gain access to Flinders Bay. This can be a very hazardous trip during a decent swell, so seek advice and play it safe before attempting the crossing. Once out in the bay there are some good whiting and herring to be caught in close, and the deeper water yields big WA dhufish, snapper, Samson fish, skippy and pike.

AUGUSTA BEACH FISHING

The remote stretch of beaches and rocky headlands following the coast east from the mouth of Hardy Inlet towards Windy Harbour, offer some fantastic fishing at times. Rough 4WD tracks make their way down to many locations along this stretch, and to the mouths of several creeks and rivers that flow into the ocean here. The mouth of the Warren River is a good example and attracts plenty of beach anglers each year, especially in late summer to autumn when the salmon are migrating along the coast. Many of these beach locations are ideal places to fish for salmon, usually with big surf rods and baits like whole pilchards on ganged hooks. Other species like sharks, that often follow the salmon schools can be hooked, as well as mulloway, flathead, tailor, herring, skippy and whiting.

WINDY HARBOUR

Situated 27 km from the town of Northcliffe is Windy Harbour, where the self-contained angler will find camping and toilet facilities. Boat launching is from the beach, allowing anglers to fish offshore. There are plenty of herring, King George whiting, squid and pike between the mainland and Sandy Island. Further out, bigger species like dhufish, snapper, sweep, Samson fish, queen snapper and blue groper can be caught. Bottom bouncing with heavy tackle is the most popular method, usually drift fishing when the conditions allow. Trolling for salmon and tailor during the summer can produce excellent results.

Boat Ramps & Tackle Stores

Many anglers take advantage of the excellent boat fishing opportunities in the expanse of Geographe Bay around the Cape and down the rugged western side towards Augusta. This area is fished all year round except for the middle of winter when the big storms bring massive swells and choppy conditions to the western side.

Autumn is a popular time for small boats trolling close to the shore for migrating schools of salmon or for bottom bouncing the deeper offshore waters on the calm days when the wind light and the sea calm.

RAMPS
Quindalup – Geographe Road
Myalup
Dunsborough – Finlayson Street and Elmore Street
Canal Rocks
Hamelin Bay
Margaret River – Prevally Park
Augusta – Colour Patch, Ellis Street and Flinders Bay
Blackwood River – Alexander Bridge and Molloy Island

TACKLE STORES

Dunsborough Outdoor Sports
Shop 3, Duns Park
Dunsborough WA 6281
Tel: (08) 9756 7222

Oceansports
Naturaliste Tce
Dunsborough WA 6281
Tel: (08) 9755 3018

Augusta X-treme Outdoor Sport
64 Blackwood Ave
Augusta WA 6290
Tel: (08) 9758 0606

Alexander's Sports & Leisure
36 Rose St
Manjimup WA 6258
Tel: (08) 9771 2758

Manjimup Sports power
6 Brockman St
Manjimup WA 6258
Tel: (08) 9777 1881

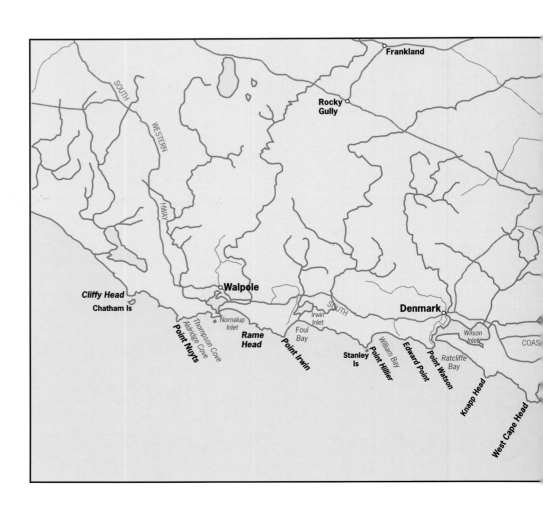

C H A P T E R 1 0
WALPOLE TO BREMER BAY

W A L P O L E / N O R N A L U P

MANDALAY BEACH

Mandalay Beach is reached by taking the road from the South Coast Highway to the west of Walpole, to the carpark near the beach. This is an impressive south coast beach with deep gutters and channels close to shore that attract mulloway, salmon, tailor and sharks. Herring and sand whiting abound in the surf and can easily be caught and used for strip or live baits for the larger species mentioned before. Heavy surf tackle is needed to successfully fish this beach.

NORNALUP ESTUARY

Like Hardy Inlet, this sheltered estuary is a light tackle fishery for a big range of species like black bream, King George and yellowfin whiting, silver bream, skippy and flathead. Walpole Inlet, which joins onto the larger Nornalup Estuary, provides the same type of fishing. Light flick rods fished from a small dinghy or trailer boat is the best way to enjoy this area; just remember to keep noise down to a minimum when fishing the shallow

water and use berley to attract the fish to the boat. A good spot to try is out from Coalmine Beach where King George whiting are often taken in good numbers and size. The Frankland and Deep rivers that flow into these estuaries are top black bream spots all along their tree snag shores.

CONSPICUOUS BEACH

This is another fantastic, white sandy beach that is easily reached by 2WD cars and provides anglers with the chance of catching salmon, herring, tailor, whiting, mulloway and sharks.

PEACEFUL BAY

This is a safe place to launch a small boat from the beach to access the bay. Bottom fishing is the most popular method of fishing for species like Samson fish, dhufish, blue groper and snapper.

IRWIN INLET

Another of the small but very fishy estuaries, Irwin also provides

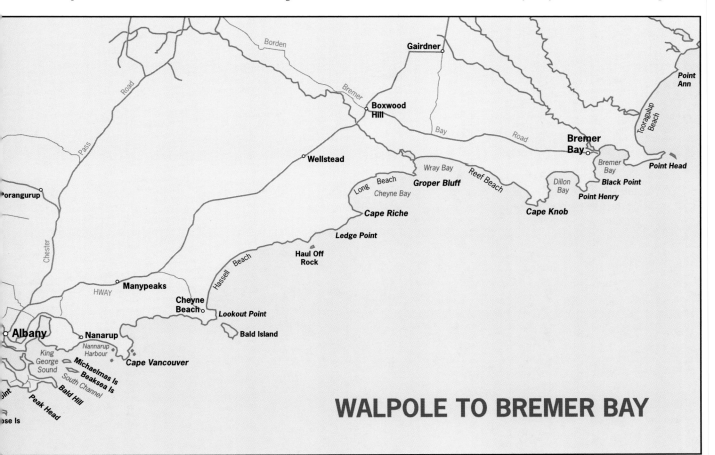

WALPOLE TO BREMER BAY

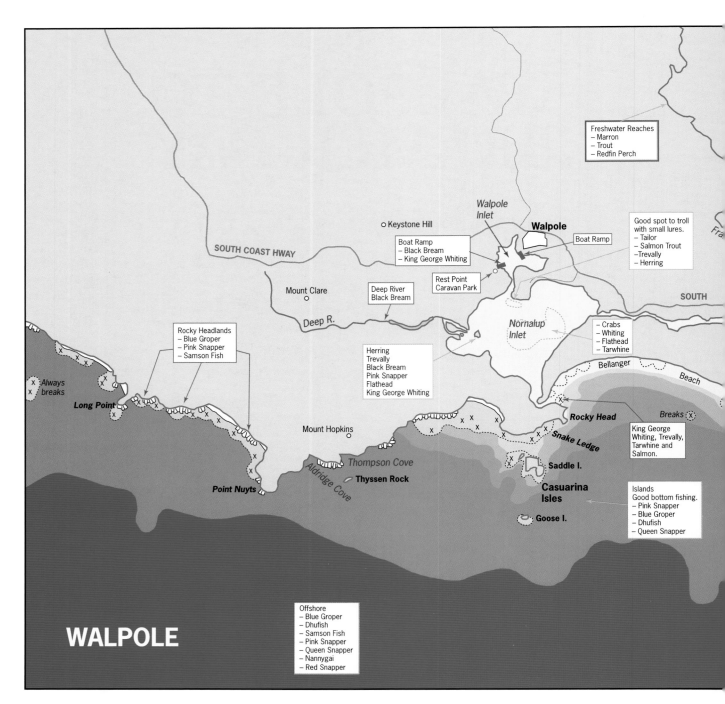

Freshwater Reaches
– Marron
– Trout
– Redfin Perch

○ Keystone Hill

Walpole Inlet

Walpole

SOUTH COAST HWAY

Boat Ramp
– Black Bream
– King George Whiting

Boat Ramp

Good spot to troll with small lures.
– Tailor
– Salmon Trout
– Trevally
– Herring

Mount Clare ○

Deep River
Black Bream

Rest Point
Caravan Park

SOUTH

Deep R.

Nornalup
Inlet

– Crabs
– Whiting
– Flathead
– Tarwhine

Rocky Headlands
– Blue Groper
– Pink Snapper
– Samson Fish

Herring
Trevally
Black Bream
Pink Snapper
Flathead
King George Whiting

Bellanger

Beach

x Always
x breaks

Long Point

Rocky Head

Breaks x

Mount Hopkins ○

Snake Ledge

King George Whiting, Trevally, Tarwhine and Salmon.

Thompson Cove

Saddle I.

Aldridge Cove

Thyssen Rock

Casuarina
Isles

Islands
Good bottom fishing.
– Pink Snapper
– Blue Groper
– Dhufish
– Queen Snapper

Point Nuyts

Goose I.

Offshore
– Blue Groper
– Dhufish
– Samson Fish
– Pink Snapper
– Queen Snapper
– Nannygai
– Red Snapper

WALPOLE

all the common species and is best fished with light tackle and berley to bring the fish to you. The two rivers—the Kent and the Bow—that flow into this estuary are well known for their black bream, which are not often large but abundant.

BEACH FISHING

Along the coast from here, access is restricted to a few tracks leading to the coast, but for those who are fit, a good walk into some of the more remote beaches and headlands will surely provide some top rate fishing.

PARRY BEACH

Found on the far western end of Mazzoletti Beach, which is part of William Bay, Parry Beach is ideal to fish from and some boat owners launch their small boats from the hard sand here to fish the inshore waters. Parry Beach is a designated salmon beach, so the commercial fisherman has priority during the summer salmon season.

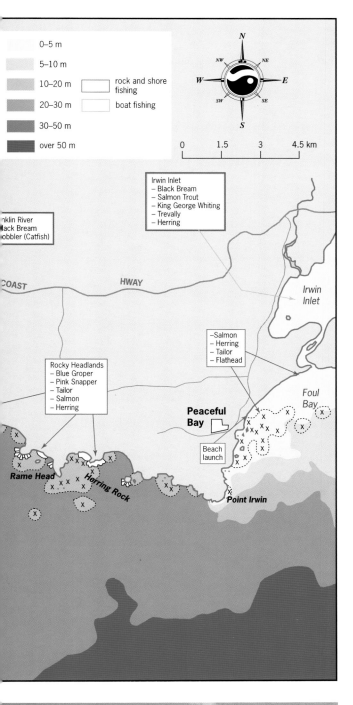

0–5 m	
5–10 m	
10–20 m	rock and shore fishing
20–30 m	boat fishing
30–50 m	
over 50 m	

0   1.5   3   4.5 km

Irwin Inlet
– Black Bream
– Salmon Trout
– King George Whiting
– Trevally
– Herring

nklin River
lack Bream
obbler (Catfish)

COAST   HWAY

Irwin Inlet

–Salmon
– Herring
– Tailor
– Flathead

Rocky Headlands
– Blue Groper
– Pink Snapper
– Tailor
– Salmon
– Herring

Foul Bay

Peaceful Bay

Beach launch

Rame Head   Herring Rock

Point Irwin

FISH FACTS

FLATHEAD

There are two common species that are often caught by anglers in Western Australia—the bar-tailed flathead and the blue spot flathead.

Bar-tailed Flathead

The bar-tailed flathead is a tropical species that has made itself at home in the Swan River, and each summer large numbers of fish are caught which average 0.8 kg to 1.2 kilograms.

Most anglers now fish for flathead in the shallows with small lures or saltwater flies that these predatory fish just can't resist. The big numbers of blowfish that inhabit the Swan River steal baits and swallow hooks and so make bait fishing for flathead almost impossible. Flathead will lie in ambush half buried in the sand and mud, waiting for a small fish or prawn to swim past. Then, in a burst of speed they will dart out and grab their prey in their large mouth. Small minnow lures, jigs or flies bounced along near the bottom will tempt most flathead and good catches are made from the big sand flats around Point Walter and Applecross. A light flick rod with 2 or 3 kg line or a fly rod capable of casting the weighted flies like Clousers (so attractive to these fish) is all that is needed to chase these fish. Bar-tails can be taken from all waters north from the Swan River.

Blue-spot Flathead

The blue-spot flathead is a bigger species that is rarely found in estuaries and more commonly encountered on offshore grounds and beaches where it favours sand and weed areas. Big blue-spots around the 2 to 3 kg mark are usually caught by anglers fishing for other species. In the Wilson Inlet at Denmark on the south coast these fish can be found stranded from the ocean each year by a sandbar. As a result anglers target the big flathead in the estuary in much the same way as the bar-tailed flathead are targeted in the Swan River, but the average size of the blue-spot flathead is well up around the 1.5 kg mark.

Flathead are often kept for the table as their flesh is very firm and tastes good. Be careful of the spines on the gills as they can give you a nasty puncture and stinging wound if you grab the fish behind the head. You are better off using pliers and a rag to de-hook these fish and they are much more passive if turned upside down on their backs to unhook them.

LEFT: Mandalay Beach, near Walpole, is a good beach to fish for salmon, sharks, mulloway and herring.

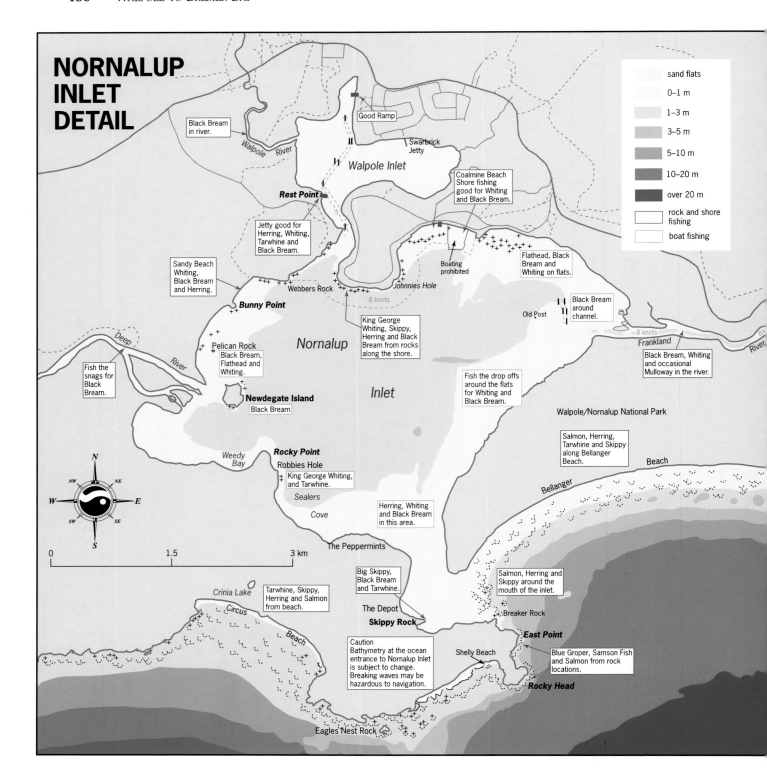

NORNALUP INLET DETAIL

Black Bream in river.

Good Ramp

Swarbrick Jetty

Walpole Inlet

Rest Point

Coalmine Beach Shore fishing good for Whiting and Black Bream.

Jetty good for Herring, Whiting, Tarwhine and Black Bream.

Sandy Beach Whiting, Black Bream and Herring.

Webbers Rock

8 knots

Johnnies Hole

Boating prohibited

Flathead, Black Bream and Whiting on flats.

Bunny Point

King George Whiting, Skippy, Herring and Black Bream from rocks along the shore.

Nornalup

Old Post

Black Bream around channel.

8 knots

Frankland

Deep

River

Fish the snags for Black Bream.

Pelican Rock

Black Bream, Flathead and Whiting.

Inlet

Black Bream, Whiting and occasional Mulloway in the river.

Newdegate Island

Black Bream

Fish the drop offs around the flats for Whiting and Black Bream.

Walpole/Nornalup National Park

Weedy Bay

Rocky Point

Robbies Hole

King George Whiting, and Tarwhine.

Sealers

Cove

Herring, Whiting and Black Bream in this area.

Salmon, Herring, Tarwhine and Skippy along Bellanger Beach.

Beach

Bellanger

The Peppermints

Crinia Lake

Circus

Tarwhine, Skippy, Herring and Salmon from beach.

Beach

Big Skippy, Black Bream and Tarwhine.

The Depot

Skippy Rock

Salmon, Herring and Skippy around the mouth of the inlet.

Breaker Rock

East Point

Caution Bathymetry at the ocean entrance to Nornalup Inlet is subject to change. Breaking waves may be hazardous to navigation.

Shelly Beach

Blue Groper, Samson Fish and Salmon from rock locations.

Rocky Head

Eagles Nest Rock

0   1.5   3 km

N NW NE W E SW SE S

sand flats
0–1 m
1–3 m
3–5 m
5–10 m
10–20 m
over 20 m
rock and shore fishing
boat fishing

GREENS POOL

This pool provides safe fishing for herring, skippy and King George whiting from the beach or rocks. The area is popular with swimmers and fishing is very poor during the day.

MADFISH BAY

Protected by out-lying boulders, Madfish Bay is used for beach launching small boats to fish the inshore waters, and for shore-based fishing for the bay's herring, salmon, skippy and whiting.

DENMARK

A picturesque small town, Denmark provides anglers with the chance to fish the rivers, estuary and ocean for most common species. Holiday accommodation is available with motels, hotels and caravan parks as well as boat ramps for boats wishing to fish the expanse of Wilson Inlet.

WILSON INLET

Cut off from the ocean during summer, this inlet gets a good flushing out each winter when the winter rains swell the height and push a channel across the beach.

This inlet is famous for producing pink snapper that move

King George whiting can be found in the estuaries, rivers and sheltered coastal bays of the south coast.

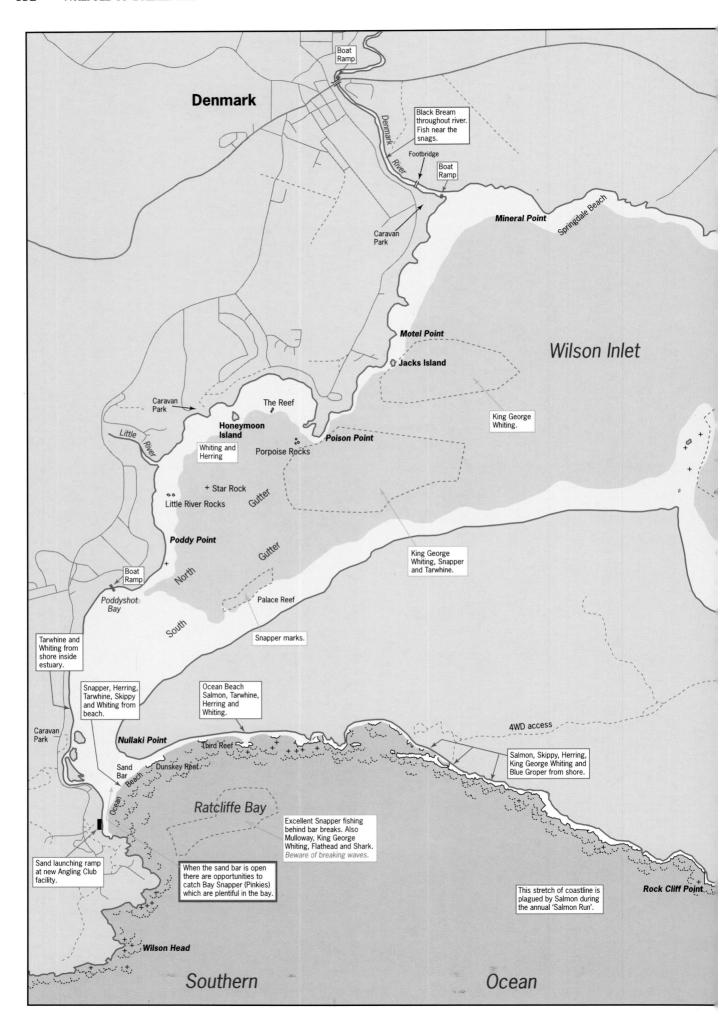

Denmark

Boat Ramp

Black Bream throughout river. Fish near the snags.

Denmark River

Footbridge

Boat Ramp

Caravan Park

Mineral Point

Springdale Beach

Motel Point

Wilson Inlet

● Jacks Island

King George Whiting.

Caravan Park

The Reef

Honeymoon Island

Poison Point

Whiting and Herring

Porpoise Rocks

Little River

+ Star Rock

Little River Rocks

Gutter

King George Whiting, Snapper and Tarwhine.

Poddy Point

Gutter

Boat Ramp

North

Palace Reef

Poddyshot Bay

South

Snapper marks.

Tarwhine and Whiting from shore inside estuary.

Snapper, Herring, Tarwhine, Skippy and Whiting from beach.

Ocean Beach Salmon, Tarwhine, Herring and Whiting.

4WD access

Caravan Park

Nullaki Point

Third Reef

Salmon, Skippy, Herring, King George Whiting and Blue Groper from shore.

Sand Bar

Dunskey Reef

Ocean Beach

Ratcliffe Bay

Excellent Snapper fishing behind bar breaks. Also Mulloway, King George Whiting, Flathead and Shark. *Beware of breaking waves.*

Sand launching ramp at new Angling Club facility.

When the sand bar is open there are opportunities to catch Bay Snapper (Pinkies) which are plentiful in the bay.

This stretch of coastline is plagued by Salmon during the annual 'Salmon Run'.

Rock Cliff Point

● *Wilson Head*

Southern   *Ocean*

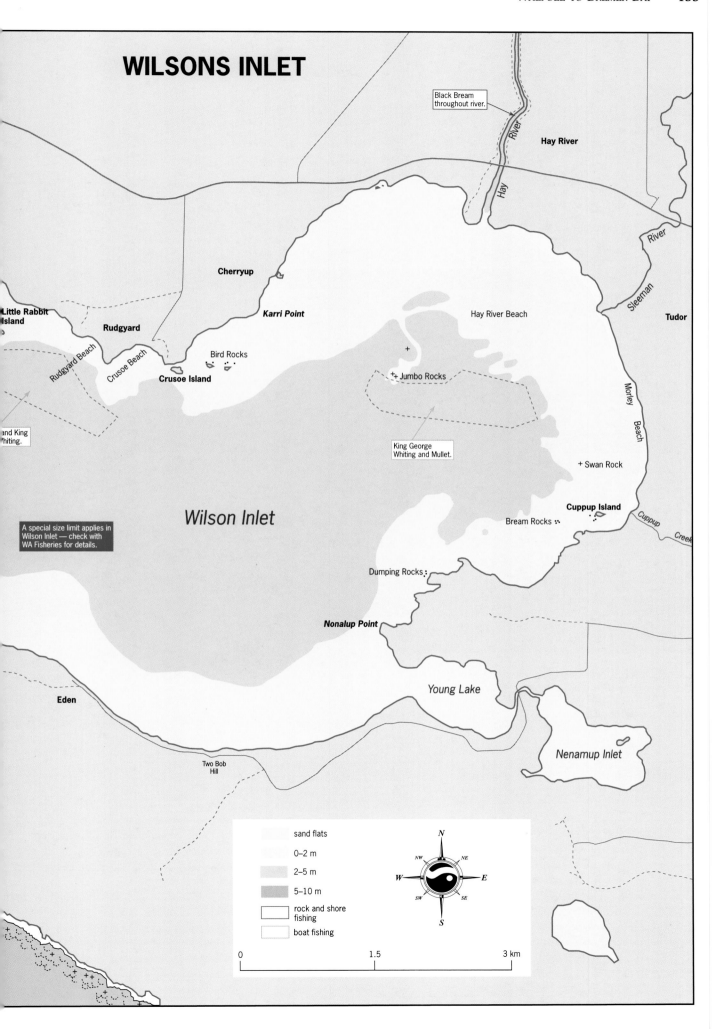

WILSONS INLET

Black Bream throughout river.

Hay River

River

Hay

Sleeman

Tudor

Cherryup

Little Rabbit Island

Karri Point

Hay River Beach

Rudgyard

Rudgyard Beach

Crusoe Beach

Bird Rocks

Crusoe Island

Jumbo Rocks

and King hiting.

King George Whiting and Mullet.

Morley Beach

+ Swan Rock

Cuppup Island

Cuppup Creek

Bream Rocks

Wilson Inlet

A special size limit applies in Wilson Inlet — check with WA Fisheries for details.

Dumping Rocks

Nonalup Point

Young Lake

Eden

Nenamup Inlet

Two Bob Hill

	sand flats
	0–2 m
	2–5 m
	5–10 m
	rock and shore fishing
	boat fishing

N
NW   NE
W   E
SW   SE
S

0   1.5   3 km

ABOVE: Madfish Bay, near Denmark, is a herring hot spot but also produces skippy, salmon and tarwhine.

RIGHT: Ocean Beach at Denmark can produce good catches of salmon in autumn, and herring and tarwhine all year round.

into the inlet when the bar is open and get isolated from the ocean when it closes. These fish rarely exceed 4 kg but occasional larger specimens have been boated. Best targeted from the deeper holes in the inlet they respond well to berley fed from the boat side.

The Inlet is also famous for producing big blue spot flathead, which, like the snapper, get isolated in the estuary and grow large on the abundant food supply. These big flathead, averaging 2–3.5 kg, are taken usually by accident on baits being fished for other species. However casting or trolling small minnow lures across the sand flats of the estuary is one way of finding a few fish. King George whiting and black bream are the other prime targets in this inlet and can be caught on light tackle all through its system and up into the Denmark and Hay rivers. Silver bream, skippy, yellowfin whiting, garfish and blue swimmer crabs are all there for the taking, especially in the warmer months.

OCEAN BEACH

Situated at the mouth of the Wilson Inlet this long surf beach is a favourite with beach anglers. A 4WD allows you to cross the shallow sandbar at the mouth in summer to explore further along the beach, or you can walk to the mouth and cast a line. Ocean Beach is well known for salmon on their annual run in late summer through to winter. Big salmon can be hooked in the surf, usually on baits such as mulies or a live herring.

Other species of fish like tailor, silver bream, sand whiting, flathead and herring are all common catches. Big baits sometimes attract mulloway and sharks, whilst pink snapper, making their way into the estuary when the bar breaks, are a possibility. From the rocks at the western end of the beach salmon, bonito, Samson fish, snapper, sharks and yellowtail kingfish have all been caught at times.

ALBANY

BORNHOLM

Bornholm is a popular beach when the salmon are running, but access is by 4WD only as the track in can become very rough and boggy after heavy use. Herring are also caught here in big numbers, while larger baits often attract the attention of sharks and occasional mulloway.

SHELLEY BEACH

Not far from the town of Albany, this beach is reached by 2WD vehicles, and fishes well for salmon.

MUTTON BIRD ISLAND

Mutton Bird Island can be reached by 2WD to the car park, or onto the beach with a 4WD where salmon, herring, whiting and sharks are all caught at various times of the year.

TORBAY INLET

This tiny estuary has a good population of small black bream in it that can easily be caught on light flick rod tackle and prawns for bait. Lure fishing, especially with small jigs and soft plastics are also worth a try for the bream. Whiting and skippy sometimes add a bit of variety to the catch here. Just keep an eye on the minimum legal size of any fish kept for dinner.

FISH FACTS

WHITING

King George Whiting

These big spotted whiting attract plenty of attention amongst Western Australian anglers, both from the shore and out in boats. King George whiting have been recorded over 3 kg in WA but from the offshore reef and sand areas fish around the 1 kg size are reasonably common. The estuaries and sheltered bays attract big schools of smaller fish that in turn often attract large numbers of anglers after a feed of whiting.

King George whiting are found along the west and southern parts of the State and many of the big fish are caught whilst fishing the offshore reefs for other species like dhufish and snapper, but are a welcome addition to the catch.

Anglers targeting these fish have found that the best King George grounds are patches of sand amongst seagrass and reef. Baits must be fished on the bottom where the whiting feed, and this is usually done at anchor with a good berley trail set up to bring the whiting around. Combination baits of squid and coral prawn are favourites amongst keen King George anglers, but at times other baits of whole bluebait or mussels will attract bites from these fish.

Once hooked, King George whiting will put up a good strong fight all the way to the surface as they roll and kick trying to free themselves. They should be despatched quickly and put straight into an Esky containing a slurry of ice and seawater. This will protect the delicate flesh and stop the fish from drying out.

In the estuaries of the south coast large numbers of smaller King George whiting are often caught, and they respond to lighter lines and smaller baits, usually fished with the aid of berley.

Whiting

The other species of whiting found in the State are popular with anglers all along the coastline. School and sand whiting are usually a pest as they steal baits intended for other species in the surf, but if targeted with small hooks they can easily be caught and turned into a fine meal. Bigger sand whiting are often found just out from many surf beaches in the deeper water, and baits of prawn pieces fished on the bottom can bring in fish around the 30 cm mark.

Yellowfin whiting have a strong following all along the coast, as they can be caught in sizes up to and over 40 cm but average 30–35 cm in many locations. These whiting just love fresh bloodworms fished on light line, but will also take whitebait, prawn pieces and squid at times.

Yellowfin whiting are found in estuaries and along coastal beaches where they seem to feed the best on a rising tide early in the morning; in the case of the Swan River it is after dark. They can be a very timid fish and are often observed finning in the shallows only to bolt for deeper water if spooked by an angler, bird or a baited rig landing too close to them.

All whiting make great eating, even if they are riddled with small bones. Some anglers prefer to fillet down bigger whiting to avoid the hassle with bones whilst others are content to cook them whole and pick through the bones.

(Map showing: Albany Aerodrome, Willyung H, Lake Powell, Werillup Hill, Torbay, Stony I., Passage Reefs, Sand Patch, Family Ro, Sharp Point, Gree, North R, North R, and a box reading "Salmon, Herring, Skippy, Mulloway and Tarwhine.")

THE SALMON HOLES

This is the most famous fishing spot close to Albany, and can be reached by 2WD to the parking area and then down a steep set of stairs to the beach. The beach itself is sheltered by a headland to the east and a reef to the west, and as its name suggests, it fishes very well for salmon during their annual migration. A deep gutter running along the beach brings the fish close to shore where they can be easily cast to with baits, lures or even saltwater flies. There are also plenty of herring caught here as well and one set out as a live bait is rarely refused if the salmon are about.

The rocks to the east are massive sloping boulders that should be fished with extreme care, as big swells and slippery rocks have washed many into the southern ocean. These rocks produce salmon, herring, skippy, leatherjackets and silver bream.

FRENCHMAN BAY

Famous for the old whaling station that is now a museum, Frenchman Bay is best fished by boat for southern bluefin tuna, bonito, salmon, queen snapper, pink snapper and Samson fish. Some good fish can be taken from the rocks around the bay by shore-based anglers.

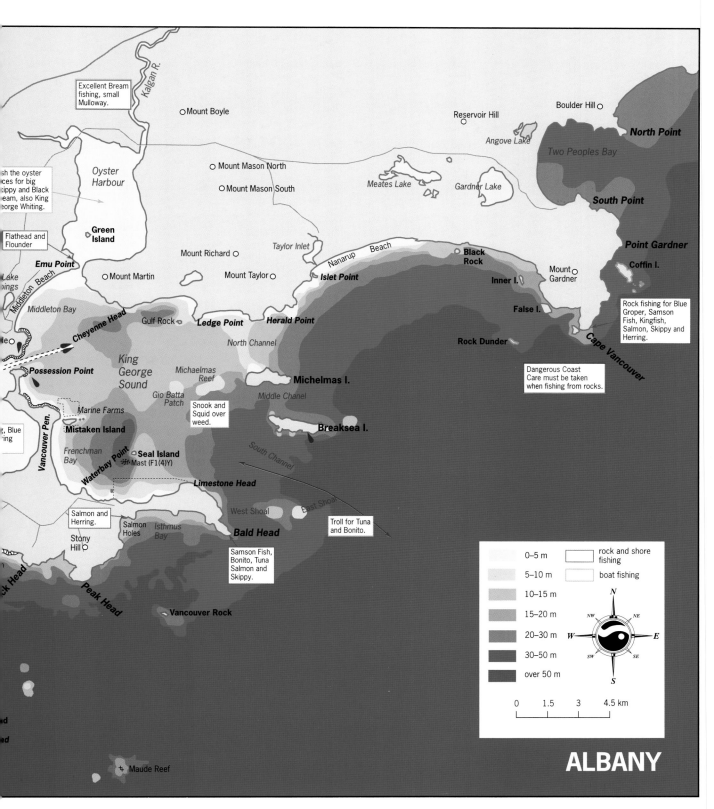

Excellent Bream fishing, small Mulloway.

Fish the oyster ...ces for big ...kippy and Black ...eam, also King ...eorge Whiting.

Flathead and Flounder

Kalgan R.

Mount Boyle

Oyster Harbour

Green Island

Emu Point

Mount Mason North

Mount Mason South

Mount Richard

Mount Martin

Mount Taylor

Taylor Inlet

Nanarup Beach

Islet Point

Reservoir Hill

Angove Lake

Boulder Hill

North Point

Two Peoples Bay

South Point

Meates Lake

Gardner Lake

Point Gardner

Black Rock

Inner I.

Mount Gardner

Coffin I.

False I.

Rock fishing for Blue Groper, Samson Fish, Kingfish, Salmon, Skippy and Herring.

Lake ...ings

Middleton Beach

Middleton Bay

Cheyenne Head

Gulf Rock

Ledge Point

Herald Point

North Channel

Rock Dunder

Cape Vancouver

Dangerous Coast Care must be taken when fishing from rocks.

Possession Point

King George Sound

Michaelmas Reef

Gio Batta Patch

Snook and Squid over weed.

Michelmas I.

Middle Chanel

Marine Farms

..., Blue ...ring

Mistaken Island

Frenchman Bay

Waterbay Point

Seal Island
Mast (Fl(4)Y)

Breaksea I.

South Channel

Limestone Head

West Shoal

East Shoal

Salmon and Herring.

Stony Hill

Salmon Holes

Isthmus Bay

Bald Head

Troll for Tuna and Bonito.

Samson Fish, Bonito, Tuna Salmon and Skippy.

...k Head

Peak Head

Vancouver Rock

Maude Reef

0–5 m	rock and shore fishing
5–10 m	boat fishing
10–15 m	
15–20 m	
20–30 m	
30–50 m	
over 50 m	

N
NW   NE
W   E
SW   SE
S

0   1.5   3   4.5 km

ALBANY

RIGHT: You need a good 4WD vehicle to reach some beach locations like the Warren Beach, but the excellent fishing is often worth the effort of getting there.

PRINCESS ROYAL HARBOUR

Small-boat anglers catch plenty of whiting, herring, gardies, skippy, cobbler, leatherjackets, flathead, flounder, crabs and squid.

OYSTER HARBOUR

This harbour produces the same species found in Princess Royal Harbour but offers a few more shore-fishing options, especially in the shallows for big flounder that can be tempted on tiny feather jigs bounced across the bottom with a light flick rod.

KING AND KALGAN RIVERS

These two rivers feed Oyster Harbour and are well known for producing some very big black bream. The best method is to fish near snags with whole river prawns, but be ready for a lock-up battle once hooked, as these fish are very good at finding cover. These big bream are also being increasingly targeted by sportfishermen using small hard bodied lures or 1/16oz jigs and soft plastic tails.

MIDDLETON BEACH

Fishing well for herring, whiting and the occasional salmon, Middleton Beach is right in town. During the peak period, whales can come right in to Middleton Beach adding something special to any visit. If not right on the beach, then the lookout on the road into town provides a good landbased whale watching spot.

TWO PEOPLES BAY

This shallow and sheltered beach, which is easy to reach by 2WD car, is a good place to fish for smaller species like herring, skippy, whiting and flathead. Some keen small-boat anglers launch dinghies off the beaches during spells of calm weather. Queen snapper, pink snapper, Samson fish, blue groper, skippy, snook, bonito and southern bluefin tuna catches can be made by boat anglers.

THE SAND PATCH

Set just behind the local prison, a tough walk down a steep set of stairs is worth the effort to reach this excellent stretch of reef where big salmon, skippy, herring, flathead, mulloway and sharks are all taken. The difficult walk back encourages a conservative approach to the excursion as a large mulloway can exhaust even fit anglers.

NORMAN'S BEACH

A 4WD vehicle is an advantage when accessing this beach, otherwise a bit of a walk is required. Norman's is a favourite salmon beach that produces good numbers of these fish as they migrate along the coast.

CHEYNE BEACH

Cheyne's Beach is one of the best salmon beaches in Australia. Anglers mostly target big skippy, salmon, tarwhine, herring and sharks from the surf when heading east to Hassell Beach from Cheyne Beach. It is a commercial fishing beach so during the peak season anglers need to give way to the salmon crews.

ALBANY ROCK FISHING

The rocky headlands are fantastic places to fish for blue groper, queen snapper, pink snapper, Samson fish and salmon, but only in calm conditions where there is little or no swell. To reach many of these rock spots a long walk is required, and you'll have to carry all of your tackle and supplies as well. On the way out you must be prepared to carry it all out again plus any fish you decide to keep. A long rope gaff is a necessity as venturing too close to the water on slippery rocks is a big mistake, especially in remote locations where help could be hours away.

For those unfamiliar with the black rocks of the Albany region, they can become like ice when wet. Rock hopping cleats are useless and only felt soles work, but if there is any weed growth on the lower reaches, even felt soles can become a liability. It is extremely important to watch the spot carefully as the Southern Ocean can be fearsome and unforgiving, with exceptional sets called king waves claiming all too many lives.

BREMER BAY

Bremer Bay offers a good boat ramp and caravan park, and has some of the best fishing the south coast has to offer. Bremer Bay is a bit off the beaten track and therefore has had less fishing pressure. The large swells mean that boat fishing, using boats launched from the ramp at Fisheries Beach, can only go out when conditions are good. Red snapper, dhufish, pink snapper, breaksea cod, groper and queen snapper are the most common targets.

Wellstead estuary offers some excellent black bream fishing on lures or bait, but the lower estuary is extremely shallow and must be carefully negotiated. There is very good fishing for mulloway when the bar breaks and salmon and herring can be caught virtually year round.

POINT GORDON

Close to town this rock fishing spot is a popular place for salmon, herring, queen snapper, blue groper, sweep and leather jackets.

Large western blue groper taken from the rocks can test an angler's strength — and stamina if they have to be carried a distance back to a car.

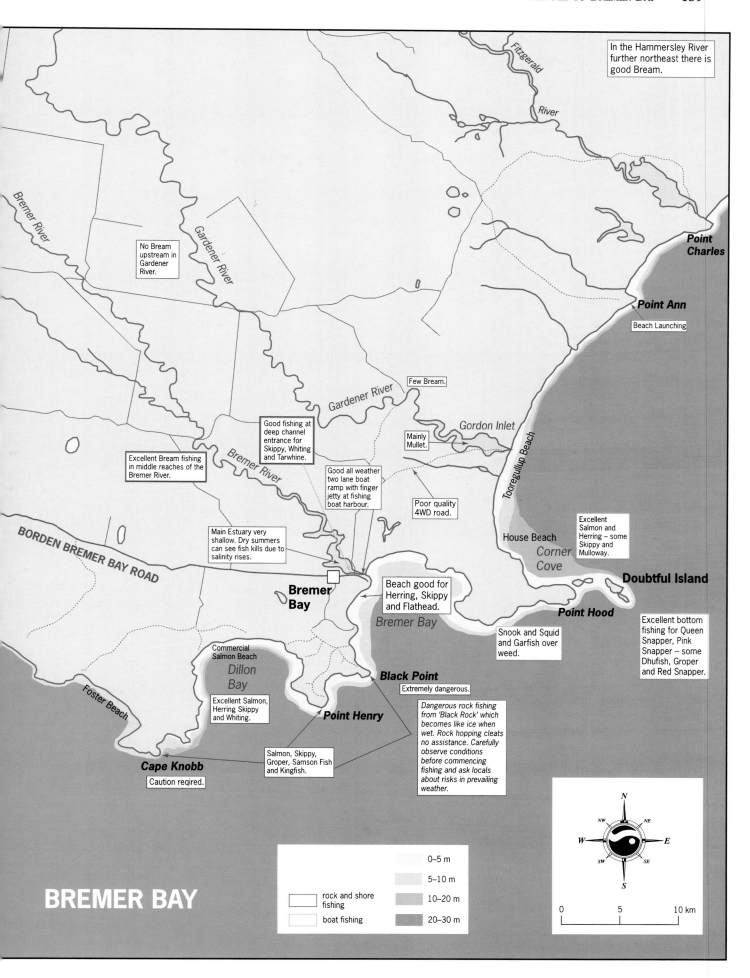

In the Hammersley River further northeast there is good Bream.

Fitzgerald

River

Point Charles

Point Ann

Beach Launching

Bremer River

No Bream upstream in Gardener River.

Gardener River

Gardener River

Few Bream.

Gordon Inlet

Good fishing at deep channel entrance for Skippy, Whiting and Tarwhine.

Mainly Mullet.

Excellent Bream fishing in middle reaches of the Bremer River.

Bremer River

Good all weather two lane boat ramp with finger jetty at fishing boat harbour.

Poor quality 4WD road.

Tooregullup Beach

Excellent Salmon and Herring – some Skippy and Mulloway.

House Beach

Corner Cove

Main Estuary very shallow. Dry summers can see fish kills due to salinity rises.

Doubtful Island

BORDEN BREMER BAY ROAD

Bremer Bay

Beach good for Herring, Skippy and Flathead.

Point Hood

Bremer Bay

Excellent bottom fishing for Queen Snapper, Pink Snapper – some Dhufish, Groper and Red Snapper.

Commercial Salmon Beach

Dillon Bay

Snook and Squid and Garfish over weed.

Black Point

Extremely dangerous.

Excellent Salmon, Herring Skippy and Whiting.

Foster Beach

Point Henry

Dangerous rock fishing from 'Black Rock' which becomes like ice when wet. Rock hopping cleats no assistance. Carefully observe conditions before commencing fishing and ask locals about risks in prevailing weather.

Cape Knobb

Caution reqired.

Salmon, Skippy, Groper, Samson Fish and Kingfish.

BREMER BAY

	0–5 m
rock and shore fishing	5–10 m
boat fishing	10–20 m
	20–30 m

N
NW   NE
W   E
SW   SE
S

0   5   10 km

BOAT RAMPS & TACKLE STORES

RAMPS

Broke Inlet
Walpole – Town ramp and Coalmine Beach
Denmark – Town ramp, Poddy Shot and
the River Mouth
Albany – Town ramps, Emu Point, Frenchmans Bay,
Misery Beach and Lower King
Bremer Bay – Boat harbour

TACKLE STORES

Ricketts Jack F & Co
2 South Coast Hwy
Denmark WA 6333
Tel: (08) 9848 1203

Albany Rods & Tackle
40 Stirling Tce,
Albany WA 6330
Tel: (08) 9841 1231

Trailblazers
184 Albany Highway
Albany WA 6330
Tel: (08) 9841 7859

The Great Outdoors
Centre
151 Albany Highway,
Albany WA 6330
Tel: (08) 9841 6818

Ray's Sports Power
288 York Street,
Albany WA 6330
Tel: (08) 9842 2842

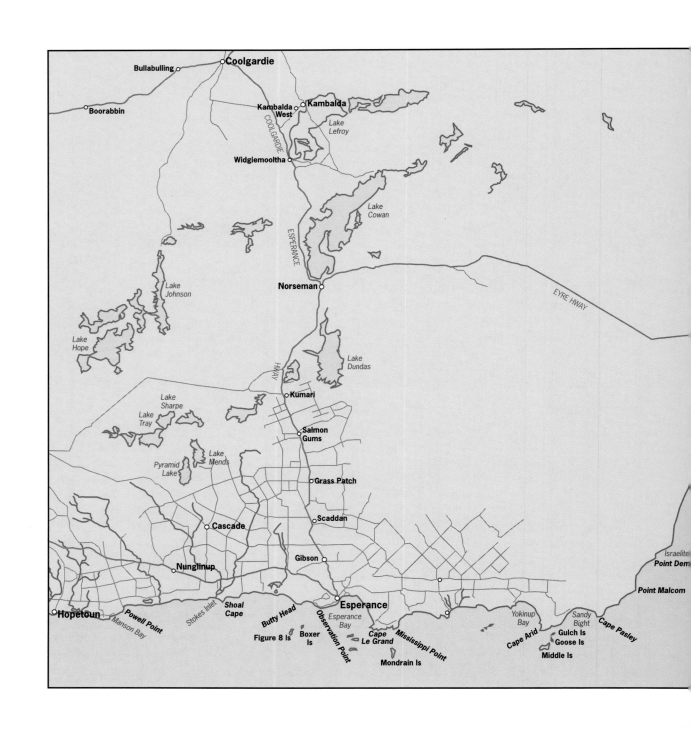

CHAPTER 11

HOPETOUN TO SA BORDER

HOPETOUN

This small settlement provides anglers with the chance to fish from beaches, rocks or by boat for many different species of fish. There is a fantastic boat ramp at Mary Ann Haven that allows safe access to offshore locations in calm weather. Bottom fishing is the most common method and provides catches of queen snapper, Samson fish, pink snapper, sweep, harlequin fish and breaksea cod. From the small jetty or rock wall at the ramp herring, gardies, whiting, skippy and squid are all caught.

There are numerous small estuaries and creeks that are often cut off from the ocean during summer. Culham Inlet to the west

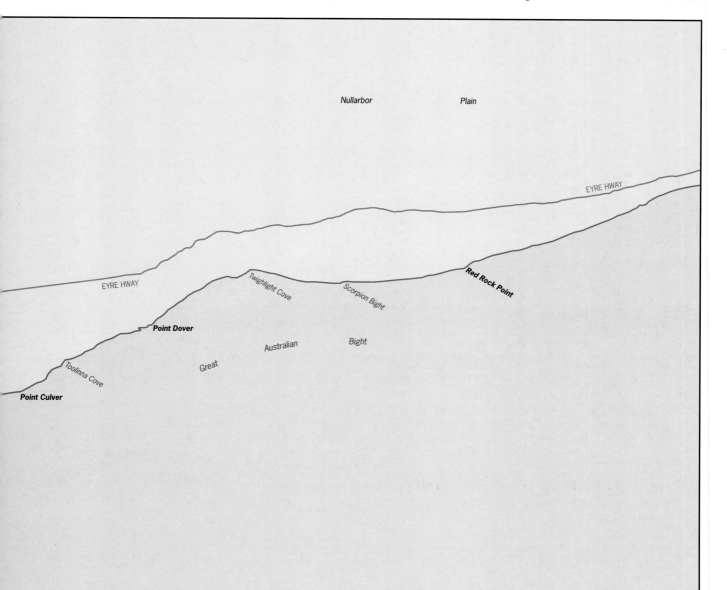

HOPETOUN TO SOUTH AUSTRALIAN BORDER

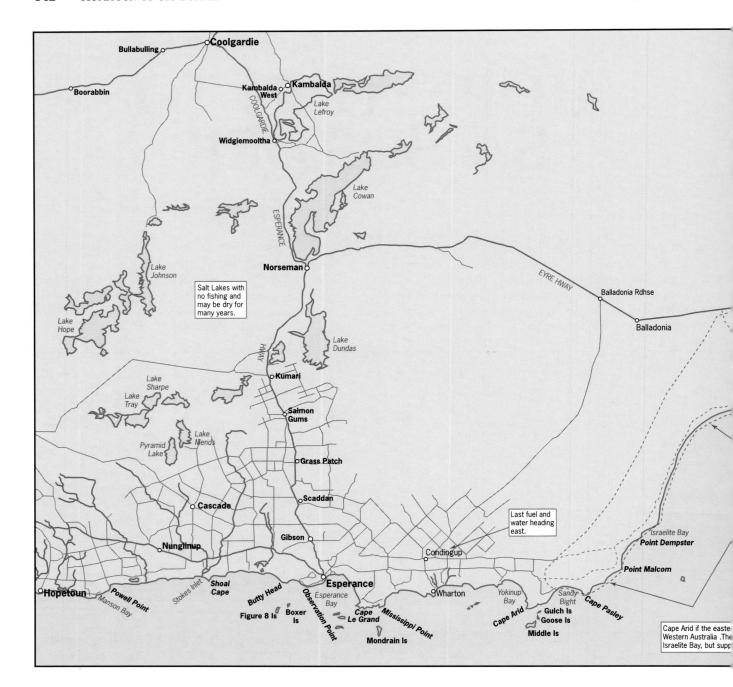

of town used to be the best bream fishery in Australia, but some incredible decisions by local authorities to put in place a low level culvert may well destroy Culham as a bream fishery in the future. The other pretty little water bodies are home to a few black bream, so if the boating weather is not good you can always spend time exploring and fishing these sheltered spots.

QUOIN HEAD

Lying to the west of Hopetoun is Quoin Head, a remote but attractive section of beach and rock headland. A 4WD is needed to reach this spot down a rough track, but once there, the fishing is worth the effort. Salmon, tailor and mulloway have all been taken from deep water from the rocks, and blue groper, pink snapper, sharks and Samson fish are all a possibility.

The beach is a great place to fish for sand whiting, skippy and herring, and a small campsite nearby makes this a great place to spend a few days.

MASON BAY AND STARVATION BAY

These popular campsites provide boat ramps and camping facilities, but during holiday periods become very crowded. The waters out from here are great for dinghy anglers chasing herring, skippy, snook, whiting and squid.

MUNGLINUP BEACH

Another good campsite but if you bring in a small boat you have to be prepared to launch it from the beach. Fish for herring, skippy, gardies, snook, whiting and squid.

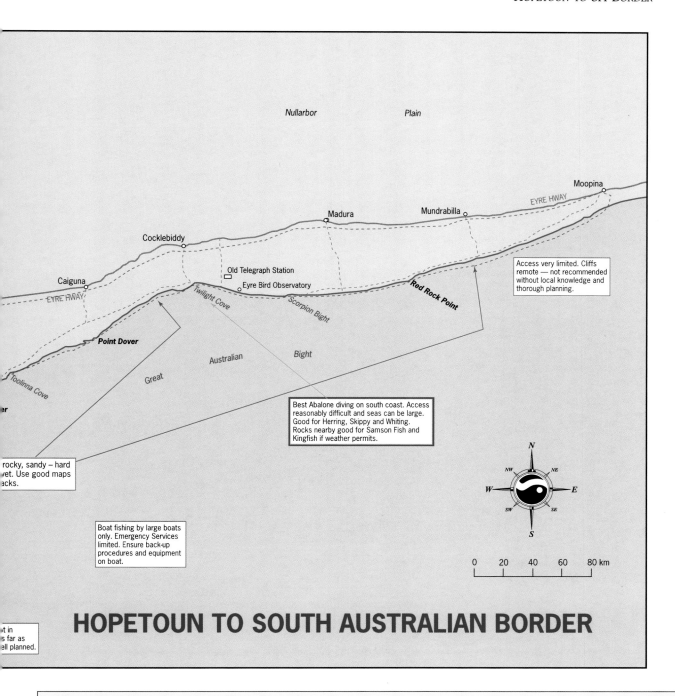

Nullarbor   Plain

Moopina

EYRE HWAY

Madura   Mundrabilla

Cocklebiddy

Old Telegraph Station

Caiguna   Eyre Bird Observatory

EYRE HWAY

Red Rock Point

Twilight Cove   Scorpion Bight

Access very limited. Cliffs remote — not recommended without local knowledge and thorough planning.

Point Dover

Australian   Bight

Toolinna Cove   Great

Best Abalone diving on south coast. Access reasonably difficult and seas can be large. Good for Herring, Skippy and Whiting. Rocks nearby good for Samson Fish and Kingfish if weather permits.

rocky, sandy – hard ...et. Use good maps ...acks.

Boat fishing by large boats only. Emergency Services limited. Ensure back-up procedures and equipment on boat.

N
NW   NE
W   E
SW   SE
S

0   20   40   60   80 km

...t in ...s far as ...ell planned.

HOPETOUN TO SOUTH AUSTRALIAN BORDER

E S P E R A N C E

Esperance is the last large town you come to along the south coast before the South Australian border, and it provides all the modern facilities to make life easy for the visiting angler. It was discovered in 1792 by the French whilst taking shelter from a storm. Then in 1802 Mathew Flinders sailed through the area mapping the south coast and naming such areas as Lucky Bay and Thistle Cove.

With spectacular beach and rock fishing locations close by and good boat ramps providing access to the offshore grounds, Esperance is a great place to spend some time fishing. Esperance is a popular fishing spot for anglers who live in Kalgoorlie, as it is situated only a few hours drive south. For Perth anglers, a distance of over 700 km has to be travelled to reach this prime spot.

BANDY CREEK BOAT HARBOUR

Situated 6.5 km along Fisheries Road you will find Bandy Creek,

a good place to fish for smaller species with light tackle. Herring, whiting and bream can be caught from the wharf on small baited hooks. This is one of the few places in WA where bream can be caught from oceanic waters, with several being washed over the ill-designed weir at the back of the harbour every winter.

TANKER JETTY

This jetty is one of the best three or four jetties in the State. It is legendary amongst those from the inland and Kalgoorlie as it regularly produces plenty of herring, skippy, whiting and squid at night. Out from the end a live yellowtail or a lure cast and retrieved is a good way to pick up bonito or snook. Even the occasional large Samson fish gets into the act from the jetty, and during the salmon run it is not uncommon to see a few fish hooked from here. Keep an eye out for the resident sea lions that often visit the jetty looking for an easy meal.

Fishing charters are also available for deep-sea trips targeting

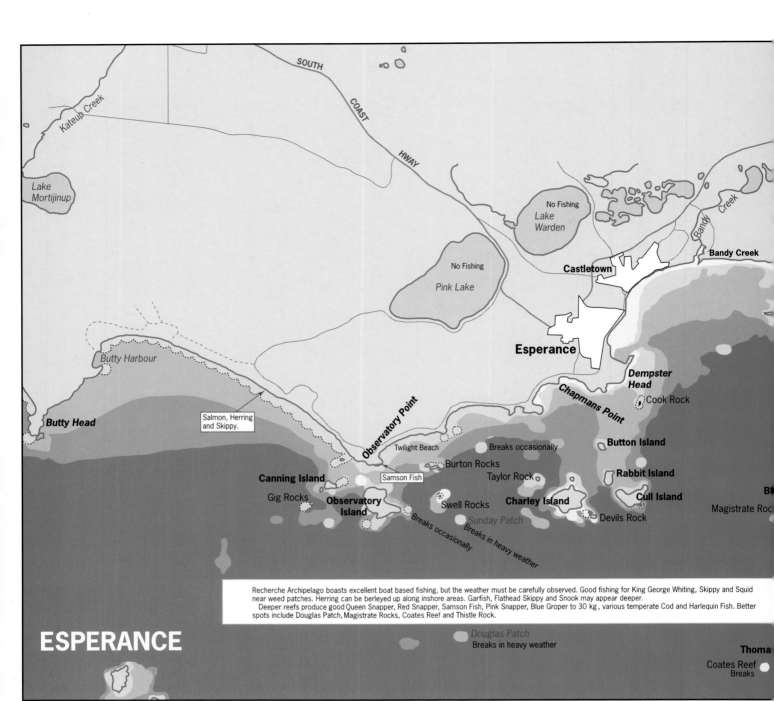

ESPERANCE

Recherche Archipelago boasts excellent boat based fishing, but the weather must be carefully observed. Good fishing for King George Whiting, Skippy and Squid near weed patches. Herring can be berleyed up along inshore areas. Garfish, Flathead Skippy and Snook may appear deeper.
Deeper reefs produce good Queen Snapper, Red Snapper, Samson Fish, Pink Snapper, Blue Groper to 30 kg, various temperate Cod and Harlequin Fish. Better spots include Douglas Patch, Magistrate Rocks, Coates Reef and Thistle Rock.

pink snapper, dhufish, queen snapper, groper, red snapper, harlequin fish and nannygai. Day or extended trips through the beautiful waters of the Recherche Archipelago can be organised.

THE STOCKYARDS

Just to the east of town, the Stockyards is a firm favourite for anglers chasing salmon, sharks, herring, skippy, silver bream, whiting and flathead.

Heading out along Twilight Beach Road to the west of town will bring you to several fishing spots such as West Beach, Hughes Step, Chapmans Point, Salmon Beach, Fourth Beach and Nine Mile Beach. Most of the common species can be caught with surf-fishing gear; sharks are an added attraction.

STOKES INLET

To the west of town you will come across good camping facilities at Stokes Inlet. The inlet is a good spot to fish for black bream, but it also contains a wide variety of species, including tarwhine, skippy, whiting, small salmon and cobbler. A camping trip in the area allows anglers the chance to fish Fanny Cove and Margaret Cove; the whole area is part of the Stokes National Park.

CAPE LE GRAND

This is a popular rock-fishing area for most common species of fish that are found along the south coast. Care is needed when fishing this area, and it pays to only fish during calm sea conditions. The beach nearby allows small-boat launching across the sand where anglers can fish for smaller species like herring, skippy, whiting and squid in close or venture out to the deeper reef areas for queen snapper, harlequin fish, sweep, pink snapper, dhufish, Samson fish and blue groper. Trolling lures through the deeper waters produces bonito, southern bluefin tuna, salmon and Samson fish.

Some of the landbased fishing spots in the National Park that are worth looking at are Hellfire Bay, Thistle Cove, Lucky Bay and Rossiter Bay.

LUCKY BAY

With a caravan park and the ability to launch small boats from the sand, Lucky Bay is a popular fishing and holiday spot. Shore fishing is from beach or rock locations for smaller species like herring, skippy, whiting, flathead and silver bream. Larger species available to beach anglers are salmon, mulloway, and

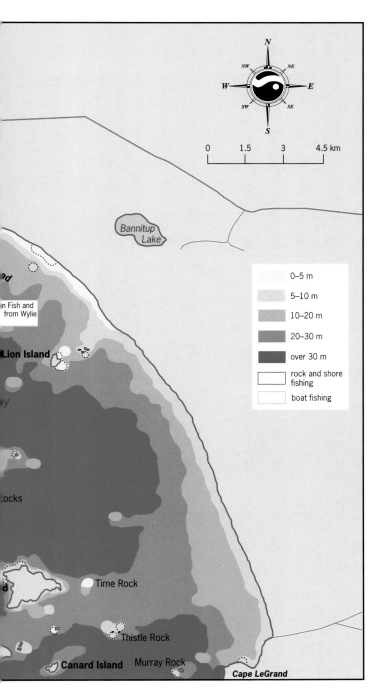

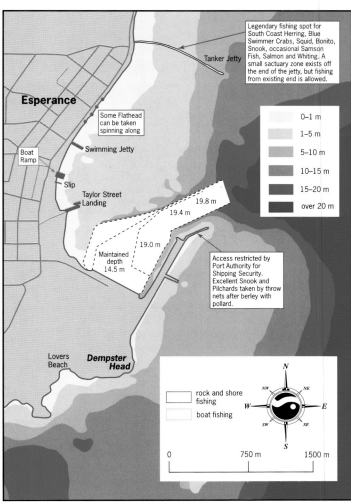

Map labels (left map)

N
NW NE
W E
SW SE
S

0   1.5   3   4.5 km

Bannitup Lake

0–5 m
5–10 m
10–20 m
20–30 m
over 30 m

rock and shore fishing
boat fishing

n Fish and from Wylie

Lion Island

Time Rock

Thistle Rock

Canard Island   Murray Rock

Cape LeGrand

Map labels (Esperance map)

Tanker Jetty

Legendary fishing spot for South Coast Herring, Blue Swimmer Crabs, Squid, Bonito, Snook, occasional Samson Fish, Salmon and Whiting. A small sactuary zone exists off the end of the jetty, but fishing from existing end is allowed.

Esperance

Some Flathead can be taken spinning along

Swimming Jetty

Boat Ramp

Slip

Taylor Street Landing

19.8 m
19.4 m
19.0 m

Maintained depth 14.5 m

Access restricted by Port Authority for Shipping Security. Excellent Snook and Pilchards taken by throw nets after berley with pollard.

Lovers Beach   Dempster Head

0–1 m
1–5 m
5–10 m
10–15 m
15–20 m
over 20 m

rock and shore fishing
boat fishing

N
NW NE
W E
SW SE
S

0   750 m   1500 m

sharks. The rocks also provide the chance to hook Samson fish, queen snapper, blue groper, sweep, skippy and leatherjackets.

WHARTON BEACH

Salmon are the main target from this beach, but herring, skippy, sharks and mulloway turn up at times. The rocks nearby provide some good fishing in calm conditions.

DUKE OF ORLEANS BAY

Coming out to the park and travelling along Fisheries Road you will eventually come to the last town before a 4WD is needed to access the bight towards the South Australian Border. The town of Condingup is a good place to stock up on fuel and supplies before heading further east. Heading south from here you arrive at the Duke of Orleans Bay, a scenic area where the Daily River meets the coast.

This bay is a very popular spot for local and visiting anglers and has a caravan park and beach launching for small boats. It is a good place to spend some time wetting a line.

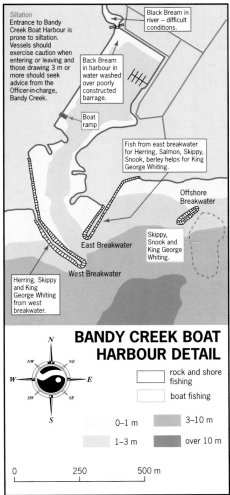

Siltation
Entrance to Bandy Creek Boat Harbour is prone to siltation. Vessels should exercise caution when entering or leaving and those drawing 3 m or more should seek advice from the Officer-in-charge, Bandy Creek.

Black Bream in river – difficult conditions.

Back Bream in harbour in water washed over poorly constructed barrage.

Boat ramp

Fish from east breakwater for Herring, Salmon, Skippy, Snook, berley helps for King George Whiting.

Offshore Breakwater

East Breakwater

Skippy, Snook and King George Whiting.

West Breakwater

Herring, Skippy and King George Whiting from west breakwater.

BANDY CREEK BOAT HARBOUR DETAIL

N
NW NE
W E
SW SE
S

rock and shore fishing
boat fishing

0–1 m   3–10 m
1–3 m   over 10 m

0   250   500 m

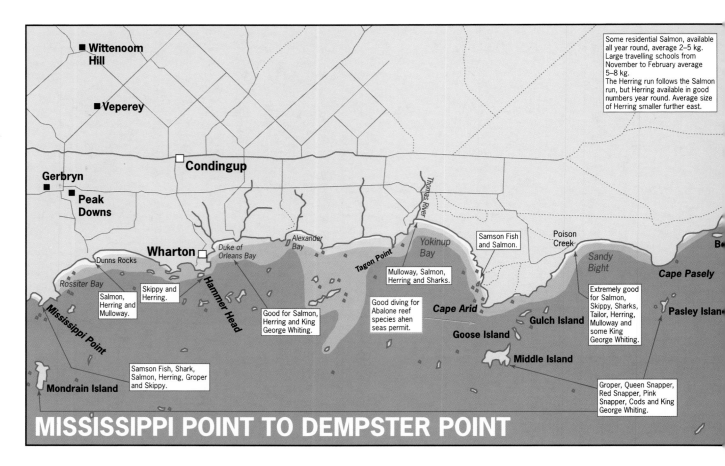

Some residential Salmon, available all year round, average 2–5 kg. Large travelling schools from November to February average 5–8 kg.
The Herring run follows the Salmon run, but Herring available in good numbers year round. Average size of Herring smaller further east.

Samson Fish and Salmon.

Mulloway, Salmon, Herring and Sharks.

Good diving for Abalone reef species ahen seas permit.

Extremely good for Salmon, Skippy, Sharks, Tailor, Herring, Mulloway and some King George Whiting.

Groper, Queen Snapper, Red Snapper, Pink Snapper, Cods and King George Whiting.

Good for Salmon, Herring and King George Whiting.

Skippy and Herring.

Salmon, Herring and Mulloway.

Samson Fish, Shark, Salmon, Herring, Groper and Skippy.

MISSISSIPPI POINT TO DEMPSTER POINT

ALEXANDER BAY

When the salmon are running, Alexander Bay is a sure place to find good numbers of these fine sport fish. The rock-fishing spots of this area also fish well for salmon, big skippy and herring.

KENNEDYS BEACH

Anglers can chase salmon, big skippy and herring at Kennedys Beach which can be reached by 4WD. Very large skippy can be tempted with whole blue sardines or mulies fished on ganged hooks. Tagon Point is the rocky headland near the beach and is well known for producing very big skippy to 5 kg from the rocks, as well as salmon, sharks and mulloway.

THOMAS RIVER

This is a prime salmon spot during the season, and the beach is also well known for producing mulloway and big skippy from the surf. This beach fishes the best after dark, especially for the large skippy.

The Cape Arid National Park starts at Thomas River and stretches eastwards to the Nysland National Park. This is the point where Fisheries Road ends and the 4WD track takes you to Israelite Bay where the remains of the telegraph station still stand. There is one house remaining, which is occupied by a professional abalone fisherman. Numerous campsites can be found in this area; many are heavily used by local anglers.

Beach launching is relatively easy with many access points to be found, and a short distance offshore you can fish for pink snapper and King George whiting. Rock fishing is much safer in this area but care still needs to be taken. Good catches of salmon, herring, silver trevally, pike, leather jackets, flathead, flounder and squid are all possible.

South is Point Malcolm where the remains lie of the first house built in the area, dating back to around 1850. There is

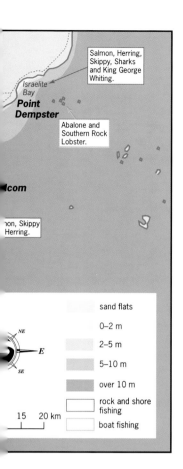

ABOVE: Australian salmon are one of the most common species taken from the beaches heading east from Esperance.

LEFT: Herring are easy to berley up and catch all along the south coast, and they make good eating when fresh.

plenty of access here to the beach and rock-fishing locations, but being more exposed to the weather this area of coastline can be very hazardous.

Poison Creek

If you had to choose one place in Australia to catch a salmon in the 6–8 kg class, then Poison Creek would have to be it. Situated in the bay between Cape Arid and Cape Pasley, a 4WD track will take you to this long stretch of beach and you can travel along it looking in deep gutters for schools of fish in the surf. Salmon are caught here in big numbers almost all year round, but best numbers of fish are caught in summer before they start their migration west.

Bait fishing with mulies or live herring is a fail-safe method of hooking any salmon nearby. Casting poppers or metal lures at schools of fish can make for exciting fishing. Big sharks are also about in good numbers when the salmon schools are there, and bait fishing at night produces some large mulloway from the deeper gutters. Poison Creek is one of the very few locations on the south coast where big tailor can be taken in reasonable quantities.

GREAT AUSTRALIAN BIGHT

Leaving Israelite Bay and heading east you travel for a short time along the telegraph line built around the 1880s before you gain access to the beach. This beach is hard but does have a problem with weed build up close to Israelite, but once past this the rest of the beach is easy to travel along at low tide.

It is about 120 km to Point Culver where the cliffs of the Great Australian Bight start. From the top of the cliffs it is possible to observe Southern Wright Whales sitting just beyond the breakers and numerous seals resting on the beaches below. About 50 km before Point Culver you reach the Billbunya sand dunes, the tallest of which is about 213.4 m (700 ft) above sea level—some of the largest dunes in Australia. Many travellers stop at this point to climb or even sand-board down the dunes.

Point Culver is very popular with Esperance anglers, and a large cave at the start of the cliffs overlooks the Southern Ocean. This area is a great place to target big salmon and mulloway from the surf. Big sharks including Great Whites patrol the deeper water at the back of the breakers and can often be seen from a high vantage point.

From the beach there is a track that takes you to the top of the cliffs where it once again follows the telegraph line. About 70 km along the top of the cliffs is Toolina Cove, where if you are game,

a climb of 106.7 m (350 feet) straight down to the beach can be made. The fishing from this location is always good with salmon, skippy and sharks making up the bulk of the catch. A strong surf rod and reel is recommended to cater for the larger species that can put up a good fight in the surf. Just remember that you must be able to carry everything with you on the climb up or down, including any fish you wish to keep. Some of the best abalone fishing is found in this area, but only commercial abalone, shark, and southern rock lobster fishermen regularly venture into this remote area by boat.

From here on, high cliffs prevent any access to much of the coastline right through to the border, so many simply depart straight up to the Eyre Highway or follow the telegraph line along to Eyre.

Recreational anglers on their trip to Western Australia can experience everything from tropical barramundi fishing to the cooler water Australian salmon and many other angling delights in between. One thing that is certain is that by the time an angler leaves Western Australia, they will already be planning another trip, either to visit places that time didn't permit or to revisit the most special places in this special State.

Boat Ramps & Tackle Stores

This stretch of coast is subject to the force of the Southern Ocean, and therefore most small boat anglers stick to the sheltered estuaries and only venture out into the open ocean when weather permits. Larger boats fish out from the major harbours at Albany and Esperance, and take advantage of the excellent fishing opportunities that exist along the southern coast. During the winter months the cold fronts pushing up from the south can keep even the largest boats from venturing out, and as a result many recreational anglers fish this area in summer.

Fishing from small dinghies or trailer craft inside the sheltered estuaries is a very popular and safe alternative for a wide range of smaller species that inhabit the waters.

RAMPS

Hopetoun

Esperance – Town ramp and Bandy Creek Boat Harbour

TACKLE STORES

Esperance Marine & Tackle Pty Ltd
30 Norseman Rd
Esperance WA 6450
Tel: (08) 9071 7373

Civic Video Esperance
Units 3 & 4 James Street
Centre Seven
Esperance WA
Tel: (08) 9071 2746

Southern Sports & Tackle
Shop 14, The Boulevard,
Esperance WA 6450
Tel: (08) 9071 3022

CHAPTER 12

WEST AUSTRALIAN RIGS

SHORE FISHING

ESTUARY RIGS FOR BLACK BREAM, FLATHEAD AND FLOUNDER

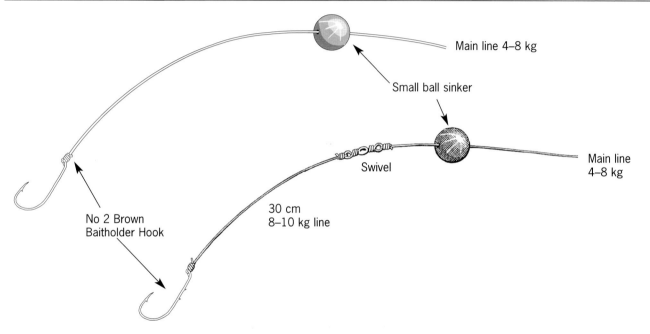

Main line 4–8 kg

Small ball sinker

Swivel

Main line 4–8 kg

No 2 Brown
Baitholder Hook

30 cm
8–10 kg line

SUIT TAILOR, FLATHEAD, BLACK BREAM, MULLOWAY AND GIANT HERRRING

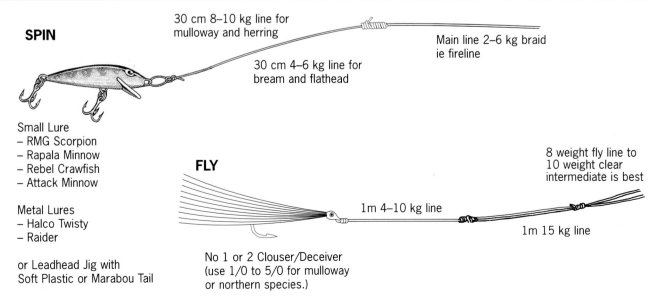

SPIN

30 cm 8–10 kg line for
mulloway and herring

Main line 2–6 kg braid
ie fireline

30 cm 4–6 kg line for
bream and flathead

Small Lure
– RMG Scorpion
– Rapala Minnow
– Rebel Crawfish
– Attack Minnow

Metal Lures
– Halco Twisty
– Raider

or Leadhead Jig with
Soft Plastic or Marabou Tail

FLY

8 weight fly line to
10 weight clear
intermediate is best

1m 4–10 kg line

1m 15 kg line

No 1 or 2 Clouser/Deceiver
(use 1/0 to 5/0 for mulloway
or northern species.)

SURF RIGS

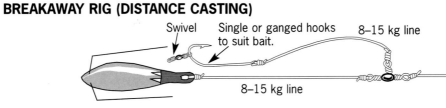

Mulloway and Tailor

15–20 kg line
swivel
10 kg line
4 x 5/0 tarpon
Use wire for 'toothy' fish like sharks and mackerel.
snap swivel
Main line 8–15 kg
Star or spoon sinker to suit conditions.

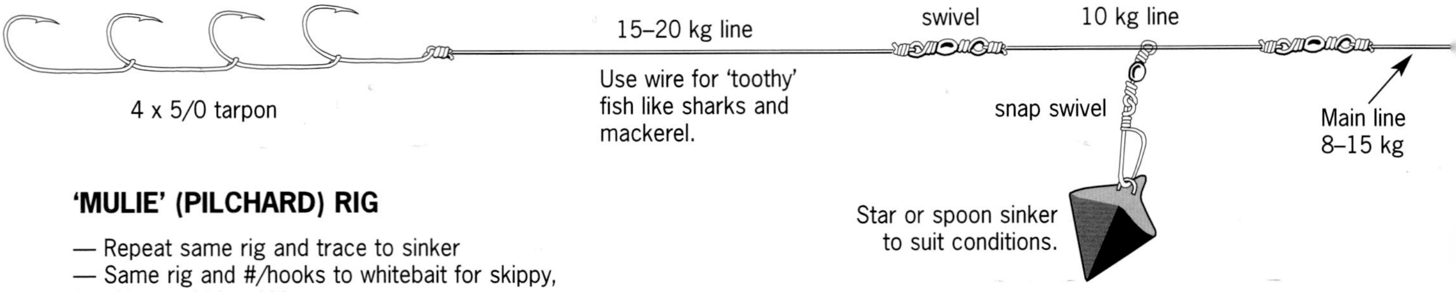

'MULIE' (PILCHARD) RIG

— Repeat same rig and trace to sinker
— Same rig and #/hooks to whitebait for skippy, tarwhine and big whiting

BREAKAWAY RIG (DISTANCE CASTING)

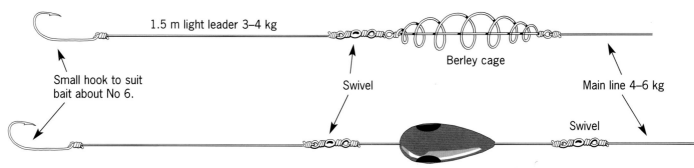

Swivel
Single or ganged hooks to suit bait.
8–15 kg line
8–15 kg line
Main line 8–15 kg
South African casting sinker No 4 to 6.

Herring, Skippy and Garfish Rig

1.5 m light leader 3–4 kg
Berley cage
Small hook to suit bait about No 6.
Swivel
Main line 4–6 kg
Swivel
Blob float with hole for burley.

REEF RIGS – SHORE FISHING

Suit Salmon and Tailor in South or Spangled Emperor/Mackerel in North

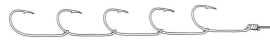

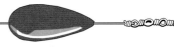

1.5 m 10 kg line
(use wire up north)
Blob float
Mulie or garfish bait —ganged 4/0 to 6/0 tarpon.
8–10 kg main line

SNAPPER/BALDCHIN GROPER

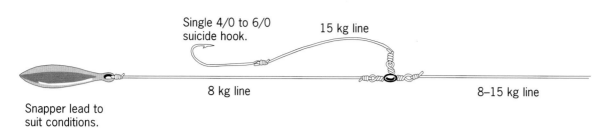

Single 4/0 to 6/0 suicide hook.

15 kg line

8 kg line

8–15 kg line

Snapper lead to suit conditions.

SPIN RIG FOR TAILOR/SALMON OR NORTHERN SPECIES

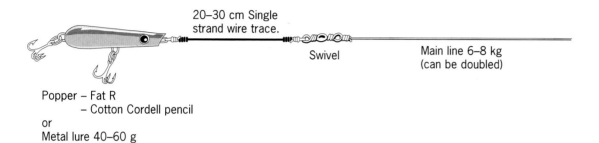

20–30 cm Single strand wire trace.

Swivel

Main line 6–8 kg (can be doubled)

Popper – Fat R
        – Cotton Cordell pencil
or
Metal lure 40–60 g
– Halco Twisty
– Raider

BOAT RIGS

DEEP WATER BOTTOM BOUNCING RIG

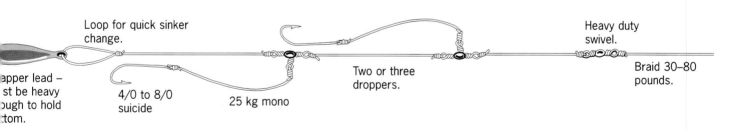

Loop for quick sinker change.

Heavy duty swivel.

Two or three droppers.

Braid 30–80 pounds.

apper lead –
st be heavy
ough to hold
tom.

4/0 to 8/0 suicide

25 kg mono

KING GEORGE WHITING

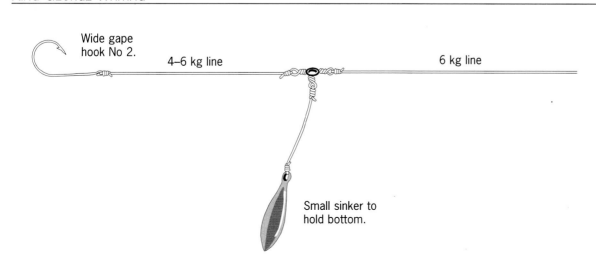

Wide gape hook No 2.

4–6 kg line

6 kg line

Small sinker to hold bottom.

KING GEORGE AND SAND WHITING RIG

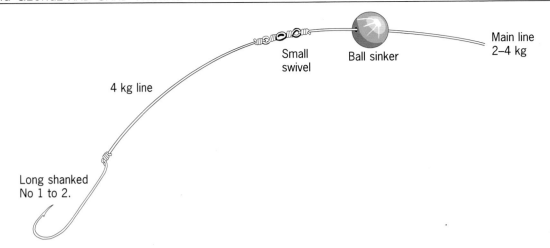

Main line 2–4 kg

Ball sinker

Small swivel

4 kg line

Long shanked No 1 to 2.

SQUID (USED MOSTLY ON HANDLINES)

6 kg main line

Prawn style squid jig.

TROLLING — MACKEREL/TUNA

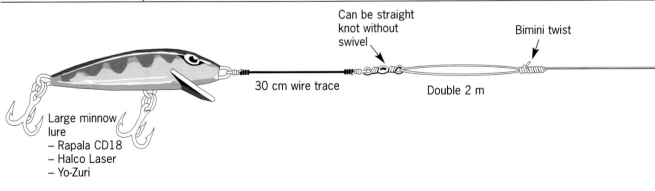

Can be straight knot without swivel

Bimini twist

30 cm wire trace

Double 2 m

Large minnow lure
– Rapala CD18
– Halco Laser
– Yo-Zuri

BALLOON RIG — NORTH WEST SHORE OR BOAT

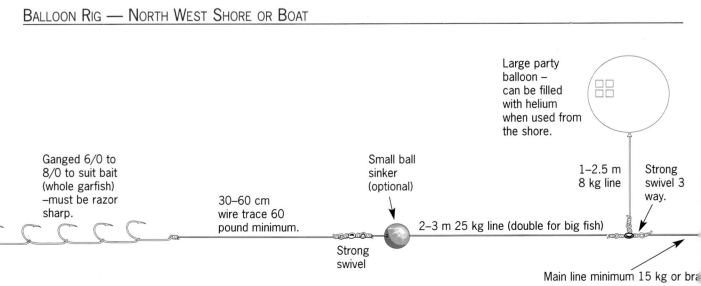

Large party balloon – can be filled with helium when used from the shore.

Ganged 6/0 to 8/0 to suit bait (whole garfish) –must be razor sharp.

30–60 cm wire trace 60 pound minimum.

Small ball sinker (optional)

Strong swivel

2–3 m 25 kg line (double for big fish)

1–2.5 m 8 kg line

Strong swivel 3 way.

Main line minimum 15 kg or bra